A Century of
Air Warfare with
Nine (IX) Squadron, RAF

A Century of
Air Warfare with
Nine (IX) Squadron, RAF

Still Going Strong

Foreword
Air Chief Marshal
Sir Stuart Peach KCB, CBE,
Deputy Chief of the Defence Staff

GORDON THORBURN

Pen & Sword
AVIATION

First published in Great Britain in 2014 by
PEN AND SWORD AVIATION
an imprint of
Pen and Sword Books Ltd
47 Church Street
Barnsley
South Yorkshire S70 2AS

ISBN 978 1 78303 634 9

A CIP record for this book is available from the British Library.

Printed and bound in England by
CPI Group (UK) Ltd, Croydon, CR0 4YY

Typeset in Times New Roman by
Chic Graphics

Pen & Sword Books Ltd incorporates the imprints of
Pen & Sword Aviation, Pen & Sword Family History, Pen & Sword Maritime,
Pen & Sword Military, Pen & Sword Discovery, Wharncliffe Local History,
Wharncliffe True Crime, Wharncliffe Transport, Pen & Sword Select,
Pen & Sword Military Classics, Leo Cooper, Remember When,
The Praetorian Press, Seaforth Publishing and Frontline Publishing

For a complete list of Pen and Sword titles please contact
Pen and Sword Books Limited
47 Church Street, Barnsley, South Yorkshire, S70 2AS, England
E-mail: enquiries@pen-and-sword.co.uk
Website: www.pen-and-sword.co.uk

Contents

Foreword

This book is about a Squadron of the Royal Flying Corps and Royal Air Force. Not just my squadron but the senior bomber squadron of the Royal Air Force and the squadron in the history of the Royal Air Force with more battle honours than any other.

The history captured by Gordon Thorburn is not about politics, machines and the context of world war, Empire or, latterly, conflicts of choice. It is about people. The author brings this out well; particularly in the context of the Second World War where the official motto 'Per noctem volamus', and the unofficial one 'There's always bloody something' applied in equal measure.

The jet age is littered with firsts for IX(B) Squadron, the B for Bomber being awarded rarely by King Edward VIII. The firsts from 1945 to 2014 demonstrate the same courage, strength in adversity, pluck and determination as in world wars.

My own links with the Squadron span thirty-two years as a junior navigator on IX(B) as the first Tornado squadron, to Squadron Commander on operations in the Middle East 1994 to 1996, and as President of the IX(B) Squadron Association from 2002 to 2014. In my view there is another book, yet to be written, on the context and complexities of IX(B) Squadron in the Tornado era. But that is for the future. This book is the story of the thousands of men and women, air crew, ground crew, support staff and families who constitute the story of this famous squadron. I commend it to anyone interested in history and the human story of warfare in the last hundred years.

Air Chief Marshal Sir Stuart Peach KCB, CBE
Deputy Chief of the Defence Staff
February 2014

Preface:
The Origins of Bombing

Hitting the right building

The Italian air force dropped hand-grenades in 1911 during a colonial war in Libya, flying over ground that would become familiar to IX Squadron crews a century later. The first self-detonating bomb to be dropped in anger, designed by an officer in the Bulgarian army, Lieutenant Simeon Petrov, was deployed on 16 October 1912 near Adrianople (modern Edirne, Turkey), in the Balkan war against the Ottomans.

For the British at the start of the First World War, bombing had not progressed beyond dropping the occasional grenade or Molotov-style cocktail should the occasion arise. Targeted, long-distance bombing missions were not really thought about until an inspirational raid by men of the Royal Naval Air Service (RNAS). After a failed attempt on 22 September, two RNAS Sopwith Tabloids set off from Antwerp, one for Cologne, one for Düsseldorf, on 8 October 1914.

The Tabloid had been built in 1913 for the civilian market, as the aerial equivalent of a sports car. It could do 90mph, far more than standard service aircraft. The RNAS pilots were in the single-seater version, flying alone right into the Fatherland with no more protection than their service revolvers. Lieutenant Reginald Marix headed for Düsseldorf. Here is an eye-witness report:

> It was a splendid feat – he took the Germans by surprise. The soldiers seeing the hostile aircraft high up in the air shot at it continually until suddenly the aeroplane started to glide lower and lower; the people were mad with joy and shouted hurrah. The soldiers got ready to catch the aeroplane as it fell when suddenly from a height of between 100 and 200 metres the airman threw several bombs, one of which reached its goal – the Zeppelin shed, in which there was the air-cruiser, the pride of Düsseldorf, which had received orders to join the army in France that afternoon. In spite of my being a good distance away, I heard the explosion, the smoke whirling high into the air, and I saw the airman escape in the common confusion.

A Bulgarian officer, possibly Lieutenant Petrov, in 1912 displays an example of the first working, purpose-made bomb to be dropped in anger. In a photograph taken after the war, we can see what bombing did to Essen, mainly in 1943. Empty shells and rubble are all that remain; everything was 'the right building'.

The German papers next day reported 'Zeppelin shed slightly damaged' and failed to mention the four army officers killed or the heap of ashes that was the remains of airship Zeppelin Z9.

While Marix's aircraft was being hit five times by rifle shots and mitrailleuse (multi-barrelled machine gun), he dropped two 20-pounders by hand from less than 600ft and changed the military outlook on bombing. As *The Times* said, under the headline 'The value of bomb-dropping': 'There has always been a little uncertainty about the value of bomb-dropping, for although it seemed possible that buildings might be set alight with incendiary explosives, it was another matter to make sure of hitting the right building. The naval pilots have now shown at Düsseldorf that this is possible.'

The Admiralty pointed out that 'in the event of further bombs being dropped into Antwerp and other Belgian towns, measures of reprisal can certainly be adopted, if desired, to almost any extent'. They also said that 'The feat would appear to be in every respect remarkable, having regard to the distance – over a hundred miles – penetrated into country held by the enemy.'

The Times added a footnote: 'Demand for air risk insurance. There was again a very large amount of insurance effected in London yesterday against the risks of damage by aircraft and bombs and shells thrown therefrom; and underwriters hardened their rates. A premium of 2s 6d per cent is now regarded as the minimum.'

Acknowledgements

With special thanks to Air Commodore 'Spike' Milligan and Squadron Leader Richard James for help with assembling the facts, and to Terry Lintin for photographs. I am grateful to all members of IX Squadron, past and present, who have contributed to the book.

Thanks to www.earlyaeroplanes.com/archive for certain images.

CHAPTER 1

The Origins of IX Squadron

Wireless in the air

Like the Italians, the French were advanced with the idea of flying aeroplanes for military purposes – the French Army Air Service, *L'Aéronautique Militaire*, had been formed in October 1910 – but most armies and navies had yet to appreciate the potential usefulness of this type of flying.

Among the British, there was perhaps an attitude between senior commanders that this American invention of heavier-than-air flight, so enthusiastically taken up by the French, could hardly be of significance to the Empire. One man who disagreed was Captain Bertram Dickson, a long-serving intelligence officer who caught the aeroplane bug in 1910. He learned to fly and decided to attach himself to the traditional annual manoeuvres occurring on Salisbury Plain. Taking sides, he would act as aerial spy for Red Force, looking to locate Blue Force. When he did find them, he landed his Bristol Box-kite and notified Red Force HQ, apparently by telephone although where he found such a thing in 1910 is not clear.

Dickson's demonstration of air reconnaissance had made an impression. During 1911 an Air Battalion was formed by the Royal Engineers, including an Airship Company and an Aeroplane Company. Four Bristol Box-kites were purchased from the British and Colonial Aeroplane Company Limited. This machine was a pusher, based on the French Voisin and the Farman III, with a huge front-mounted elevator and a top speed of 40mph. To modern eyes it would look more like a market stall on a windy day than an aeroplane, British or colonial – but it was a beginning.

In November 1911, Prime Minister Asquith commissioned his Technical Sub-Committee for Imperial Defence to report on the military potential of aeroplanes. The Committee asked Bertram Dickson what he thought and,

A Farman III, close forerunner of the Farman Longhorn (see below) and the model for the Bristol Box-kite, with its elevator out front in the manner of the Wright brothers' first successful machine.

despite suffering from injuries sustained in the world's first mid-air collision, from which he would later die, he made a quite remarkable prediction:

> In case of a European war, between two countries, both sides would be equipped with large corps of aeroplanes, each trying to obtain information on the other. The efforts which each would exert in order to hinder or prevent the enemy from obtaining information would lead to the inevitable result of a war in the air, for the supremacy of the air, by armed aeroplanes against each other. This fight for the supremacy of the air in future wars will be of the greatest importance.

Someone was listening, because numbers 1, 2 and 3 Squadrons and the Central Flying School of the Royal Flying Corps (RFC) were established in May 1912 but No. 1 Squadron didn't have aeroplanes. They took over the balloons, airships and kites of the Royal Engineers at Farnborough. By September of 1912, with the formation of No. 4 Squadron, the RFC had three-dozen assorted aeroplanes, mostly French and all powered by French engines. The German Army Air Service had confused priorities, as the influence of Count Zeppelin and the Kaiser placed too much emphasis on the Zeppelin Luftschiff, but still had over a hundred heavier-than-air machines.

By August 1914 and the outbreak of hostilities, *L'Aéronautique Militaire* was the leader in strength and technology, with 132 machines in 21 escadrilles. Altogether about 400 aeroplanes were operational militarily in Europe, roughly half on each side. The Germans had 8 main marques and several minor ones, about 220 machines, including some of the Fokker Spin (Spider) type. The Belgians had four squadrons of Farmans.

The British had fifty or so aircraft in France, four squadrons, nominally with twelve machines each. Nos 2 and 4 Squadrons had mostly BE2 types with a few Farman Shorthorns; 3 Squadron had the Blériot XI and the already obsolete Henri Farman F20; 5 Squadron had F20s, Avro 504s and BE8s.

The BE designation for machines built at the Royal Aircraft Factory, previously the Balloon Factory, stood for Blériot Experimental. You could argue that all aircraft designed in 1912 were experimental, but the nod to the great Frenchman was partly to his method of propulsion, a tractor design, with the propellor pulling from the front, rather than the Wright/Farman method of pushing from behind. Partly also it was because there had been no intention to design new machines. The BE series, initiated by the young engineer Geoffrey de Havilland, had begun with a Blériot reconstruction.

Regardless of maker's name, these monoplanes and biplanes were broadly similar in what they could do. The science of aeronautics was little understood, so designs were based on whatever had gone immediately before with a few empirical improvements. They were all fragile, martyrs to the weather and unreliable in the extreme. That anyone, Italian, Bulgarian or otherwise, would be willing to go to war in one must excite astonishment in every modern airman.

Most of the time, most of them were unserviceable, so numbers were important if any operations were to be flown. A single type of machine for a single squadron was a thing to be desired, by pilots and mechanics alike, but there was no requirement for formation flying. In the chaos of the early days, any aircraft would do if you could get it.

In Britain, there was no aero-engine industry. It was easier to buy French than design new engines, a factor that severely handicapped British aircraft development for much of the war. Some components were not made in

Britain; it had been usual practice to buy magnetos from Germany. Also, there were no factories geared up for mass production. All sorts of firms had been building aeroplanes, as and when a few orders happened to come in, but nobody in a position of power had foreseen the need for great numbers so there had been no pressure applied, and no planning.

Kitchener ordered a display of formation flying at Farnborough featuring four aircraft, but was told by Colonel Trenchard, OC the RFC, that such a thing was impossible, because 'The machines are all of different types and different performances; we cannot fly in formation. It cannot be done.'

That all the machines were slow and underpowered was not thought to be necessarily a bad thing. These were tools of reconnaissance and nothing more, and a sedate pace allowed for better observation.

Flights of 50 miles into enemy territory could be reasonably contemplated but, despite Dickson's predictions, there was very little notion of them doing any actual fighting. Bomb-dropping experiments had been tried, for example by Major Musgrave's technical section (see below) at Netheravon, but that was all. Surprisingly perhaps, neither had aircraft's value in directing artillery fire been deeply thought about.

Aircraft, it was understood, would be able to observe and operate where the cavalry could not, to espy enemy positions and numbers. The pilot would report to HQ on landing or, where matters were more pressing, write a note as he was flying along and drop it attached to a weight.

On the first day of war, 4 August 1914, as the German army crossed the border into Belgium, no French, Belgian or German aircraft was armed. Guns were not in the specification. Only one British aircraft was fitted with a gun and that was a private experiment by its pilot.

To quote from Sir Walter Raleigh, *The War in the Air*:

In early days, officers often took a revolver, a carbine, or a rifle, into the air with them, but machines designed expressly for fighting and armed with Lewis or Vickers Guns did not appear in force until it became necessary to counter attacks made by the Fokker on our observation machines. Then began that long series of dramatic combats splendid in many of its episodes, which fascinated the attention of the public, and almost excluded from notice the humbler, but essential and no less dangerous, duties of those whose business it was to observe.

If shooting the enemy pilot with a hand-held gun didn't work, there was one other way to gain a victory. By buffeting and generally threatening to bounce and bash, and using the turbulence caused by close approaches, it was occasionally possible to win a submission. The first instance of this was on 25 August, when three BE2A aircraft of No. 2 Squadron forced a Taube to land.

The first British aeroplane purpose-made to carry a gun did not arrive on the Western Front until December 1914. This, the Vickers Fighting Biplane Mark V (FB5), AKA 'The Gunbus', had a pusher engine so its extra man, the observer, could fire the machine gun forwards. Anthony Fokker, the Dutch pioneer working for the Germans, was experimenting with a copy of a synchronisation gear to allow a machine gun to fire through the propellor, a device invented in 1913 by a Swiss engineer, Franz Schneider, but not then pursued by the German authorities. Thus equipped, the Fokker Eindecker would arrive in May 1915 to terrorise Allied airmen.

Meanwhile, in other types of aircraft, as Raleigh says, the pilot took pot shots with his service revolver while the observer, if there was one, had a go with a rifle. When machine guns were later fitted to those aircraft capable of taking them, such as the Farman Shorthorn, their propensity for jamming and inconvenience in reloading made victories in aerial combat very difficult to achieve.

This was the status quo as war broke out. Aeroplanes were a substitute for cavalry as scouts, there was no need for them to be armed, and messages from them could be passed on to HQ when convenient.

It only took a few weeks of the war for the combatants to realise that several new uses of aircraft were desirable, if not yet routinely possible. Flights over roads crowded with troops and equipment showed obvious targets. Hand-held grenades did little damage. Big bombs would be good, but there were none, and no means of carrying them had been devised.

Efforts were being made but the poor load-carrying abilities of the aircraft were a limiting factor. One type available at this time was a shrapnel bomb, painted red, weighing 10lb, with a small parachute attached to give it directional stability. Another new type, called the Mélanite bomb, weighed 26lb and had a striker in the nose to detonate it. It was a converted French shell, and was soon withdrawn as being unsafe. The 10-pounders were carried in racks on the fuselage beside the pilot, who had to unload them by hand. The Mélanite was tied to the aircraft with string; the pilot cut the string with a knife and pushed the bomb overboard.

Photographs would be good too, for analysis at HQ, and leaning over the side of the aircraft with a press camera made clear the need for a purpose-made camera fixed to the aircraft and a mobile laboratory to develop the pictures.

The greatest eye-opener of all was the new message technology, the wireless telegraph, and the RFC had the only two military aircraft fitted with it.

Back in April 1914, a few aircraft and officers from RFC headquarters had been placed at the disposal of Captain (temporary Major) Herbert Musgrave of the Royal Engineers, a decorated Boer War veteran, a hugely important aviation pioneer and communications visionary. He would become the first commanding officer of IX Squadron. For the moment, he supervised technical work at the curiously named 'Concentration Camp', Netheravon, in all manner of subjects including meteorology, bombing and gunnery but, above all for Musgrave, wireless.

Wireless had been carried in airships since at least 1912. Airships could cope with the

Herbert Musgrave, first CO of IX Squadron, as a young army officer with his Boer War ribbons before joining the RFC and learning to fly. He saw the potential of airborne wireless telegraphy and did not let senior officers' lack of vision stop him developing it.

weight, but flimsy little aeroplanes struggled with the massive sets available at the time. Certainly there was no possibility of carrying a wireless set and an observer. He was left behind, so the pilot had it all to do.

On his staff, Musgrave had more Royal Engineers, in particular two men who would also be greatly significant in the early days of IX Squadron, Lieutenants Donald Swain Lewis and Baron Trevenen James, who became pilots. This small group made good progress with no encouragement from the great majority of those above, who largely regarded aeroplanes as fancy toys and airborne wireless as an unfathomable and irrelevant mystery.

Lewis and James made a trip in June 1914 of 30 miles, flying 10 miles apart, communicating wirelessly by Morse code all the way. What use that might be entirely escaped the generals.

Events overtook Musgrave. Lewis and others were transferred to No. 4 Squadron and to France on 13 August. They were the squadron's wireless section, not thought to be especially important and, at first, the only aeroplane-borne military wireless in the world could do little to change that view. Equipment was lacking and no more could be had. Wireless only worked if there were ground stations not too far away, but the Allies were in retreat and none could be properly established.

Lieutenant Lewis set out from St Quentin on 6 September in a BE2A fitted with wireless. On the official opening day of the Battle of the Marne, Lewis was working with 1 Corps. As the German commander von Kluck wheeled his First Army to meet the attacking French and British, he opened a gap between his own forces and the German Second Army. At its widest, this gap in the enemy lines was 30 miles or so. Lewis saw it, and sent a wireless message reporting his observations. The response was immediate, with British commanders sending their troops to join the French in charging through the gap.

This is the first record of a wireless message being sent on active service from a British aeroplane, to be received and acted upon, and so the first record of its kind altogether. Its significance was deeply appreciated. With one transmission, Lieutenant Lewis had changed the opinion of hundreds of generals on both sides of the war and made immediately necessary the introduction of fighter aircraft. From the German point of view, Lewis and his ilk had to be stopped, and not just because of their reports on troop movements.

It was a small step from reporting on troops and enemy installations, to the idea of target marking with wireless. You fire your artillery, I'll tell you where your shells are landing, you alter your aim accordingly. All very well, but the pilot was alone with his heavy, inanimate passenger and had to transmit Morse while flying, a full-time occupation in itself, with constant adjustments having to be made to keep his frail machine where the pilot wanted to be.

At first, the messages were what you might expect: 'A little short, left a little. You have them. Hit. Hit. Hit.' Later, maps with grid references would be in use, and codes devised on a clock-face plan so that a few Morse letters and numbers could indicate so many yards to the west, north or whatever of the bullseye, and the wireless sets would be light enough to afford an observer to send the messages.

Meanwhile, the solo pilot, flying his kite in the wind, being shot at, did everything. Perhaps it was just as well that the sets could not receive, so there were no questions or instructions from the ground. Those flyers without wireless, that is the great majority, had to signal with Very pistols, or flash messages in Morse code with a lamp.

As was often the way, progress was made because of the vision and determination of a few individual officers. In between original thinking and organisation to cope with a set of problems nobody had confronted before, and flying on operations, Lewis and James would go to Paris to buy wireless kit.

After initial scepticism at messages arriving by Morse key rather than horse, the artillery grew to love it. By 27 September, a Headquarters Wireless Unit had been formed at Fère-en-Tardenois, in Picardie, with Major Musgrave in charge. This was really no more than No. 4 Squadron's wireless flight with a new name, but growth was the intention. The demand for this kind of air co-operation already vastly exceeded the supply.

During the first Battle of the Aisne, starting on 13 September as the Germans, retreating from the first Marne battle, turned to face the Allies and thus begin four years of almost immobile trench warfare, stability of positions meant that it was at last possible to organise fixed ground stations for wireless.

General Sir Horace Smith-Dorrien reported in a telegram to GHQ dated 27 September:

> Today, I watched for a long time an aeroplane observing for the 6-inch howitzers of the 3rd Division. It was, at times, smothered with hostile anti-aircraft guns, but nothing daunted, it continued for hours through a wireless installation to observe the fire and, indeed, to control the battery with most satisfactory results. I am not mentioning names as to do so, where all are daily showing such heroic and efficient work, would be invidious.

The general was deeply impressed but there is more to his praise than is immediately apparent. He was writing to an informed audience, who knew that the ideal artillery spotter was a stationary one, the better to report accurately as firing progressed. This was why balloons and kites had been initially favoured. The unnamed pilot, almost certainly Lewis, had to try and maintain his position relative to where the shells were aimed, which also made him a stable target for the enemy.

There was also indiscriminate small-arms fire from British troops, which led to the application of a Union Jack to the wings' undersides, but this was easily mistaken for a German cross, so the French system was copied, with the colours changed around. From December 1914, the RFC and the RNAS flew with the red, white and blue roundel. Manfred von

Richtofen, the Red Baron, at this time in the trenches, said that he and his fellows never realised that aircraft carried distinguishing marks and so used to fire at all of them.

With such foundations laid, the ninth squadron of the RFC was formed on 8 December 1914 with headquarters at St Omer, the first RFC squadron to be constituted overseas. This was twenty-two days before the eighth squadron was formed.

The CO was the British army's most enthusiastic and successful wireless man, Herbert Musgrave, and among the officers were Lewis and James, now captains, commanding 'B' and 'A' Flights respectively. This heroic and efficient pair would fly many, many missions but would not last the war. Captain B T James MC, by then of No. 6 Squadron, would be killed on 13 July 1915. His CO would report:

> [Captain James] was observing from the aeroplane alone as he generally did. He was ranging a battery and was being heavily shelled. His machine was hit by a shell and was seen to dive to the ground from a great height. The Germans dropped a note from one of their machines saying that he was dead when he fell. He met the end I am sure he would have wished for – if it had to be – suddenly, alone, and doing his duty.

On Lewis, a fellow officer noted in his diary: '[He] came in from spotting with his machine shot full of holes. I believe he likes it.' In February 1916, Lieutenant Colonel D C Lewis DSO, OC Second Wing RFC, co-operating with the Second Army in the Ypres Salient in a Morane Parasol, would be brought down by a direct hit from anti-aircraft guns.

With no serious bomb load possible on these little aircraft, and with the low-flying risks necessary for accuracy in dropping from the hand, the chief objective of air warfare remained scouting for the artillery and spying in general, with some active but non-strategic support for the infantry.

To start with, No. IX's main aircraft type was the BE2A, but there were Blériot XI monoplanes too, and Farman Longhorns and Shorthorns. Fitting these with continuously redesigned wireless sets of at least three different basic types was a challenge to be met by a very scarce resource, trained wireless mechanics. The few there were worked under canvas and slept in barns, trying to fit in some training of others while meeting the non-stop demands of the artillery and wishing some help would turn up soon.

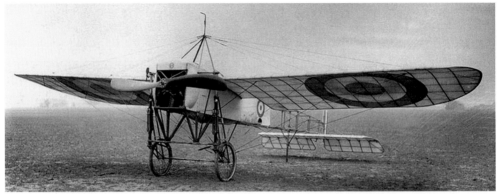

The Blériot XI monoplane, not greatly different to the 1909 Channel-hopper, the Farman MF7 called Longhorn for its front-mounted elevator held by elongated skids, and the Farman MF11, called Shorthorn because it wasn't a Longhorn, were among the original equipment of IX Squadron. The Shorthorn could climb to 3,000ft in 15 minutes; both Farman types were nicknamed 'Rumpty'. All three were French designs with French engines – the Farmans had the Renault V8 70hp, the Blériots had the 80hp Gnôme (rather than the 25hp Anzani three-cylinder as originally fitted).

As the new year turned, the squadron had nineteen officers and eight aircraft. Two of their BE2As, one Longhorn and three Shorthorns had been wrecked in one way or another not involving the Germans, the Farmans all on the ground by a storm. The airman's slang for an aircraft, 'kite', was highly appropriate for these lightweight machines of wood, wire and fabric, and tying them down with guy ropes and pegs was only effective up to a point.

Even in these circumstances, the pressures of war forced rapid development of wireless sets which soon shrunk to make room for an observer again who, from above enemy positions with a pilot concentrating entirely on flying, could send comprehensive information to his fellow soldiers on the ground.

Major Herbert Musgrave was awarded the DSO and went back to the Royal Engineers, where he would serve as Deputy Assistant Quartermaster General. He would be killed in action, aged 42, in June 1918.

Royal Flying Corps soldiers earned 2s a day (10p, worth about £5.50 in today's money) as an Air Mechanic Second Class, up to 6s for a Sergeant and a few bob more for officers and those trained as Flyers, 'with Free Clothing and Necessaries, quarters, rations, fuel and light'.

The British army commanders decided that all their squadrons should have wireless flights, and so No. IX became the supply centre. As flights were formed, trained and equipped, they were sent off to other squadrons until there was one left, C1 Flight, flying Shorthorns under the command of Captain Hugh Caswell Tremenheere Dowding, later Air Chief Marshal Lord Dowding GCB, GCVO, CMG, head of Fighter Command in the Battle of Britain.

The squadron's first casualties were not due to enemy action. A flying accident at Neuve Chapelle, where it was briefly stationed on reconnaissance for the General Staff, killed two men of C1 Flight, pilot and flying school instructor Lieutenant Albert Ernest Morgan, aged 25, and observer Second Lieutenant Aubrey Gordon Irving, South African, aged 27. Irving had served in the Boer War at the age of 16, took a double first in engineering at King's College, Cambridge, and had almost completed his qualification as a doctor at St Thomas's when the war began.

That Flight was transferred to 16 Squadron on 22 March, and No. IX was briefly no more. Dowding went back to England with half a dozen men to reform at Brooklands on 1 April 1915 and, under his command as Major, No. IX became the de facto wireless school of the RFC.

Individual officers and extempore methods were still the routes to progress. Among the wireless contingent of the Cumberland and Westmorland Yeomanry, seconded to IX Squadron, was Lieutenant Prince who deeply impressed his CO, first by acquiring large quantities of wireless components from non-military sources, and then by devising an airborne wireless telephone. Dowding, second in a long list of IX Squadron commanding officers, was thus the first man to receive the spoken word transmitted from a mobile phone in the air. The receiving set, however, was much too heavy to be described as mobile.

Those powers responsible for the allocation of aircraft and pilots seemed to view No. IX as a technical establishment not requiring very much of either, and over the early summer Dowding had to make do with a small collection

The wing-warping BE8, here in prototype, was a very basic aircraft, or 'general purpose', we might say. Compared to those earlier, open-frame designs like the Farman III, and with ailerons added in the BE8A model, it did offer a more stable and reliable platform on which to learn to fly more adventurous machines.

of the older types of machine. Posted to Dover in a dual role, air defence and pilot training, the squadron had a couple of BE2Cs and a Martynside Scout for the former job and five BE8As for the latter. The BE8A was the pre-war BE8 that was steered by warping wings, but fitted with BE2C wings which had ailerons. If it was ever meant for action it never saw any, but it served well as a trainer.

The Martinsyde Scout was a single-seater that could manage almost 90mph. It was converted to fighter by adding a single .303 Lewis gun, mounted on the top wing and firing over the propellor, which was very difficult to aim and fire and even more difficult to reload.

All this, however, was about to change. From being the pioneers, professors and tutors of wireless in the air, No. IX Squadron was to be re-equipped with the best available aircraft and sent to the Front.

CHAPTER 2

Life and Death in France

Wireless, camera, action

By December 1915, in the charge of Major J A Wanklyn, No. IX was back in France as an army co-operation squadron, working at the front line, mainly in reconnaissance and artillery spotting, and giving air support to ground-force attacks. The equipment was a full complement of twelve of the C version of the BE2, usually called The Quirk. While the BE2 was indeed experimental when it was selected for the British army in 1912, by the time the men of IX Squadron made their first bombing raid on 17 January 1916, in seven BE2Cs flown solo with two more as escorts, the experiment was over and the 'Fokker Scourge' was at its height.

The BE2C was IX Squadron's main aircraft for most of 1916. The power unit was usually the Royal Aircraft Factory RAF1, basically a 90hp version of the Renault V8 70hp, which produced a little over 70mph at service heights (80mph at sea level) and took the machine up to its maximum 10,000ft in three-quarters of an hour. Although a considerable improvement on earlier BE types, with new wing and tail designs making it a very solid and stable flyer, those pre-war priorities for reconnaissance made the BE2C vulnerable to the first German fighter aircraft and a sitting duck for the later ones.

The Quirk had a British version of the Renault V8 engine giving 70mph or so at 6,000ft, more at lower altitudes. Because it was almost impossible to fire a gun productively from the observer's cockpit, the best armament was two .303in machine guns mounted offset on the fuselage. Quirks could also carry a few bombs, experimental ones, on experimental racks under the wings. The definition of a large or heavy bomb then was one of 22lb or 10 kilos.

Compared to the new German fighter, the monoplane Fokker E Series called Eindecker, the BE2C was slower by 15mph and built for stability rather than aerobatics but, even more importantly, the Fokker could fire its Spandau machine gun forward through the propeller by means of its synchronisation gear. The advantage this gave was a revelation, and the mechanics of it were so precious to the Germans that pilots were forbidden to fly across the lines in case they were shot down and their secret discovered. *The Times*, 6 January 1916: 'The Fokker is a monoplane, expressly built and contrived for fighting and for pursuit of the enemy, to which duties its activities are by strict order confined, and for which it is specially adapted on account of its high speed.' The first of the E Series could do 87mph. Later models were faster. *The Times* continues: 'The Fokker's machine-gun, being fixed, and fixed on the same plane as the body of the machine, fires through the propeller. Such bullets as miss the propellor naturally carry straight to the front; while such as are intercepted by its blades are dispelled by angled and bullet-proof "deviators" attached to the back of these blades.' Either the press really believed the Germans were using this tried-and-disproved French method of deflecting bullets, or they were forbidden from telling the truth. One RFC officer wrote: 'We have not got the mastery of the air. We have the pluck, but we have not got the machines nor the organization.' He added that most of our machines were too slow to cope with the Fokker.

Such a new and deadly facility meant that the Germans, including early aces such as Immelmann and Boelke, could devise hit-and-run tactics so effective that the RFC reconnaissance squadrons like No. IX were severely restricted in what they could do.

By March 1916, with No. IX well into its duties over enemy lines – sometimes with one of their few Bristol Scout fighters flying shotgun – this message was sent from GHQ to the War Office: 'Under existing conditions, it is essential to provide protection in the form of patrols for machines employed on artillery work. Information can no longer be obtained by despatching single machines on reconnaissance duties. The information has now to be fought for, and it is necessary for reconnaissances to consist of at least five machines flying in formation.'

However, in those early months of 1916, German air superiority was gradually reduced and reversed as new French and British fighter types came into service that were more than a match for the Eindecker, and the slow and steady Quirks were back in business.

The Times visited the Front on 1 March 1916 and reported the business of RFC squadrons such as No. IX:

> There was never anything so little suggestive of effort as the landing of an aeroplane by a good pilot. It is the effort of organization, or specialization which makes the miracle possible. The fleet of aeroplanes derives its strength from the storehouses and workshops which have sprung up around it.
>
> In the storehouses, you will find every imaginable spare part, from engines to struts; in the workshops there are Army carpenters hard at work repairing the wooden lace of damaged frames, tailors sitting cross-legged stitching away at wing repairs which cannot be tackled by the sewing machine; electricians fitting wireless apparatus into the

The German front line in the early winter months of 1916 is seen here in a photograph taken from a IX Squadron BE2C. The camera, set into a hole in the floor of the observer's cockpit, was operated remotely by the pilot while the observer changed the plates, up to eighteen of them. They crossed the Front at 10,000ft, taking half an hour to reach that altitude, and would spend a further half hour on their work, perhaps 5 miles behind enemy lines.

machines, operators taking wireless messages from distant aeroplanes, mechanics seeing to the guns carried by the craft, and testing engines.

The task of the military airmen is three-fold and relates to strategy, tactics and artillery. For routine work at all events, it is under these three headings that the air is divided. In the first class come the flights covering some 30 miles of country behind the enemy trench line. The photographs and reports furnished by the airmen over this area enable the General Staff to have early information of big movements of troops and to gain some knowledge of the main line of the enemy's intentions. The second zone, which stretches for about 10 miles behind the trench line, is that in which more immediate tactical movements are prepared. The third area is along the front. Here the airman notifies changes in the enemy trench line, the position of enemy batteries, giving his own artillery the range.

All this work, this organization of detail, has but one aim – to give the Army eyes where formerly it had none.

The army generals' minds were concentrating hard on the forthcoming Somme offensive, and the IX Squadron portion of their eyes in the sky, now based at Allonville, was increasingly and intensively active, in photography and, in that third area along the front, 'notifying the position of the enemy's batteries'.

Extract from Royal Flying Corps Communique No. 31, 12 March 1916:

A Helping Hand. Lt. F W Lervill (IX Squadron) on leaving the ground in a BE2C lost one of his wheels. Capt. Egerton went up after him in a Bristol Scout to attempt to warn him. The machines collided in the air. For a short time they glided down together, but afterwards assumed a steeper dive and crashed, wrecking the machines and injuring both pilots. Both pilots are progressing satisfactorily.

Lervill progressed satisfactorily right through the war. Bob Egerton, ex-Sandhurst and Royal Irish Fusiliers, had been awarded the Military Cross in March 1915 and invalided home as unfit for any more trench work. He learned to fly, was posted to IX Squadron in December 1915, flew scores of operations and was sent home again after his attempt to warn Lervill. Five months later he was the first CO of the newly formed 59 Squadron at Narborough and was back in France in February 1917. Major Robert Egerton

The Bristol Scout was designed as a reconnaissance aircraft, but its excellent agility and high speed – up to 100mph – saw it armed and promoted to fighter. No. IX Squadron had the C version for escort duties in 1916.

MC was killed on 23 December 1917, when his aircraft, an RE8, partly collapsed in mid-air and went in, nose first.

The Bristol Scout was a nippy little fighter, even ahead of its time as an aircraft and certainly a better machine than the Eindecker, but without the German's ability to fire through the prop it could not reach its potential. No. IX Squadron was allocated four Scouts to act as escort to their BE2Cs; only one was still flying in June 1916.

Activities of No. IX in 1916, on allocation to 13 Corps on the far west of the British line, were largely dominated by the Somme offensive. By late May, the squadron had eighteen aircraft, twenty pilots and sixteen observers, the latter being trained on the job. Most observers joined the RFC without ever having been near an aircraft; getting them up to scratch was an urgent matter. The squadron had only been able to field six trained observers back in February.

One such became a IX Squadron hero, a Canadian backwoodsman and sharpshooter, William George Barker, who had been in the trenches before being accepted as an NCO for observer training, perhaps because of his great skills with a machine gun. He joined IX Squadron and from the rear seat of a BE2 he shot down a German machine by killing the pilot, and a few weeks later claimed another. He qualified as a pilot, which apparently took him less than an hour, so he had clearly learned a lot as an observer, and finished the war as Major Barker VC, DSO and Bar, MC and two Bars, plus a Mentioned in Despatches (MiD) for his kills with No. IX, and fifty accredited victories in all.

Through June, the squadron flew non-stop counter-battery operations; in fact, apart from a few routine patrols, they did nothing else. They even tried it at night, although without much success.

In the week leading up to 1 July, there was a massive artillery bombardment of those German positions discovered by the reconnaissance squadrons, and No. IX contributed 60 flying hours a day, weather permitting. Such artillery spotting was especially hazardous; if they flew above the trajectories of the shells, the smoke and haze made accuracy impossible, so they had to go down where they could see the shells landing and, incidentally, watch them go past.

When the Battle of the Somme began on a long, long summer's day, the squadron was in the air from 4am to 9.30pm, spotting for the guns, spying on troop movements, photographing and bombing the German trenches. The recce and camera missions often had fighter escorts from other squadrons, although the chief danger in 'contact patrols' – very low flying following the progress of infantry advances on 'battle days' – was from ground fire. For those on artillery wireless duty, without fighter escort, being hit by a British artillery shell always seemed more likely than being attacked by any German keen enough to join them in the two-way traffic of flying metal.

Of course, no form of flying was as dangerous as being a British army infantryman on that day, with almost 40,000 wounded and 20,000 killed.

So great was the volume of shells landing on the opening day that the wireless crews could give general information only and, seen from single aircraft of an individual squadron, the enormity of the Somme was not apparent. Their war was a series of small incidents, seemingly contributing to success but, it has to be said, in the great scheme of things not having a major influence.

Still, there was heroism, ingenuity and aggression in plenty. One No. IX wireless pilot called down artillery fire on a column of troops and vehicles with no result, so he attacked the column on his own. Captain Whittaker and Second Lieutenant Scaife were watching the enemy advancing in the sunshine when a support battery began firing. Whittaker took his BE2C down to 700ft, Scaife raked the battery with machine-gun bullets and the battery stopped firing. They also attacked a column of troops, and Scaife meanwhile drew a map showing the limits of the Allied advance in that sector which, it turned out, was the greatest of the day. With IX Squadron's help, 13 Corps had moved forward 1,500yd.

This observer, Thomas Earl Gordon Scaife, ex-Dragoon Guards and an original member of IX Squadron in the move to France, would become something of a legend over the next few months, earning the Military Cross for 'conspicuous gallantry and skill when on contact patrol work during active operations, often flying low under heavy fire' (*London Gazette*).

On one occasion, with petrol leaking at an alarming rate after being hit in the tank, he managed to stop the holes, although with what it is not known, so the machine could make it back across the lines and home. On another, he watched with his pilot Lieutenant Pollack as British soldiers left their trenches, forced the Germans to retreat, but were held up by a machine-gun crew. Pollack flew down for Scaife to silence the machine gun so the British could move forward again.

These contact-patrol aircraft had a klaxon, with which to signal to advancing British infantry and, provided the pilot flew low enough in all the noise and mayhem, the soldiers might hear and understand the codes being tooted to them by the observer.

Scaife would fall a few days after his MC was announced, to a direct hit from an anti-aircraft shell on his BE2E, killed with his pilot Lieutenant Bernard Tarrant Coller, another IX Squadron original, 22 years old, on 26 September 1916.

To have lasted so long was in itself a remarkable achievement. Taking IX Squadron figures over the whole war after the landing in France, December 1915, less than 5 per cent of air crew managed nine months like Coller and Scaife. A third lasted less than one month, of whom almost half were war casualties, the rest being hurt or killed in accidents, sick for some other reason, transferred to other units or sent back home as unsuitable.

Equipment was changing, with the arrival of the D and E versions of the BE2. The D was an odd design, basically a C with an extra set of controls for the observer, and larger fuel tanks. It was slightly faster than the C in level flight but the increased weight gave it a much slower rate of climb, so it was swiftly relegated to training duties only. The BE2E was meant to be a great improvement on the C, in response to the C's poor reputation against German fighters, but it was still using the 90hp engine, was only 10mph faster and was no match against – for instance – the German Albatros D2 that could make over 100mph and climb at twice the rate. Nevertheless, this was the best that could be had and so IX Squadron and many others had to go to war in it, whatever the risks.

During the Battle of the Somme, the squadron moved to Chipilly, sharing with a French escadrille, then to Mourlancourt, and it was from this base that the squadron's aircrew saw tanks in their first deployment, at the Battle of Flers-Courcelette in September 1916. These fearsome new weapons had been rushed to the front too early and in too small numbers. They proved unreliable

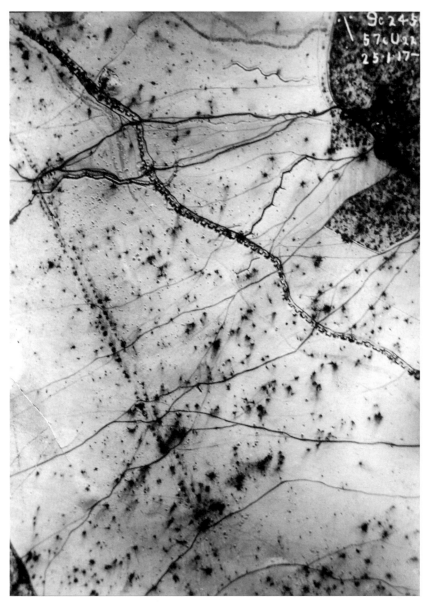

On this day, 25 January 1917, the Germans attacked at Verdun and moved the French back a mile or so, and at night the German navy shelled Southwold, Suffolk. Here, on the west of the line photographed by No. IX and manned by 14 and 15 Corps, things seem quieter.

and, bogged down in the awful terrain, could not punch the hole in the German lines that Haig had hoped for. Their hour would come; meanwhile IX Squadron had another new weapon, the hundredweight bomb, 112lb, roughly one-hundredth of the weight of the Tallboy bomb that IX Squadron would use to disable the battleship *Tirpitz* in 1944, see p. 162. Two IX Squadron crews took two hundredweight bombs each, the limit for the aircraft to carry, to drop on Roisel railway station.

The weather dominated the rest of the year, with stalemate in the Somme while the usual round of flights was being made when conditions allowed, with the usual casualties, including Stanley Mann, an observer on the Roisel raid, aged 21, and his pilot Second Lieutenant Arthur Wynn, aged 20, shot down behind enemy lines on 1 November 1916.

In the new year, with a new CO in Major I A E Edwards, the weather remained unkind to flying but jobs were done when at all possible, one of which led to a historic opportunity that, alas, was largely missed by the Allied generals.

The final version of the Blériot Experimentals, a IX Squadron BE2E, is seen here in early spring 1917. This one, No. 7189, survived four months, long enough to be replaced by the new equipment, the RE8.

Morlancourt, near Amiens, was IX Squadron's base from September 1916 to April 1917. Of their twenty-one different homes in the First World War, only Proven in Belgium provided a longer stay.

General Ludendorff, nominally the second in command of the German forces to von Hindenburg but really the prime mover, had ordered a strategic retreat of his armies on the Western Front, to provide time and opportunity for reorganisation, replenishment and refreshment. That there had been such a retreat, in fact to the Siegfried (Hindenburg) Line, was discovered by IX Squadron pilot Captain E L H Williams, who was surprised to find, on a reconnaissance flight at the beginning of March, that there were no Germans anywhere.

This led to a flurry of activity in support of cavalry units attempting to keep in touch with the disappearing enemy, an interesting development of modern warfare, with these Johnny-come-lately flyers instructing ancient regiments of horse about where to go next. 'C' Flight of No. IX was dedicated to this task and was moved forward to a tented base at Mons-en-Chaussé, while 'A' and 'B' Flights carried on with their scouting and messaging for their army masters, now 14 Corps.

This Corps' withdrawal for rest coincided with a new programme of formation flying for the squadron, with daylight bombing raids in mind. There was also one night-flying practice; thereafter, the squadron would often supply a machine and crew to joint night raids, usually on railway stations.

The plan for the daylights was much more ambitious. Six BE2Es were to be escorted by six each of FE2B fighters and Sopwith Scouts, known as Pups, from other squadrons. The Sopwith Pup had the synchronising gear that allowed it to fire through the prop and, for a while anyway, it was superior to anything the Germans had.

The FE2B, Farman Experimental 2, was, like the BE2, designed by Geoffrey de Havilland at the Royal Aircraft Factory, the Farman in the name only meaning that it was a pusher. It had forward and backward firing machine guns operated by the observer. It had been an important factor in reversing the Fokker Scourge but it had had its day by now. The observer stood on his seat to fire his forward gun, and got out of the machine altogether to stand on the rim of his cockpit to fire the backward one.

Bombing was a highly controversial matter, with all those doubts still about 'hitting the right building', illegally destroying private property and, worst of all, injuring and killing civilians. Extract from the diary of a Belgian priest, 4 December 1916:

> At midnight, a German plane flew over Reningelst by moonlight. At the d'Hemelstrate Inn, on the Poperinge road, it dropped three bombs. One fell on the Bulteels's house and exploded in the attic. It was a terrible disaster. Four children were sleeping there. One of them, aged four, was killed instantly. A girl of thirteen was hideously wounded and died the same night . . . boy of nine, also badly injured . . . recovered . . . another son escaped unhurt . . . (downstairs, the youngest child) was hideously mutilated and died.

The FE2 was not the only aircraft living beyond its prime. The Quirk, in its E version but still basically the same aircraft designed in 1911, was not up to the job now assigned to it – bombing, and, in contemporary terms, heavy bombing at that.

The squadron's first ventures in organised bombing were not an unqualified success. The 20-year-old Captain Reginald Lowcock, who had led 'C' Flight on its cavalry and camping assignment, was given charge of the inaugural raid, 4 April, the aircraft carrying two hundredweight bombs and no observer, but the weather was too bad to press on. Next day was better, when IX Squadron and more machines of 4 Brigade (of which No. IX was part) were led by Lowcock to the railway junction south of St Quentin. They got there, more slowly than expected as a headwind would not permit the planned speed of 65mph, but the bombs were dropped and there were no losses.

Another raid was mounted the following day but this time the wind was so strong that no headway could be made and they could not get across the front line. After an hour of flying on 11 April, the bombers still had not managed to join up with the fighter escort and so had to come home. They tried lightening the load, with six 20lb bombs each, which was satisfactory as far as it went, but when five Quirks of IX Squadron set out on 24 April, only two came back.

One of these was a new one, just arrived, and they kept coming, and they were sent on more bombing raids up to the last week of May when the move to Nerlu and re-equipping with the RE8 was complete under a new and very popular CO, Major Jack Hunter, whose speciality was flying in the worst weather, to check if operations might be possible for his pilots.

RE8 A4366 lasted two weeks of August 1917 on IX Squadron. Here it is on 21 August, its demise being officially noted as 'force landed', possibly after engine failure, possibly after supporting a small British advance near Lens.

The officers of IX Squadron assemble with their CO, Jack Hunter, seated sixth from the left, 20 October 1917, at Proven. George Fuller (see p. 27) is second row standing, fourth from right, and Captain 'Rosie' Hilton (see p. 33) is two along from him. Third from the left in that row, looking slightly questioning, is Lieutenant Robert Cameron, an observer for whom the daily danger became too much (see p. 31).

Reginald Lowcock, with his observer Lieutenant Leach, in the last days of the BE2E, proved that it was still a worthy chariot in the right hands. They were famous for coming home from contact patrols with many bullet holes after flying very low indeed.

Major Reginald John Lowcock, DSO, MC, still only 21, would be killed in an accident in England, flying a Bristol F2B fighter, on 22 July 1918. His Military Cross, awarded in December 1916 when he was on No. IX, was for beating off an attack by four enemy machines while continuing his artillery ranging, and for flying at below 1,000ft in a zone full of 'friendly' shells, to silence a German battery. His DSO was also awarded for his work with IX Squadron. The citation said:

> For conspicuous gallantry and devotion to duty in carrying out artillery observation with great skill and success, in spite of very unfavourable weather and strong hostile opposition. On one occasion, although attacked by five hostile machines, he carried on with his work until his machine was riddled with bullets and he was wounded in the leg. He then succeeded in landing safely, having destroyed one of the hostile machines. He has also done some exceptionally fine contact patrol work.

So, in flew their new machines, the Royal Aircraft Factory's RE8, Reconnaissance Experimental 8, which was an improvement on the BE2 but not much. Early models of this machine had shown a strong tendency to spin, which caused many accidents with inexperienced pilots. Modifications solved the problem but the poor reputation of the aircraft stuck for some time. It could do 100mph at 5,000ft with its twelve-cylinder engine and could climb to 13,500ft. If it stayed at such a height, having taken 45 minutes to get there, the pilot and observer in their open-air cockpits with no oxygen would have been near incapacitated in the winter cold.

A list of winter flying wear is provided by a IX Squadron RE8 observer, Lieutenant George Fuller: heavy woollen underwear, silk socks underneath wool socks, bedroom slippers with felt-lined leather soles and woollen uppers, overshoes, silk gloves under combination leather gloves with adjustable fur-lined mitts to cover fingers, Sidcot suit, woollen balaclava under fur-lined helmet, fur-lined face mask and goggles.

Even with all this kit, exposed parts could still freeze, and flying in an open cockpit could have much in common with Arctic exploration. It was especially hard on the observer, who had no benefit from the heat of the engine, and it was not unknown for him to fire his gun so he could warm his hands on the barrel, otherwise he would not be able to change his camera plates or operate his Morse key.

The specified armament was two machine guns and 260lb (118 kilos) of bombs, or about a quarter of one standard RAF bomb as used in the Second World War, although it was more usual on the squadron to carry two 20-pounders on patrol, to drop should a target present itself.

The RE8, called Harry Tate, was the most commonly used British aircraft on the Western Front and, despite it being a paradox, that is both experimental and obsolete at the same time, was still in service at the end of the war.

Here is the beginning of the list of RE8s coming into service with IX Squadron in May 1917, and what happened to them: A3103, crashed; A3208, missing; A3233, in use; A3245, burnt; A3255, direct hit, anti-aircraft fire; A3406, missing; A3407, wrecked. The following 6 entries are crashed, crashed, crashed, crashed, shot up, missing, and the list goes on for another 150 or so.

Even so, the RE8 was considered able to withstand a lot of punishment, which was as well because they were about to enter the Third Battle of Ypres. In mid-June, as part of the preparations, the squadron moved yet again, to Proven, western Flanders, near Poperinge, an airfield that was itself a cause of many losses. One IX Squadron man wrote: 'During the whole time I was there, it was a rare sight not to see an aeroplane in an unnatural position somewhere on or near the aerodrome.'

Part of the problem was the RE8's specified landing speed of between 70mph and 80mph, below which it would stall. The member of IX Squadron continues: 'This was all right on a big aerodrome but Proven was very small and one approach was over a belt of trees.' Another hazard was the hop poles that fringed the field.

> There were very many crashes, especially on landing. My pilot developed some nervous trouble that affected his landings. We crashed eight times coming into land and then the next crash was on taking off downwind, into a petrol store and onto a hangar where the machine turned upside down and I fell out and then the whole contraption descended on me.

By a near miracle, there was no fire. The pilot had a scratch on his nose and the observer here quoted had a broken arm which was accidentally set for him by his rescuers dragging him out of the wreck by his wrists.

Right through Ypres, the squadron flew spotting missions for the big guns, trench strafings and troop-movement reconnaissances, contact patrols and ad hoc bombing, with many sharp encounters, many losses and all to no strategic avail. The high command still believed that the effects of prolonged artillery bombardment before an attack outweighed the advantages of surprise. The real effect was to render the ground more or less impassable for the attackers and to give the enemy plenty of time to prepare his defences.

The bombardment before Ypres was especially heavy. The squadron's crews, out every day, twice a day, on long patrols plotting enemy batteries, again feared British shells as much as enemy action. During the whole of this Ypres period, No. IX suffered fifty-seven casualties, of whom twelve were killed by 'friendly fire'.

The advance began on 31 July with bad weather preventing the planned air support, and by the middle of August the army was stuck, waiting for the rain to stop and the ground to dry out. Squadron crews continued with their low-level reconnaissance and artillery registration through September, with no formal bombing raids, so intense was their army support activity.

Arriving on squadron as a probationary observer was Canadian Second Lieutenant George Fuller, after less than four weeks' training rather than the seven of the full course, including an hour on aircraft recognition. Having failed in pilot training, he did at least have a little more aerial experience than just that short time in school at Brooklands.

> I arrived, met Major Hunter, and was posted to 'C' Flight, which had two observers left after heavy casualties. I went into lunch in the large

tent that served for officers' messing, and was told I was going up on my first trip over the lines that afternoon. I was issued with a Lewis gun, introduced to my pilot, 'Titch' Turner, and up we went. My training had been mainly about wireless, with some photography and various other matters in theory, but there had been almost nothing on what to do when flying as an observer in a Harry Tate.

You sat with your back to the pilot, Morse key to one side, ammunition drums behind in racks. Your gun could be elevated, depressed and rotated on its ring mounting, the latter motion achieved by the weight of your body as you swung yourself around on your little upholstered stool.

The only way of communicating with the pilot was by tapping him on the shoulder. He would turn around and, if the message was complicated, throttle back the engine so he could hear you. Otherwise, we had a system of signals. For example, pointing and clenching the other hand meant a German machine. Pointing and tapping your chest meant it was one of ours.

Communication with the forces on the ground was also elementary:

Our wireless sets could not receive, of course, so our messages were answered by flashing lamp, called *panneau* (French for sign), which we could see if we were low or flying in the dark, or there was a coded system of strips of white cloth laid out. A simple straight strip, a dash as it were, meant message not understood. The letter L was guns ready, K was yes, N was no, and T was go home.

Our method for counter-battery work, called flash patrols, was to head firstly towards the target, the enemy artillery battery that had been decided upon, and check it. Meanwhile I wound down my aerial, a long, braided copper wire with a lead weight on the end, held in my cockpit on a wooden reel and let out through a hole in the floor. We then flew towards our own battery and give them the signal to fire, watched for the gun flash, and turned towards the German battery to see where the shell landed. We turned again, I sent the correction, waited ten seconds, and gave the signal to fire again. Our hope was always that we should complete the job before any hostile fighters turned up.

Sometimes we had fighter escorts, sometimes not. Occasionally we would have extempore protection from near-by 70 Squadron's fighter patrols, which would have been better if we could have kept

29

up to speed with them. On some artillery observation flights, called 'shoots', especially on our section of the Front, the German fighter squadrons were so active that the pilot had to do all the observer's work as well as his own, while I reverted solely to air gunner, to protect him.

On the way back from all these flights, except the photographic ones, we dropped our four 25lb bombs on a nominated target, often troop huts. These huts, we found later, were concrete pill boxes, so even if we'd hit them we'd have had no effect.

The rains came again on 7 October, turning mud into slurry. The crews of No. IX watched as artillery shells disappeared into the morass without exploding as British troops tried to advance at Poelcapelle on, 9 October, making a short gain and then having to pull back. This 'battle day' was a bad one for the squadron too, with three aircraft shot down and Lieutenants Sogno, Torry MC, Brasington and McMurchy killed.

Captain Alfred Youdale earned his MC and two Bars to it with No. IX during the Ypres and Passchendaele battles. Youdale was one of the first among equals, but his citation describes what amounts to the everyday duties of the squadron:

> Working in conjunction with our infantry, he rendered valuable assistance to the attack, flying several times through our heavy barrage and using his machine gun at very low altitude. His work has been consistently skilful and fearless during the whole of the operations, especially when engaged in contact patrols and in attacking enemy infantry from low altitudes.

Thus the *London Gazette* noted his MC on 9 January 1918; his first Bar was published on 18 March 1918: 'On one occasion he attacked from the rear, from a height of about 150 feet, the enemy that were holding up our infantry.' His second Bar, awarded for locating British positions at Passchendaele from 200ft in a snowstorm, was not published until 5 July 1918, by which time Captain Youdale was long dead, killed on 23 December 1917 after transferring from IX to 21 Squadron. George Fuller knew him:

> I was standing in front of the hangers one evening when Youdale and his observer, Ashcroft, came in. There were bullet holes in the machine and, as Youdale discovered, one in his flying helmet. It had gone right through, just under his chin, and his tie fell off onto the ground, cut as neatly as by scissors.

At last, the guns fell largely silent on the marshland burial grounds of Ypres. Many, many thousands of men on both sides had died, with a net gain to neither. The Americans were now in the war and the expectation was of new aggression and, perhaps, an end to it all, but while the Allied commanders and politicans argued about what to do next, Ludendorff – one man in charge of everything – planned a new advance.

This time, he would forego the usual mighty barrage in favour of surprise. He would assemble his troops, his poison-gas artillery and all the rest under concealment, whenever possible moving forces up to the Front at night.

Such great manoeuvrings could not be kept entirely hidden. Between October 1917 and March 1918, No. IX flew many, many reconnaissance patrols under a new CO, Major James Rodwell, to reveal the build-up of troops. One such patrol, on 22 October, spotted fifty-five enemy positions in a flight of over 2 hours.

A new duty for the squadron now was propaganda. A leaflet had been devised in London, showing a fat German in cook's garb, holding a plate heaped with buns. The caption translated as 'Just think of it – buns with currants', and the text extolled the virtues of surrender. Someone had gone to a lot of trouble because there was another leaflet with photographs of happy German POWs, gardening and playing football, and extracts from letters home telling how well they were being treated. These various travel brochures were bundled up, tied with pink string, and dropped by the observer through his camera hole while under close attack from archie (anti-aircraft artillery).

When a crew from 11 Squadron was captured with leaflets in its aircraft encouraging German soldiers to desert, the crew was court-martialed and sentenced to ten years. This dispute over international law was resolved when the men were released after reprisal threats, and the Chief of Staff ruled that such matter would henceforth only be dropped from balloons.

Pilots had the celebrity and most of the medals, but observers had a doubly dangerous position. They were the ones with the guns, so attackers paid them special attention and, if the pilot was killed in the air, the observer almost inevitably became a casualty too. There were rudimentary controls the observer could reach but these could be of use only if the pilot was out of business temporarily.

One man's death is a tragedy, or all in a day's work, depending on the viewing position. Lieutenant Robert Cameron, aged 21, had had plenty of excitement in his few months with the squadron. He had flown with several different pilots of varying competence – he'd survived four write-off crashes – and had driven off aerial German attacks on at least three occasions. On

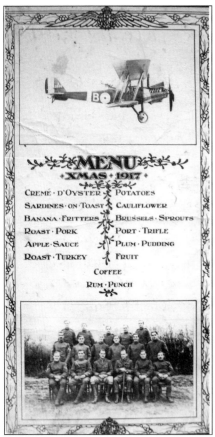

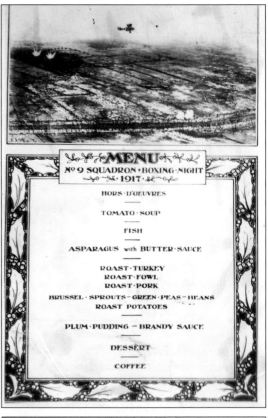

MENU
XMAS 1917

CREMÉ · D'OYSTER · POTATOES
SARDINES · ON · TOAST · CAULIFLOWER
BANANA · FRITTERS · BRUSSELS · SPROUTS
ROAST · PORK · PORT · TRIFLE
APPLE · SAUCE · PLUM · PUDDING
ROAST · TURKEY · FRUIT
COFFEE
RUM · PUNCH

MENU
Nº 9 SQUADRON · BOXING · NIGHT
1917

HORS · D'OEUVRES
—
TOMATO · SOUP
—
FISH
—
ASPARAGUS with BUTTER · SAUCE
—
ROAST · TURKEY
ROAST · FOWL
ROAST · PORK
BRUSSEL · SPROUTS — GREEN · PEAS — BEANS
ROAST POTATOES
—
PLUM · PUDDING — BRANDY SAUCE
—
DESSERT
—
COFFEE

The new CO, Major Rodwell clearly believed in doing things properly in the Mess, no matter how trying the circumstances, although 'Cremé d'Oyster' is still puzzling French scholars. RE8 A3930 arrived on squadron on 23 October 1917 and crashed on 22 May 1918 while based near Abbeville on the River Somme, possibly after a bombing raid on the railways at Liège. Meanwhile the plane was selected to decorate the Christmas Day dinner menu. Rodwell or no, that's his predecessor Jack Hunter in the photograph below. A different sort of notice for the Mess board ordered that bomb-dropping and machine-gunning will be carried out assiduously, and it is expected that a record number of bombs and machine-gun rounds will be expended.

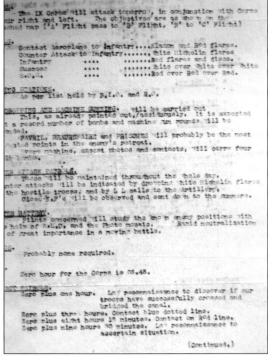

the morning of 7 January, seemingly confused and unwell, he went up with Captain Cripps and leaped from his cockpit, a thousand feet above the ground, to be classified as killed in action.

Captain 'Rosie' Hilton wrote that he had two of his observers killed and two more wounded, in the year he was a pilot with No. IX:

> I had several air fights, mostly unsatisfactory. Once I was attacked by two enemy scouts and my observer cried like a child and refused to fire, though they fired about 200 rounds at us. Foolishly I did not report this as I rather pitied his terror, which was akin to my own but more wantonly and stupidly expressed.

George Fuller noted that of his intake of seven observers, after six months he and one other went home hale, three had been sent back wounded and two were in the churchyard. Altogether in that time, the squadron had 157 killed, wounded or missing, enough to man a squadron more than 3 times over.

The somewhat elderly warrant officer (with stick, also seen thirteenth from the right, second row in the whole squadron picture, see p. 37) poses with his IX Squadron NCOs and some captured German artillery. It was common practice to transfer experienced men like him from regiments of the line to instil discipline into these fly boys of the RFC.

CHAPTER 3

Peace and the RAF

When the German offensive came in early March, the squadron's role switched to direct attack, including night bombing on railway targets and ammunition dumps and daylight raids on infantry, but a move back from the battle to GHQ Reserve had been planned for 11 April and that went ahead regardless of the situation at the Front.

This was really a two-month R&R withdrawal, to Calais, where flying was practised away from peril. The highlights were friendly dogfights with 70 Squadron's Sopwith Camels and exercises with the US 77th 'Statue of Liberty' Infantry Division.

The squadron went back to war on 6 June, based at Argenvillers, still classified as a Corps squadron but not allocated to any particular unit. The daily round of reconnaissance was replaced by formation bombing, at first with half a dozen machines carrying six 25-pounders each or two hundredweight bombs, later rising to twice that number, sometimes flying together, sometimes splitting into two attacks of six.

In July, with the German advance paused, the squadron moved to Quevenvillers and kept on with the bombing, while heavy Allied reinforcements, including tanks, moved up. German air superiority was finished by this time. The squadron in their RE8s could mount their bombing raids with fighter support, fairly secure at least from aerial attack. The new generation of British fighters – Sopwith Camel and a de Havilland design, the Royal Aircraft Factory SE5A, were as superior to the German craft as the Germans' had been to the BE2s. In 1918, the German air corps was putting around 350 new pilots on duty every month, to replace losses.

Ingenious new uses were being discovered for aircraft in war. As Allied troops prepared to advance, IX Squadron practised supplying them from the air, by parachute. No parachutes were issued to Allied airmen themselves, except for observers in tethered balloons, at any time during this war, and not only because of the old worry among the generals that air crew might prefer to jump and save themselves rather than continuing a fight or trying to land their precious aircraft. There was as yet no practical chute – presumably because the men running the war didn't see the need for such a development – that was small and light enough in the pack to fit beside or beneath the flyer. It was also thought that the parachutes of the day were bound to become entangled with a falling aircraft.

The Germans did devise one, and used it successfully towards the end of the war, but when IX Squadron went forth on 4 July 1918, the only parachutes they had were attached to the ammunition they dropped.

Twelve aircraft set out for an advance landing ground at Villers Bogade, where their modified bomb racks were fitted with metal drums containing the payload, two to each machine, which were to be dropped from 800ft. As the troops advanced, they would signal their new positions, and the aircraft would return to their forward base to pick up more drums.

Over this remarkable day, with many officers, junior and senior, doubtless wondering why nobody had thought of it before, around 100,000 rounds of rifle and machine-gun bullets were supplied, with IX Squadron crews each making 3 and 4 trips. There was a cost. Lieutenants S E Harris, W Knowles and Harry Riekie were all killed by small-arms fire from the ground, and four more were wounded.

By the time the Fourth Army attacked Amiens in early August, it was a matter of competitive pride among IX Squadron air crew to see who could drop the ammunition drums right into the trenches.

Another novel airborne tactic successfully tried in this attack was laying smoke screens for the Allies' terrifying new weapon, the tank, now being used in large numbers. The squadron sent six machines to drop phosphorus bombs, four 40-pounders each, screening the advance of the Fourth Australian Division, while hiding the flying ammunition-droppers from the enemy too. So successful was this ploy that sixteen crews went the next time.

Meanwhile, the squadron was flying low offensive patrols against troops and anti-tank guns, until 15 September when there was a move to Athies and duties were reassigned to reconnaissance ahead of the offensive against the Siegfried Line. Over the next fortnight, crews flew mission after mission, supplying information which was to direct the artillery barrage preceding the great attack. The squadron, if not the crews, had been here before; it was the same hunting ground as in 1916/17.

The Allied advance was unstoppable, and No. IX moved several times to improvised airfields to keep up and ahead. The weather interfered with some

The whole squadron poses for the camera in 1918. Note the mixture of RFC and RAF uniforms.

of the work but it was, at last, all over. During the final few months, seven Distinguished Flying Crosses and two Bars had been awarded to squadron officers.

After the Armistice, the squadron had their RE8s replaced by Bristol Fighters and an SE5A, and moved to Germany, where they had a fairly relaxed time. Some privileged officers stayed at Ludendorff's country house near Cologne, while a special detachment was based at Spa, Belgium, returning to their origins of wireless development, attempting to prove that air crew could receive messages from the ground.

Flying was like rehearsing for the war that had been, with reconnaissance, photography, formation practice and general co-operation with 9 Corps, the squadron's last army colleagues. There was also rugby, football and riding, and why not?

At the start of the war, when No. IX was formed, the understanding of air warfare, of the design and construction of flying machines, even of flying itself, was primitive to say the least. By the Armistice, 200,000 aircraft had been built by the combatants and something like 75,000 air crew had been killed, wounded or captured.

The early machines had been 50mph motorised kites, looking to modern eyes like a joint venture between a seamstress and a bicycle mechanic. Considering such a starting point as a Maurice Farman Longhorn, we should marvel at the speed, sophistication and agility of fighters such as the SE5A, the Sopwith Camel, the Fokker Triplane and so on, only four years later. But what of the bombers, of IX Squadron's future reason for being?

Here is Ronald Birnn, a lieutenant colonel in the American air corps, writing in retrospect: 'Aircraft were used mainly in World War One as adjuncts to the older arms. Commanders employed them very largely for observation aloft, carrying out in greater detail and increased mobility, the sort of work that balloons had been used for in earlier wars, in the Crimea, and by the union forces in the [American] Civil War.' So? Would aircraft always be an adjunct to the older arms? Another expert, writing anonymously, said:

A navy acts mainly by economic methods, through control of overseas communications; the result of this will not usually be apparent for a considerable time.

An army ultimately brings pressure to bear by occupation of the enemy's country but cannot do this until it has disposed of the enemy's army, usually a slow and costly process both to life and property.

An air force acting separately can contribute its share of pressure in several ways; by dislocation of the normal life of the people, by deprivation of supplies through attacks on transport systems, by bombing the centre of government. Many of the objectives which an air force can attack at the beginning of a war, could, prior to the advent of aircraft, be reached only after prolonged fighting. This power of bringing direct pressure to bear upon its enemy from the start of a war, is a deciding factor in reducing the time required to compel an opponent to come to terms.

Britain had that aerial ability to act separately; she had the Royal Air Force, the world's first independent air force, formed on 1 April 1918 out of the RFC and the RNAS. As the war ended, that force was 188 squadrons, more than 22,500 aircraft and 290,000 servicemen, the greatest in the world.

This had been the war to end all wars, the country was in dire financial straits, and massive reductions in the armed forces had to be made. Additionally, the top brass of the Royal Navy and the army were quite certain that the RAF was unnecessary, and any bits of it that might be useful would be better re-incorporated into the 'older arms'.

It was less than five years since General Haig had said that it would be foolish to think that aeroplanes could be usefully employed in reconnaissance. Even with all the experience of the war, there were still senior military men who were unbelievers. Aircraft ferried people and things about, did some reconnaissance to help out the cavalry whose job it really was, and spotted for the artillery. The pilots were a lawless gang of playboys and hotheads for whom a spell in the trenches would have done the world of good. Aces of the RFC had had their dogfights with the Red Baron's circus but that was on a par with hunting, shooting and fishing. It was nothing to do with force of arms or the course of a war. It was no more than duelling between offended officers. Where was the power in that? If you wanted to make a big mark on a battle, on land or sea, you needed big guns to do it.

They were right in a way. Where were the big guns?

By the end of 1920, the RAF had been reduced to one fighter squadron and four army-co-operation squadrons at home; five Imperial policing squadrons in Egypt, four each in India and Iraq and one in the Far East. In round numbers, 23,000 officers, 21,000 cadets and 227,000 other ranks had been demobilised and the Women's Royal Air Force (WRAF) disbanded.

The RAF now consisted of 3,280 officers, 25,000 other ranks, most of it overseas. Under Trenchard, and through the foresight of Winston Churchill (a great believer in air power and the possibilities of bombing), it had to become the core of a new kind of war machine, one that, as Trenchard said, could 'grow larger and larger, and become more and more the predominating factor in all types of warfare'.

Although No. IX had been one of the 160-plus squadrons to be dissolved and dismissed, the disappearance was temporary. The rebirth and growth would be entirely to do with that philosophy, to an extent that could not have been dreamt of by anyone.

The intervening period, between disbanding in 1919 and reformation at Upavon, Wiltshire on 1 April 1924, was characterised by attacks on the RAF itself, by the two other services and by those politicans and others who thought it too expensive for Britain to afford. Its success in policing the Empire in a most economical fashion and, curiously, government concerns about the intentions of the old enemy, France, which had retained a much bigger air force, ensured the survival of the RAF and a plan to build it up to fifty-two squadrons for home defence over five years.

That plan never materialised in peacetime, but that part of it which was implemented, Trenchard made sure, included the capacity for offence, for strategic bombing. A large and powerful bomber force would be a deterrent to aggressively minded potential enemies, and so would ensure the peace as well as ensuring the continued existence of the RAF.

Here is a French expert, Georges Prade, writing in 1916. He classifies four uses for, and therefore types of, military aircraft: reconnaissance scouts, artillery observation machines, battleplanes (fighters or chasers) and bomb-droppers.

> The bomb-dropper is the Dreadnought of the air. (It) must include among its qualities a certain minimum of speed, climbing power, and manoeuvring capacity to enable it to escape from the fire of anti-air guns. As for chasers, bomb-droppers must not be expected to defend themselves against these. They must be escorted by squadrons which have nothing else to do. Bombarding fleets always include several squadrons, operating on well-determined itineraries, known in advance, at fixed hours. Thus, convoying them is easy. It has been found possible to group in this way 50 machines, which, flying in a triangle like wild duck, have gone as far as the large cities of South Germany. These machines must therefore have powerful motors – 200 h.p. – a large range of action, and large fuselage, permitting the well-aimed dropping of bombs by special apparatus. They should also carry a machine gun.
>
> This is the most difficult machine to construct, and the task of he who pilots it is both ungrateful and perilous – long raids over enemy territory.

CHAPTER 4

The Dreadnoughts

They should also carry a machine gun

The Italians had been flying a three-engined bomber, the Caproni CA32 carrying about 1,000lb load and three crew, since August 1915. The Russians had had the amazingly sophisticated Sikorski Murometz six months before that. The Murometz could carry 1,750lb of bombs and had a 300-mile range, and was probably the inspiration behind the Zeppelin-Staaken Riesenflugzeug, the Giant Flight Device which, with the Gotha, took over German bombing from their airships.

The first 2 Gotha raids, on Folkstone and London in the early summer of 1917, had caused 250 deaths and tremendous panic, but not the popular revolution against the war that the Germans hoped for. The French had had

The Vickers Vimy, produced at the end of the First World War, was the original equipment for the reformed night-bomber squadron, No. IX.

a fast light-medium bomber from the summer of 1917, the Breguet 14, a very successful design, top speed 112mph, top load 560lb of bombs (256 kilos). The Belgians used it too, and the Americans.

The British had given a certain modest impetus to building a big bomber, or a 'bloody paralyser of an aircraft' as Royal Navy officers put it to Frederick Handley Page soon after war broke out. The result was a long time arriving. The demands of the Western Front came first in almost all matters of aircraft development and production, and air superiority was deemed essential by Trenchard and Haig before large and slow bomb-droppers could be risked against the nimble chasers of the enemy. In any case, there were innumerable technical problems to be resolved by engineers working beyond their knowledge in designing aircraft with a hundred feet wingspan.

While most bombing continued to be in support of the army, the Gotha raids on England made retaliation a political necessity. The Handley Page O/100 became available towards the end of 1917 and raids were mounted against Germany with them and with DH4 and DH9 machines until June 1918, by which time the rather better aircraft, the O/400, was also in France, and that could carry the biggest bomb of the war, 1,650lb.

A new 'Independent Force' commanded by Trenchard was established in May 1918, to operate in strategic bombing without regard to the war on the ground. The results served to illustrate the potential of offensive air power, provided that, one day, the problems would be solved of navigation, target planning, communications, aircraft defence – in sum, once it was known how to mount an air raid effectively, especially at night.

Until the Armistice, Trenchard's bomber force went to Cologne, Mannheim, Frankfurt and other cities, looking for chemical works, steel works (easy to see in the dark), railways and aircraft factories, finding the job more and more difficult as the Germans increased their home defences – which, in turn, made matters less difficult at the Front.

It was not possible at the time to gauge exactly what effect the bombing had on its targets, or on a nation weary of war, dispirited by battlefield sacrifice and impoverished by naval blockade, but post-war evidence suggested that 550 tons of bombs dropped in 239 raids – a mere 2.3 tons per raid average – had given extremely good value, especially in terms of lowering civilian morale and the reassignment of military resources. If Trenchard needed any more convincing of the need for a powerful bomber force in an independent RAF, these few months at the end of the war provided it.

Contemporary technology still could not produce instruments to guide a pilot accurately through darkness or cloud. Airmen navigated by eye, map and compass, and sometimes by sextant. There were no powerful and reliable engines to fly high and far and fast enough with a really heavy load, nor a bomb or a bombsight that could enable hard strikes with repeatable surety. Nevertheless, there were aircraft.

The Vickers Vimy, named for the Battle of Vimy Ridge and first flown in November 1917, came too late to contribute to the war effort although it had been scheduled to bomb targets in Germany flying from mainland Britain, if allowed free and uninterrupted access and most of a fine day to do it.

The Vimy was smaller and neater than the O series, with a wingspan of 68ft as against 100ft, but it could carry a similar load much higher and slightly faster, and it could reach 5,000ft in 13 minutes as opposed to 23. Even so, it was a typical large biplane of the time, with a fixed four-wheel undercarriage and its two engines mounted between upper and lower wings. It could do 100mph (more with a following wind, see below) carrying 2,500lb of bombs but, with a range of 900 miles carrying rather less, it would have been flying on empty coming back to England from Germany. The crew would have been cold, too. The two gunners stood in open galleys like pulpits, one at the front and one amidships, and the pilot and observer also were free to air. Still, Alcock and Brown crossed the Atlantic in one, modified admittedly, averaging 118mph, with Brown climbing out onto the wings half a dozen times to chip ice off the engines with a knife.

Two Avro 504K collided in mid-air, 16 December 1925. One trainee pilot, Leading Aircraftman Dunn, was killed; the other, Leading Aircraftman Parrish, survived and continued his training. Another Avro 504K went out of control on 23 July 1926, forcing the squadron's first parachute jump when the same Leading Aircraftman Parrish was able to prove the effectiveness of this new equipment.

This was the machine to equip the reformed ninth squadron of the RAF, designated a night bomber unit, part of the RAF's long-range bomber group. At first, as with the three other 'new' squadrons, Nos 7, 58 and 99, the idea of long-range bombing, at night or otherwise, came a poor second to the realities of collecting aircraft, organising facilities to support same and training air crew and ground crew.

It was a case of teaching themselves to be a squadron. In May, No. IX set up at Manston with two Vimys and several Avro 504s, and began a programme of training flights, air testing and camera-gun practice with the 504s as attackers. As more aircraft were assigned and more flying instructors and students turned up, formation flying could be attempted, and some serious long-range endurance tests undertaken. The first such lasted 5½ hours.

At the end of 1924, there were fourteen pilots on the strength, eleven of them officers. In the new year, the Vickers Virginia Mark V began to arrive (earlier marks were basically prototypes), and a year later the squadron could say it was properly established, with a wing commander as CO, two squadron leaders as flight commanders, four flight lieutenants and eighteen flying officers.

The Vimy and the Virginia were not the shape of things to come. It was as if bomber design – and bomber thinking – had stopped in 1917. The Virginia in its final version, the all-metal Mark X, was slightly faster – it could overtake a Vimy at about 5 miles an hour – and could carry more – 3,000lb rather than 2,000lb – and further, 1,000 miles rather than 900. It had a better climb rate too, but it still never met the original Air Ministry specification.

As any aeroplane at all would be, it was adequate for chugging over restless natives in the noonday sun, for instance in Mesopotamia, modern day Iraq, and dropping a few bombs on them to keep them quiet, rather than the more expensive and dangerous option of sending in troops. The natives in question, armed only with rifles, did not shoot down many aircraft. As an anonymous contributor wrote in a contemporary edition of *Encyclopaedia Britannica*, 'Aircraft have proved of the utmost value for the control of semicivilised or uncivilised countries and for carrying out those classes of wars which may be grouped under the term of tribal operations'.

Being part of the home-based bomber group, No. IX was never called upon to do that and the situation in Mesopotamia, many years hence, would be rather different for the squadron in fast jets and the Gulf wars.

The British government's emphasis on Empire, the general economic situation and the national lack of enthusiasm for any new wars, would mean that No. IX would fly Virginias for a decade.

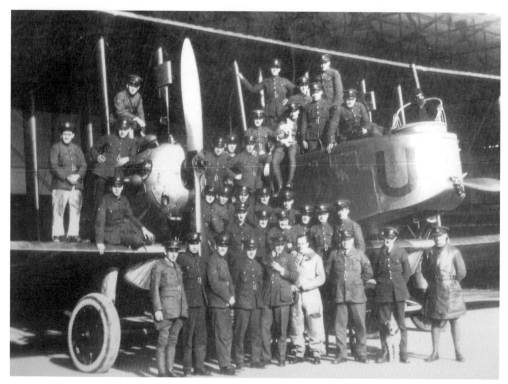

Rather than build always from new, Virginias were often remodelled to bring them up to the latest specification. A Mark VI like this one would be returned to Vickers to have its wings swept back and be reinstated at No. IX Squadron as a Mark VII. Virginia J7439, a Mark V that crashed in the sea in April 1925 with two fatalities, went back to Vickers, returned as a Mark VI, went back again, was given new, lighter metal wings and a fuselage with all-metal framework as the prototype of the Mark X, and reappeared at the squadron in that guise in October 1931.

The first Virginias were found by the pilots to be quite unstable compared to the Vimy, and a severe trial in awkward weather. That no one ever fell out was something of a surprise to all. Modifications to the wings – increased dihedral and giving a sweep back of 6 degrees – much improved stability in the Marks VI and VII, some of which the squadron had until 1930. The maiden flight of the Mark VII, with all its improvements, was made by a IX Squadron man, Flight Lieutenant Markham, rather than the Vickers test pilot.

The squadron spent 1925 training and practising in their difficult machines that required constant adjustments by pilots in everything but the calmest conditions. There was night flying, bombing, gunnery, landing on one engine, cross-countries and height tests. The theoretical ceiling of the Mark X would be given as 15,500ft. In a Mark VI, one IX Squadron pilot took her up to 12,200ft but that was the limit as the engines vibrated alarmingly.

The highlight of the year was the burgeoning excitement of the Hendon Pageant, an important and sociable component in the process of establishing the RAF in the minds of the people. No. IX flew Virginias in formation with Nos 7 and 58, which was the first time the public had seen the aircraft.

Another part of that agenda was the long-distance flights the squadron made, for example one by five Virginias in September, leaving Manston at night, climbing to 11,000ft and reaching Leuchars just under 7 hours later. Operations Record Book (ORB): 'Preparations for refuelling these had already been made and 1,625 gallons of petrol were put into the machines in 2 hours, together with the requisite amount of oil and water.'

The flight back, with a tail wind, took only 4½ hours. ORB: 'A letter of congratulation on this successful flight was received from the Air Council.'

The wind was very important in a flight, and there was no means of measuring its effects accurately from the bomber. In a strong crosswind, for instance, an aircraft behaved like a boat on a swiftly flowing river, heading for a specific point on the far bank but constantly drifting off course and having to make corrections. Any small difference in the expected wind, the wind by which the navigator made his calculations, and the actual wind could have fatal consequences if the difference was not noticed. The only reliable way of noticing was to see pinpoints on the ground, so this was a problem frequently unsolved, and it remained so even with the much more advanced and powerful bombers of the Second World War.

The routes of these flights were planned to pass over as many centres of population as possible, and the Virginias' excessively noisy Napier Lion twelve-cylinder engines made sure that everyone heard them go, as well as rendering the crew half-deaf for several hours afterwards.

By 1926, half of the promised fifty-two RAF squadrons had been established, and a scheme was well underway for training pilots on squadron from scratch. No. IX had had five of these pupils arrive in 1925, all Leading Aircraftman rank. One had been killed in a flying accident with another, W E Parrish, who survived his injuries and came back into training. The squadron's Avro 504s were the learner machines, and Parrish's went into a spin, on 26 July 1926, when a stray leather strap caught around the control column in the empty instructor's cockpit while Parrish was executing a loop over Margate. With his controls hopelessly jammed, he jumped out and parachuted to safety, while the crowds on the beach watched him float down and the machine crash to earth.

This was remarkable for several reasons. It would surely have been the first time those holidaymakers had witnessed an emergency parachute descent, since it was only the second time it had happened so far in the RAF. Although parachutes had been recently issued to the squadron, pilots did not usually bother to strap them on for routine flights, but Parrish had done so and was later called to the Air Ministry to describe his escape. A few weeks later, a full complement of chutes was drawn from the Eastchurch stores and fitted to all the Virginias, and thenceforth a different attitude prevailed towards them.

This happened after Hendon, on 3 July, when IX Squadron and, seemingly, all the bombers in the country took part in a long-distance trial and a bombing display.

Returning to normal duties had two new features. Defensive searchlight batteries had been set up to protect London against any potential European foe, which must have been the French at this stage, and the squadron flew many runs over them to give the operators some practice, but the greater novelty was the new radio beacons at direction-finding stations. Practice with the wireless telegraph was intensified and listening watches were kept on many flights, but the promised bearings were not often obtained.

The potential of IX Squadron's aircraft as war machines in Europe is illustrated by an incident on 2 January 1927, when Sergeant Richardson, flying a Virginia from Spitalgate, near Grantham, Lincolnshire, to Manston, in Kent, got lost above the clouds. The W/T bearing he received, perhaps meant for another crew, sent him to Oosterhout, near Breda in the Netherlands.

Pilot error in a Mark VII Virginia proved that ditching might be preferable to parachuting when Flying Officer R H Barlow, not realising that he had two petrol cocks turned off, believed his engines had failed over the Thames estuary, on night of 21/22 March. Unable to call for help other than by Very pistol and shouts, the crew of four sat on top of the machine for 6 hours before being discovered by a passing fishing boat. The Virginia stayed afloat to be towed into Sheerness, whence it was returned to Vickers and reissued to the squadron in serviceable condition three months later.

It was about this time that the question of a squadron badge and motto arose. The motto, *'Per noctem volamus'* ('We fly by night'), was less of a problem to the educated officers of No. IX than the badge which, it was decided, should be that unerring nocturnal aviator, the bat. A model for the artist was required and so, in the true spirit, those same scholarly fellows would go out in the gloaming and shoot one. Many cartridges later, a sufficiently entire specimen was obtained and its likeness transferred to the centre of the badge, in green, which was the night camouflage colour of the time.

The squadron's secondary motto, 'There's always bloody something' (possibly '*Semper aliquid cruentus est*') did not come about until much later.

Small duralumin bats were made by a man at Vickers and fitted to the aircraft and to officers' cars. The Mark VIIs were given names, after the kings and queens of Wessex, as the squadron was in the newly designated Wessex Bombing Area, and large metal nameplates commemorating Caedwalla, Ceawlin and others were attached.

ORB, 19 April, 1927, concerning the squadron's last Mark VI, which had been received in July 1926: 'Vickers Virginia J7714 crashed at Eastchurch as a result of striking another machine on taking off. The pilot, Flying Officer Kelly and the crew consisting of Pilot Officer Dowdeswell, Flight Sergeant Alderton and AC2 [Aircraftman Second Class] Daniels were killed.'

ORB, 29 June 1927: 'Photographs were taken of the the Eclipse of the Sun from a machine, which was flown to Catterick on the evening of the 28th. The results were satisfactory and an excellent view of the Corona was obtained from over Darlington.'

There was Hendon too, and continuous training and exercises. The squadron's two Flights were each sent on an intensive course at North Coates Fitties, featuring high-level bombing (8,000ft) by individuals and formations, air-to-ground gunnery from 200ft, air-to-air firing, night cross-countries and a final bomb-dropping exercise with the hundredweight bomb, one per crew. Over the whole course, the best average bombing error was 240yd.

When landing at night, where there was no flarepath or an inadequte one, pilots had to use a First World War aid, the Holt flare, invented by RFC Captain F V Holt. These were magnesium-fired lights, slung under the aircraft, operated by an electric button at the last minute so the pilot could check his landing ground. Surprisingly, perhaps, these devices rarely caused accidents, although IX Squadron did lose a Virginia Mark X in November 1935 when the flare failed to release and set the plane on fire.

Meanwhile, minds had been exercised about the poor defences of the Virginia against fighter attack, and the result was the prototype Mark VIII, which the squadron was asked to test. It was fitted with Rolls-Royce Condor III engines, 670hp, but that was not the essence of the matter. Two open gun turrets had been built into pods on the trailing edges of the upper wing. Thoughtfully, the pods were streamlined, to reduce their influence on speed, but the gunners stood with their upper halves exposed, aiming machine

Guests at a Manston station tea party enjoy a flypast by IX Squadron Virginias, 1928.

The Mark VIII Virginia was modified to provide extra defensive power although, at no more than 100mph with all three gunners in the open, it is difficult to imagine with much hope of victory. The gunners (from left): Leading Aircraftman Newton, Flying Officer Harvey and Leading Aircraftman Andrew of No. IX Squadron, had to clamber out to their turrets after take-off, wearing parachutes, via a ladder and catwalks. Comments coming back from the squadron resulted in senior officials trying it, and the Mark IX appeared without circus act.

guns at fighters coming in from behind and above. If they came in from behind and below, the gunners could do nothing without hitting their own tail.

The squadron's air crews thought very little of this machine, and said so, especially those deputed to man the guns, who had to climb to their turrets while the machine was in flight, via a ladder from the fuselage to the centre section of the wing, and thence outwards along a strengthened catwalk, and all the while wearing a parachute.

Officials of the Wessex Bombing Area, bravely deciding to find out for themselves what IX Squadron was complaining about, tried out this circus act of ladder and wing-walking while a squadron pilot kept the aircraft as steady as possible. With all opinions confirmed, the one and only Virginia Mark VIII was passed on to 7 Squadron, and from there to the dustbin of history.

The much more sensible idea of a rear gunner was incorporated in the Marks XI and X, by means of a turret, open of course, fitted between the tailplanes. The gunner could get into this before take-off.

Another innovation was the combined formal training of wireless operators as air gunners, the beginnings of the crew designation w/opAG that would last well into the Second World War. The squadron drew the extra flying pay for an establishment of eight gunners but generally had twice that number, and so divided the cash up between all who managed to scrounge a minimum of 4 hours flying a month by hitching lifts with pilots on practice flights.

They, and everybody else who flew for no matter how short a distance, had to take with them their shaving kit, in case of forced landings. Only two men in the RAF were permitted beards, one of whom was the 1926 CO of IX Squadron, Wing Commander Vivian Gaskell-Blackburn DSC, AFC, a notable First World War flyer who had also built his own machine to compete at Brooklands in 1913.

As a Flight Sub-Lieutenant, RNAS, Gaskell-Blackburn had taken part in the famous Cuxhaven raid on Zeppelin sheds, Christmas Day 1914, and won his Distinguished Service Cross for his reconnaissance flying over Turkish forces at the Battle of Kut-el-Amara, 1916. Tornado crews of IX Squadron will know this place as the city of Al-Kut, 100 miles south-east of Baghdad.

Gaskell-Blackburn, being ex-navy and so celebrated a figure, by some secret process was allowed to keep his senior-service adornment, during his IX Squadron posting and all others, and he still had it in 1941, as can be seen on his portrait in the RAF Museum.

That the Virginia was the RAF's main bomber for so long, twelve years and more, was entirely due to government spending priorities. In the same year as the comical Virginia VIII experiment, 1927, the Air Ministry issued specification B19, looking for a new bomber. It was hardly the most ambitious vision of the future, requiring a machine that could fly at 115mph for 920 miles, carrying 1,546lb of bombs. The spec looked even less enterprising in 1933, when the first machines to come from it began service. Meanwhile, with more muddle, and more failure to keep up with technical developments, it was apparent to the Ministry that no new bombers would be arriving soon and so fifty more Virginias were ordered. The RAF would still have a hundred or so of them going into 1936.

And so the round of training and exercises went on, with more tests of the London defence scheme, now with listening posts and anti-aircraft guns as well as searchlights, which the squadron flew over at 3,000 to 6,000ft. In one such foray, the squadron flew twenty-six bombing raids on London in three days.

There was a special display at Hendon for the Emir of Afghanistan, featuring Virginias of No. IX and Bristol Fighters of No. 2 Squadron. The display went off all right but in the rehearsal a fighter collided with a Virginia, killing the No. 2 Squadron crew, and on the way to Hendon a Virginia's starboard engine burst into flames. Flight Sergeant Grantham climbed out onto the wing with an extinguisher and was still getting the fire under control as the pilot landed the aircraft.

From 1930 there was an annual exercise at Catfoss, in the East Riding a few miles inland from Hornsea, where there were gunnery and bombing ranges. These detachments and all other flying were highly susceptible to the weather. Rain and cloud could make bombing and night cross-countries impossible and on one occasion, in 1929, night bombing had to be practised in daylight. Things had hardly improved by 1935 when the CO, Wing Commander G H Cock MC, watched the Virginias take off from Boscombe Down into a strong head wind, set off for Catfoss in his car and was there to greet his men when they landed.

Hendon 1930 had a special element, when the squadron was issued with three Vickers Victoria Mark V troop transports. There was to be a Troop Transport Event at the display but there was a shortage of pilots to fly these machines, which were a compilation of Virginia Mark X wings and tail and a metal passenger fuselage, with sufficient room inside for twenty-two fully equipped men, while the two pilots of course were in an open cockpit. The wings folded, so that smaller hangers in Empire outposts would be able to take them.

Over 100 of the Mark X Virginia were put into service with the RAF. Most were replaced in 1936, eleven years after IX Squadron took delivery of the earlier models. The Mark X was no faster but did have a better climb rate and higher ceiling. Note the tail-gunner's cockpit between the tailplanes.

The squadron only had the Victorias for a few weeks, long enough to practise for the display, and the same thing happened for Hendon 1932.

No. IX had moved to Boscombe Down in November 1930, and that would be home (shared with No. 10 Squadron) for the next five years, flying the all-metal framework Virginia Mark X. Like the Mark IX, this had a bomb-aimer's Perspex panel underneath the nose, below the front gunner's cockpit, and a tail-gunner's turret.

Various modifications were made to the Virginias, such as a new type of compass, and Handley Page slots, a patented addition to the leading edge of wings that altered airflow to allow better handling at low speeds. Also coming in were the first automatic pilots, which, it seemed, were an improvement on their human equivalents as better scores in bombing practice were achieved.

The tail-gunner's position, considered so vulnerable and especially dangerous in later years, proved to be the safest in crashes. ORB, 4 November 1930: 'Virginia J7561 [a Mark X] crashed near Manston and was completely destroyed by fire. First and second pilot, Flying Officer Goad and Sergeant Roberts were killed and AC2 Edwards, who was in the tail cockpit, was slightly injured. This aircraft had no slots.' The tail-gunner escape was not an isolated incident (see below).

There was a big change to the routine in mid-1932 when the results of the 1927 B19 specification were sent to the squadron for testing. Four designs had been approved. The Fairey Night Bomber, the Handley Page Night Bomber and an enhanced Virginia with different engines came to Boscombe, but the fourth competing proposal, the Avro 613 night bomber, was never built. ORB:

> In the summer [of 1932] pilots of the squadron tested experimental night bombers made by the following firms: Vickers, Handley Page, and Faireys. The census of opinion was in favour of the Vickers. The H.P. was nice to fly and easy to handle but doubts were expressed concerning the strength of the undercarriage. This collapsed at Upper Heyford for no apparent reason. After repairs the machine was crashed by F/O Matthias of No. 10 Squadron at North Coates Fitties. It caught fire and was burnt out. The Fairey was returned to the makers as the controls were found inadequate. The gliding angle was considered too flat for night flying on small aerodromes.

This may have been a case of 'better the devil you know'. The Fairey was a low-wing monoplane and so of startlingly different appearance to its biplane contemporaries. It eventually appeared as the Hendon, of which only fourteen ever entered service. Specification in round numbers: 150mph, range 1,400 miles maximum, bomb load 1,600lb.

The Handley Page may have had a collapsing undercarriage in prototype but it became the Heyford and RAF front-line equipment. No. IX Squadron would have twenty-one of them, and would still have five of them in May 1939, with three months to go to the Second World War.

The Vickers, known as the Type 150, came back for more tests in September, and was to be developed as the Vanox, which the squadron would test the following year.

ORB, 2 February 1933:

> Three machines of 'B' Flight endeavoured to carry out a camera obscura exercise at Bicester in adverse weather conditions. The first machine to leave the ground was J7129 with the following crew: Sgt R A Allen 1st pilot, F/O T P Pilcher navigator, Cpl C Smith wireless operator, AC2 E C Sholl wireless operator (upper turret), LAC Hipwell

rear gunner. This machine, in negotiating the high ground just north of Tidworth, struck a tree and crashed to the ground. All the occupants of the front cockpits were killed, trapped in the wreckage and burnt, the machine catching fire as it struck the ground. LAC Hipwell, who was in the tail cockpit, was thrown out into the flames but was able to escape with superficial burns.

Camera obscura exercises were normally done in clear weather, whether night or day, as good visibility was really a requirement, from the ground and from the aircraft. The bomber did dummy runs over a small building, a hut usually, which had a wide-angle lens fitted in the roof. The light coming through the lens became a picture of the sky on a flat table inside the hut. When the bomber dropped its imaginary bomb on the hut, it flashed a light, and the judge inside the hut marked the time and place and calculated the target error. The aircraft was usually fitted with its own camera too, so photographic evidence could be combined to give a reasonably accurate report. It was a long way from dropping bombs while under attack from fighters and flak guns but they had to start somewhere.

While Sergeant Hartley was having to make a forced landing in a field near Lincoln with a fuse box on fire, and again later with a boiling engine, the squadron had the revamped B19/1927 Vickers Vanox to test. It was a modified, slightly smaller Virginia, the only one ever built, and the modifications, of which it had many, were its downfall. ORB, IX Squadron, May 1933: 'It was found to be too unstable fore and aft to make a good bombing platform, and bombing was particularly difficult in hazy conditions. It offered no greater difficulty than a Virginia for machine gun firing. Successfully flown at night under full war load.'

The Station Sports in June were won by 10 Squadron, with No. IX second and Headquarters third. ORB: 'The result was largely due to Sgt Thomas, of 10 Squadron, who has been a member of the Olympic Team.'

Also on that day, a young sergeant pilot, Ian Borley, reported for flying duties. How Virginia experience would count when flying a Wellington under fire from Messerschmidt 109s, we shall see.

In searchlight co-operation exercises, 'cloudy weather hampered the programme to a considerable extent'. The recently arrived pilots 'gained valuable experience of flying in searchlight beams', but otherwise 'no new lessons were learned'. Air crew from the classes of 1939–1945 might have managed a wry smile at that, thinking of their experience of flying in searchlight beams, over Berlin.

Observer Corps duties were also cut short by the weather, likewise the first night of the Air Defence of Great Britain exercise. On the second night, 18/19 July, seven Virginias of the squadron, plus the Vanox, crossed the coast at the Needles and headed for Stratford-upon-Avon, where they were to bomb the bridge. No results were reported from the camera obscura.

Extensive co-operation exercises with the anti-aircraft brigades, who were using searchlights and sound locators, had mixed results. When the bombers glided in to their targets, they didn't make enough sound to be located and, according to the ORB, in the lights, 'It was found sometimes that, when two Virginias were flying close together, one would screen the other.' If the gunners thought this a great opportunity to get two old birds with one volley, or the pilots thought it an effective tactic, is not known.

Although the higher ceiling of the Vanox proved a benefit in such searchlight practice, it wasn't sufficient to persuade the authorities that the model was worthwhile. In any case, there was no real point in keeping on with it when the Heyford and the Hendon were already ordered and in production.

In May 1934, three Virginias of No. IX were scheduled to attack a fleet of Royal Navy ships, anchored at night off Portland. A flying boat was to discover the fleet's position and signal same to Boscombe Down, whereupon the three bombers would take off, plus two more Virginias each carrying a VIP observer, respectively an admiral and an air marshal. All went to plan so far. The intention now was for the leading bomber to illuminate the ships with parachute flares while two others bombed and two observed. As there was cloud down to 1,000ft they couldn't do any of it and had to go home.

It would seem, looking across all the different exercises, that good weather was essential for war, so many were cancelled through 'adverse weather conditions', although on one occasion the reason was the anti-aircraft gunners being redeployed to put out heathland fires. On consecutive clear nights, the squadron's full complement of ten Virginias bombed the Air Ministry, the House of Lords and Wormwood Scrubs prison, scoring five hits, 'though a great many raids were interrupted by defending fighters in the searchlight zone, both on the outward and homeward journeys', as reported in the ORB.

As well as fighter interruption, another drawback of night flying, it was found, was the need to reset the flarepath if the wind changed, and this could take an hour or more. Still, in daylight at the annual Hendon display and the Tidworth Tattoo, the bombers could fly in low to drop bags of flour in an attempt to knock over some giant skittles. ORB: 'This event seemed to be very popular with the crowd.'

In front of the all-metal Virginia Mark X, pilot Sergeant Stanley Byrne (third from right) stands ready to take his place in the open cockpit above. The officer pilot, third from left, clearly goes to a better tailor than the rest of them but it was Sergeant Byrne who was presented to the Prince of Wales (later Edward VIII) at Hendon, 1934, after the flour bags and skittles.

There was a review by King George V at Mildenhall, and the squadron moved to Andover in October 1935, where 'B' Flight was reconstituted as 214 Squadron, and thence to Aldergrove, where in March 1936 they took delivery of their new aircraft, the Handley Page Heyford Mark III. This machine, originating in that 1927 specification, ceased production in the same year.

The Virginias of No. IX had a final fling, on Empire Air Day at Aldergrove, when a large crowd in May sunshine saw a brilliant flying display, including parachute drops with dummies, a dive-past and dogfights, which had Westland Wallaces as attackers. The Wallace, successor to the Wapiti, was a single-engined, general-purpose biplane and the first aircraft in the RAF to have an enclosed cockpit.

The bombers were planned to lose the fights, and their defeats were signalled by flares under their wings. Trailing flames and smoke, they limped away at zero feet, to be given a last gasp of life in the hands of 214 Squadron.

By this time, the threat from Germany was becoming more obvious. The RAF went into a period of expansion, the number and frequency of exercises for IX Squadron increased greatly, and the new RAF Commands were formed – Fighter, Bomber, Coastal and Training.

Radio direction-finding, the early form of radar, was being installed at stations around the country, and one of the squadron's many tasks was to help the engineers calibrate their equipment, by repeatedly flying over the stations at set directions and speeds. Once satisfied, the engineers had their capabilities tested by the Heyfords flying in with groups of fighters. The squadron did much the same thing with the Royal Navy, co-operating in exercises with ship-borne radar.

The transition from Virginia to Heyford was effected without much trouble. It was just another biplane after all, if one requiring the pilot to take off and land in a cockpit 18ft above the ground. Defensive armament comprised three .303in machine guns – one in the front turret, one in the dorsal turret and one in the retractable 'dustbin' underneath. As with the facilities for pilot and observer/second pilot, the two gunners' cockpits were open which, given that the fuselage was fixed to the upper wing, meant that all had a fine field of vision. The other side of that coin was visibility to the enemy. The front gunner especially must have felt vulnerable, standing there, seen from the waist up, swinging his gun around and changing magazines when he ran out of bullets. The man in the dorsal turret could at least drop into the fuselage when he wanted to get into his dustbin, but once he'd wound that down and out, he was exposed again. One of the gunners operated the wireless when not under fire.

The Heyford's fuselage was metal clad at the front, fabric covered behind, and all the flying surfaces were fabric on metal frame. It could carry a 3,500lb bomb load but that would have to be halved if it was to reach its top speed of 142mph and maximum range of 920 miles. It allegedly had a ceiling of 21,000ft. On one petrol test, a IX Squadron Heyford reached 15,000ft where the temperature was measured at minus 13 °C.

In the matter of bomb carrying, it marked a kind of interim stage between the exterior racks of earlier craft and the bomb bays of Second World War machines. The centre section of the lower wing took the bombs, ready fused, in closed cells that were clicked into place by armourers lying on their backs on the ground, then plugged in to the electrical circuit ready for use. The

The Handley Page Heyford III resulted from a 1927 Ministry specification, a 1930 prototype and a 1933 Mark I. It was the last biplane bomber in the RAF. Although still on the strength in 1939, thankfully it never had to fly against a modern enemy. This one, IX Squadron's K5189, was written off during a training exercise in May 1938; no one killed.

crew, in their quarters built to the upper wing, could not get at the bombs once airborne.

More weaponry could be attached to conventional racks on the lower wing, outboard of wheels that had huge spats, streamlined in a futile attempt to make the thing go faster.

In October 1936, King George V officially approved the squadron badge and the squadron moved to Scampton, which wasn't quite ready for them so some of the admin accommodation was in tents, many of which blew away in a gale on the 25th. Six of the old No. IX Virginias, now belonging to 214 but without hangars, were also wrecked in this storm.

Through much of the Vimy and Virginia period, the squadron had been commanded by ex-RFC officers and most of its air crew had trained for a war that would never be fought in their time. All that was changing. The new men coming in, like Peter Grant, Robert Turner, Tom Smalley, Harold Rosofsky and the South African Peter Torkington-Leech, would carry on month after month with similar training in similar machines, but with an ever clearing view of the end to which that training might be put.

The talk everywhere was of real war, and a war that would have the squadron in the front line, taking the fight directly to a well-equipped and determined enemy. Even so, good relations had to be maintained on the surface, and No. IX took five of their Heyfords to Mildenhall in October 1937, to show to a visiting party of German air force staff officers. We can only imagine the Germans' thoughts as they contemplated the RAF's main bomber, knowing that the Messerschmidt 109 was even then being delivered to the Luftwaffe, an aircraft that would set a new speed record of almost 380mph the following month. All parties also knew what the Luftwaffe, in the guise of the Condor Legion with a mixture of old and new types of aircraft, had done at Guernica and other places in the Spanish Civil War, admittedly largely unopposed but terrifying nonetheless.

The Germans used the Civil War (July 1936–March 1939) to give their airmen experience. There were about 3,000 Luftwaffe air and ground crew in Spain at any one time, but the force was rapidly rotated so that perhaps 30,000 men had training on the job. The conclusions generally were that wholesale bombing of cities did not of itself bring victory, but the use of bombers, especially dive bombers, as artillery in support of ground forces, was very effective.

The German high command in any case believed that strategic bombing would not be necessary in the forthcoming European war, as Britain would not be involved. The fall of France would come about through defeat of its army, its now poorly equipped air force being almost an irrelevance, and so 'co-operation' types of aircraft were the ones on which to concentrate. Although there was a brief surge of emphasis on heavy bombers for the Luftwaffe, and various prototypes were designed, their chief proponent, General Wever, had been killed in an air crash in 1936 and the enthusiasm died with him.

The high command could not allow limited production capacity to be diverted from their favoured fighters and co-operation fast bombers, to a type for which they could as yet see no use. The mistake was not rectified and Germany never would have a significant force of heavy bombers. Focke Wulf FW200 transport planes would be converted to bombers for the 1940 Norway campaign, and Heinkel He177, with four engines and two propellors, would see service in 1943 against sea-going targets, but that was all.

By the summer of 1938, the squadron was established in another new home at Stradishall, sharing with No. 148 who were equipped with a rather different aircraft, the Vickers Wellesley. In September, with Austria annexed by Germany and obvious threats being made to do the same with the Sudetenland region of Czechoslovakia, the bomber squadrons were put on permanent stand-by, but the operation planned, should the situation worsen,

Posing with a Heyford in 1938 are the pilots of IX Squadron. Most are not identifiable but names that feature in our story include Pilot Officer Peter Grant, third from right, Pilot Officer Bob Turner standing centre, Sergeant Charles Bowen standing sixth from right, Flying Officer Tom Smalley, seated first right.

was a raid on Berlin, and Heyfords were not considered capable of the job. Eleven front-line RAF squadrons had Heyfords and yet, at the first inkling of their possible employment in the task for which they were designed, they were no use.

The squadron had been practising night flying and bombing almost non-stop, with dummy raids over industrial centres where lights had been dimmed in expectation, and more attacks on areas of Greater London such as Enfield and Walthamstow. Now, when the alarm went off, aircraft and crews were not good enough.

All of IX Squadron's trained wireless operator/gunners were temporarily attached to No. 148, to fly in the Wellesleys, single-engined monoplanes, faster and with a much longer range than the Heyford, that were made ready for the raid on Berlin should the Czech crisis not be resolved. All were loaded with three 500lb bombs, carried in torpedo-shaped pods under the wings.

The range and the load meant that the return journey was unlikely to be completed and crews expected to parachute into the Netherlands as they ran out of petrol. Being armed only with one machine gun fixed to fire forward in the starboard wing, and another in the dorsal turret, return would have been made even more doubtful should they have been intercepted.

The first British modern bomber, the Wellington, was still a while away but the Wellesley was an intermediate design on the road to it, with enclosed cockpits and a retractable undercarriage. It was also the first aircraft using Barnes Wallis's geodetic construction. Mathematically, a geodesic line is the shortest possible path between two points in a curved space or, to put it another way, a geodesic curve is one of which the tangent vectors remain parallel when transported along it.

To put it more simply still, Wallis, thinking of the basket-weave of metal in the airships he'd worked on, devised a system of criss-crossing curved metal ribs, in effect a lattice or net of duralumin members, which was light yet very strong. He called it geodetic, to distinguish it from geodesic proper, and the engineering principles of stress and torsion at work in it meant that large pieces of the structure could be removed while the load-bearing abilities of the whole remained. As No. IX would experience many times in the approaching war, Wellingtons could limp home with seemingly fatal amounts of damage, enough to cause other aircraft to break up in the air.

As it turned out, Czechoslovakia's allies backed away from the threat of war, gave in to the Germans, and Prime Minister Neville Chamberlain came home from Munich famously waving his piece of paper and declaring peace in our time. The bomber squadrons were stood down and debombed, all except one Wellesley of No. 148 that the armourers forgot. This aircraft was flown for another four months before its extra load of 1,500lb was discovered, the pilots meanwhile regarding it as a rogue machine.

CHAPTER 5

Getting Ready

Modern aircraft at last

The chiefs of the Allied armed forces had all been through the Great War that had finished only twenty years before. Nobody could contemplate such a thing happening again, years of struggle between opposing armies going nowhere, with millions of dead. The next one would be a different kind of war, surely, although quite how different nobody knew, except possibly the Germans. One thing all could be certain about. Air power was bound to be a major factor.

It was the view of Winston Churchill, soon to be Prime Minister, that he who held the skies held the ways and means of military success. Current PM Neville Chamberlain didn't seem to have a view. So, what were the chances of Britain holding the skies and thence taking the war to the enemy? We had two superb fighters in the Hurricane and the Spitfire, but they were for defence. What about attack? What about the bombers?

It was obvious to bomber strategists that their job would be a hard one. All thought was of precision targets; that meant going in daylight because long-distance targets could not be found at night. If they were to go in daylight, the only way they could reach their targets would be if they could defend themselves against fighter attack and somehow avoid the shooting from the ground.

Flying in close formation, with cloud cover, could be the answer if it were possible to keep formation in the clouds when bomber crews couldn't see each other. Keeping formation while attacking, and while under attack would also be difficult, which made things doubly questionable when the tight formation was the given means of defence.

Flying too quickly for the ground gunners would also be an asset, if only there were an aircraft that could go that fast. Having long-range fighter escorts would also be very welcome, if only such were available.

Here was a most ingenious paradox: Stanley Baldwin had said the bombers would always get through, and maybe they would if there were any bombers that could do it. The RAF certainly didn't have any. Added to that, they had no real idea about the defensive strengths and abilities of their likely opponents in Germany, in the air or on the ground.

Of course, the Germans didn't have any bombers either, at least, not ones suitable for strategic bombing of Britain from aerodromes in the Fatherland. Hitler saw the Luftwaffe as a dramatically effective addition to the army, the *Wehrmacht*, not as an offensive force on its own. Besides, he had no intention of going to war with Britain, at least until 1942.

In America, the prototype 300mph Boeing B17, the four-engined Flying Fortress, had flown in 1935 and was about to come into service with the USAAF. The first British four-engined bomber, the inadequate Short Stirling, was being developed but would not fly in anger until February 1941, the Handley Page Halifax shortly after, while the Avro Lancaster hadn't been thought of yet.

According to Air Ministry figures, the airspeed of bombers progressed thus in ten years (given in mph):

	1929	1934	1939
Light	Fox 160	Hart 184	Battle 257
Medium	Sidestrand 144	Overstrand 152	Blenheim 295
Heavy	Virginia 104	Heyford 142	Hampden 265
		Hendon 156	Wellington 265

The definition of a heavy bomber was really little more than the heartiest twin-engined beast available at the time, and obviously does not compare with the later four-engined heavies. None of the 1934 bombers could have reached a target in Germany with a worthwhile bomb load and got home again. Why the Blenheim was classified as medium is not clear.

Not on the above list but regarded as modern enough for war in 1939 was the Armstrong Whitworth Whitley, AKA the flying barn door. It was a twin-engined monoplane, it did have a retractable undercarriage and it did have enclosed, movable gun turrets front and rear. It was classified as a night bomber and so its lack of speed (max. 230mph) and agility were not considered so important at the time, and it compared very favourably with the biplane 'heavy' bombers it was replacing.

Likewise, the Handley Page Hampden, the flying suitcase or the flying tadpole, entered service in late 1938, a daylight medium bomber with two engines. It was fast for its time – 265mph maximum – and could carry 4,000lb of bombs, and it was much more manoeuvrable than the Whitley. Its defences were its weakness; one fixed and one movable gun up front, and one (later twins) under the tail boom and on its back.

The Hampden was really obsolete before it went into action and should never have been used on long-range raids, which it would be when the bombing war began in earnest after the fall of France. If it was carrying a 2,000lb bomb load it could stay in the air for 10 hours. The trip to Berlin and back for an aircraft of the Hampden's speed was 9 hours minimum, assuming good weather and favourable winds, and many a Hampden would be lost at sea as its petrol ran out coming home.

Also fast were the Bristol Blenheim – the Mark I was faster than most of the fighters flying in 1936 – and the single-engined Fairey Battle, an elegant machine looking rather like a stretched out Spitfire or Hurricane. These two were both light bombers, carrying a maximum of 1,000lb armament, although the Battle could carry another 500lb on wing racks.

The Bristol Blenheim had curious origins, deriving from a fast passenger aircraft first ordered by Lord Rothermere as his private transport. The military version was, like the Battle, poorly armed with a fixed gun in the port wing and another in a dorsal turret. Speed would be its defence, which was a sound enough policy at the time.

Best of all by far was the Vickers Wellington, designed by Barnes Wallis. It doubled the Heyford biplane's performance, taking 4,500lb of bombs 1,500 miles at 240mph, and it could reach up to 18,000ft although its ceiling in practical terms was rather lower. It was equivalent as a bomb-carrier to the B17 Fortress but, with much less defensive armament, two engines fewer and its fuselage made of geodetic metal net covered in fabric, it was a great deal cheaper to build.

Exercises were stepped up after the Munich Agreement. In December, No. IX Squadron fielded eight Heyfords 'with full crews to take part in the No. 3 [Bomber] Group Monthly Tactical Exercise. Owing to inclement weather however, no raids were attempted', according to the ORB. The squadron CO, Wing Commander Smith MC, had recently been killed when his Heyford hit a tree at night and burned out, but the squadron was brought back to full establishment of sixteen aircraft, twelve to be kept in readiness and four in reserve. The squadron had been expecting Wellingtons for several months but the first one didn't arrive until 31 January 1939. While they waited, pilots had been instructed by 148 Squadron members in Wellesleys, in the matter of flaps, retractable undercarriages and the Bristol

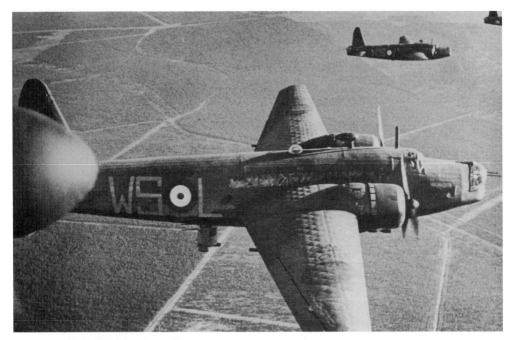

L4260 was one of the first of the Wellington Mark Is to be delivered to the RAF, in January 1939. It never flew an op, being transferred to training duties in the October. Barnes Wallis's fabric-covered geodetic construction can clearly be seen; note the extended 'dustbin' turret underneath.

Pegasus engine, and on 24 April the sixteenth up-to-strength machine was delivered.

Exercises and formation practice were intensive, all the more so after IX Squadron was informed that it was to provide the main British entertainment at the Military Aviation Meeting in Brussels, at the Évere aerodrome. The ORB recorded: 'Ten machines were to go; nine for the display and one as a spare. Training was commenced immediately by the Squadron, and flying crews were provisionally chosen so that the personnel would have the maximum opportunity of getting used to one another.'

Having become so used, they would fly past in several formations – vic (that is, in a V), line astern, echelon to starboard and, seeking to impress as was clearly the purpose, they would make figure-of-eight runs while thus arranged. It was hardly the Red Arrows but it would be nerve-racking enough, knowing that the world was watching.

The display date was Sunday 9 July. After many difficulties in finding sufficient spares for ten operational Wellingtons, and a delay in departure due to bad weather, the squadron loaded up (40lb luggage allocation for officers, 30lb for airmen) and arrived at Évere on the evening of the 8th, to find that the doors of the hangars were not wide enough to take a Wellington straight in. During a sweaty battle of an hour and a half, the aircraft were pushed and pulled and swung back and forth until they were safely housed, and the officers could repair to their hotels:

> for our first glass of continental biere. Our thirst quenched, we went to our rooms where we were, it is to be confessed, a little staggered by the luxury, and a trifle surprised by the absence of valets de chambre and the presence of femmes de chambre. Resolving firmly not to be surprised at anything, we changed into Mess kit for the Banquet in the Salle des Glaces, Palais d'Egmont.

Sumptuous and tediously long though the banquet was, the spirits of the RAF representatives were not cast down, and 'the whole squadron sallied forth with the Belgian officers to taste the night life of Brussels'.

Next day there was a truly magnificent display of flying, although the Germans and the French were not showing their hands in their latest types of aircraft. The French did complex aerobatics in Morane Parasols, First World War machines now used for training, and the Germans similarly flew their advanced trainer, the very agile Bücker-Jungmeister, a single-engined biplane that would go on to dazzle air-show crowds for many years. The Belgians flew Gloster Gladiator biplane fighters, and one RAF Hurricane put on a high-speed array of aerial tricks and turns to complement Europe's first look at a modern RAF bomber squadron. There was a crash. A German pilot overdid it in his Jungmeister and was killed.

Another formal dinner that evening was followed by a tourist day in Lièges, and a Guest Night at a chateau organised by the Belgian officers. ORB:

> Here a most enjoyable and rather hilarious evening was spent, greatly aided by the presence of a great deal of beauty in the form of the girlfriends of Belgian officers. It has been rumoured that English officers, unable to speak a word of French at 20.00 hours were, by the small hours, conversing fluently in that language.

The august editor of *Aeronautics* magazine, Oliver Stuart, was at the same show:

> The general impression made by the show was that the newest and most interesting types of aeroplanes and engines were being held back. However, this is no wonder, given the international situation.

Wellingtons of IX Squadron take off to impress the crowds at the Brussels air show, 9 July 1939.

The largest machine at the show was the Vickers Wellington which has a span of 86 feet. . . . amazing spectacle of a completely fabric covered large high-speed bomber . . . It has been compared to a basket or a crab-pot with gloves on but its speed of 265mph indicates that it is a basket of very special shape and refinement. It was notable as being the only twin-engined type at the show whose wheels completely disappeared behind doors when retracted.

After this extravagant affair, the squadron relocated yet again, to Honington, a grass airfield (of course) off the Ixworth/Thetford road in Suffolk, where crews were able to practise with the Lorenz blind-landing system. This was actually a German product which, by radio signal, put the pilot onto a flight direction coinciding with the centre line of the runway or flarepath. To port of this line, he heard short pips like Morse dots; to starboard, he heard dashes. Right on the mark, the signals blended into a continuous tone. As the squadron would soon find out, this signal could be picked up as far away as the Dutch coast, at 12,000ft, provided one was not too far off track to start with.

The Air Ministry demanded one more display of aerial might, and that was the 'Showing the Wings' initiative, when all available Wellingtons – known universally as the Wimpy, named for the character in the Popeye cartoons, J Wellington Wimpy – of Bomber Command 3 Group would fly over France, on 18 July 1939, in formation to Marseilles. That was the intention, at any rate, and they all took off from their home bases and assembled north of London with IX Squadron in the lead. South of the capital, the weather was worsening and every aircraft was sent instructions to reroute along the English south coast. Further orders, to return to base, were received by some squadrons before others, resulting in two-way mid-air traffic that would have been even more horrifying for the crews had they been able to see very far.

Only two squadrons, No. IX and No. 214, were deemed to have shown the discipline and skill required in a large formation and, it must have been noticed, for the daylight air raids to come, and so they were selected to show their wings in a more modest way, a flight of eighteen aircraft going to Marseilles and back the next day.

Another flight to Marseilles, 23 July, had formation-keeping as a secondary consideration to petrol consumption. The ORB recorded:

The consumption figures showed improvement, one machine attaining 3mpg (from 2.6mpg). We were informed that this was the last of the flights over France. S/Ldr Cole made a forced landing at Lyons owing to fabric stripping off the aircraft; and P/Offr Rosofsky made a landing at the same place owing to an opened pilot's hatch. A good time was had by all. They returned to Honington the following morning.

This was followed in early August, the 5th and 6th, by Bomber Command Tactical Exercises. Those on the 7th were cancelled because of bad weather. The next three days were devoted to the RAF Annual Home Defence Exercise, in which 1,300 aircraft took part, to test the air and ground defences of Great Britain against air attack and the efficiency of the forces engaged.

A line was drawn from Withernsea to Bournemouth to provide an area to be defended by anti-aircraft guns, searchlights, balloons, and 800 aircraft of which 500 were fighters. The attackers were 500 bombers; in the words of the time, 'their raids were presumed to have come from territories located east of the operational area'. There was to be a full-scale black-out, monitored by ARP wardens, during the night of 9/10 August but unsuitable weather postponed it to the following night, when it was considered effectively carried out on the whole.

Rain, poor visibility and low clouds frequently interfered with the work of both attackers and defenders, although the attackers seemed to suffer less and many of the bombers reached their targets and were not intercepted. The bombers used the cloud to avoid the fighters, some of which were not allowed to take off in case the weather caused collisions. The anti-aircraft gunners claimed to have hit some of the bombers.

The Air Minister, Sir Kingsley Wood, praised everybody and congratulated all on the most valuable experience gained. He also profoundly regretted the loss of several fine airmen who had met with fatal accidents (none from No. IX). And that was that.

The RAF now had some aircraft capable of attacking targets in Germany. There were nowhere near enough for an all-out war nor were there men to fly them should there ever be enough, nor yet a cohesive system for fully training such men. There were no navigation aids beyond the old methods of map, compass, landmarks, stars and dead reckoning to help crews find their targets in bad weather or at night. There was no stratagem of aircraft combining together to hit a marked target, and no devices for target marking had there been a stratagem. Worse, there had been no serious thinking about how these matters might be resolved.

The idea that bombers could defend themselves successfully against enemy fighters had not been tried, much less proved and, Wellingtons apart, there were surely no war-winners among the rest of Bomber Command's equipment, even though a full-scale offensive of strategic bombing against Germany was the official policy.

Air Chief Marshal Sir Edgar Ludlow-Hewitt, Commander-in-Chief of the bomber force, had had a brilliant career in the first war, starting as a pilot of high repute and ending as a 31-year-old brigadier, RFC. That he had a superb brain and exceptional talent for administration and analysis was never in doubt, though his abilities as a front-line commander were less apparent to some of his senior colleagues.

He had been appointed to the top bomber job in 1937, when all the facts (as outlined above) soon became horribly obvious to him. His pleas for more resources did not resonate loudly enough with the Air Ministry, preoccupied as most officials and politicians were with the requirements of Fighter Command, and, in any case, there was that general belief that the bombers would always get through. There was also opposition, or inertia, among those who objected to the whole business of bombing a country into submission. The RAF's plan for destroying industrial targets in the Ruhr was initially met with a ministerial objection that factories were private property.

Ludlow-Hewitt saw that, if he were asked to mount that offensive, Bomber Command would be totally destroyed. He calculated that his current force would be annihilated within eight weeks. That force consisted of fifty-three squadrons of five types of aircraft – Wellington, Whitley, Hampden, Blenheim and Battle.

His realistic assessment was reluctantly accepted but he was viewed as a pessimist and, probably, despite his cold and distant demeanour, too soft-hearted to be a warlord. He would soon be replaced. A message from President Roosevelt urged the future combatants, Britain, France and Germany, to exercise restraint in the use of their bombers and to avoid civilian casualties. Not wishing to offend the Americans, Britain and France agreed right away and Germany too a few weeks later, once it became unnecessary to bomb Poland.

The British and the French found the Roosevelt stricture convenient, for the time being. The French greatly feared a bomber war, having an air force, mostly equipped with obsolete aircraft, quite unable to resist. The RAF could not fly bomber missions from Britain over neutral Belgium and the Netherlands, nor yet over France for that matter, so attacks on Germany would require some circuitous routing.

The great bomber offensive was off. Twenty of Bomber Command's squadrons were assigned to training roles.

In any case, according to the Germans, the whole thing was impossible. German periodical *Der Adler*, 22 August 1939: 'The invisible wall, the Air Defence Zone West, is unsurpassable. Raiding machines will either be brought down entering German territory, or leaving it. Large industrial plants of the Ruhr district are protected by 30 and more balloons which, in case of stronger winds, are replaced by kites.'

A German newspaper had this to say about the defence of Berlin, 1 September 1939: 'Anti-aircraft defence in National Socialist Germany is no longer a technical problem; it is a spiritual one. It proves the maturity of a nation which knows its destiny is in excellent hands.'

Mobilisation of Bomber Command was ordered on 1 September 1939 and most of the Fairey Battle squadrons flew to France, leaving 23 squadrons as the entire British-based operational force, being 6 of Wellingtons, 6 each of Hampdens and Blenheims, and 5 of Whitleys, while the Luftwaffe could attack Poland with 900 bombers and dive bombers.

The Blenheims could not be considered serious bombers for attacks on Germany, so 17 squadrons can be counted as capable of taking a worthwhile quantity of bombs to enemy territory and coming home again, roughly 170 aircraft serviceable and ready at any given moment. Even so, Ray Norman, Parliamentary Correspondent of *Aeronautics* magazine, could write in August 1939:

Our first line strength is already well over 1,750 machines, which means that we can keep that formidable number in the air almost indefinitely, whatever the losses.

And I hear that a new long-range, fast bomber is being developed, capable of looking after itself in all circumstances, and of carrying the war very far indeed into the enemy's camp.

IX Squadron ORB, 2 September: 'Squadron standing by for orders. Four [navy] Observers attached to Squadron for recognition of ships.'

The enemy's camp, in the sense of targets on land, was forbidden so only the German navy was a legitimate aiming point, provided it was at sea. If it was in harbour, civilians might be hit, but out on the ocean, well, Mr Roosevelt could not object to that. To find and hit warships, operations would have to be in daylight, so that let the Whitleys off the hook but brought the Blenheims back into the reckoning. There would be no fighter escorts, despite Ludlow-Hewitt saying they were essential, because the RAF did not have fighters with sufficient range to reach the areas where the warships currently were stationed.

On the morning of Sunday, 3 September at 11.15, war was publicly declared by Prime Minister Chamberlain on the BBC, speaking to you from the Cabinet Room at number 10 Downing Street, saying that no such undertaking had been received and that consequently this country was at war with Germany.

The expectation in Bomber Command was all-out war, probably, with squadrons on a three-week cycle: maximum effort one week, sustained effort (roughly half speed) one week, rest one week. The Luftwaffe was not thought to be as good a fighting force as the RAF even though it was numerically vastly superior.

IX Squadron would have to wait until the next day to feature in the first blood-and-bullets operations of the Second World War, but there was some activity before that. Less than an hour after Mr Chamberlain finished his speech, an attempt was made to carry the fight to the enemy by the only means possible, by air. The offensive against the Third Reich began with a single Blenheim Mark IV of 139 Squadron, sent from RAF Wyton across the sea towards Wilhelmshaven to reconnoitre ship movements.

The crew of three – pilot, wireless operator/gunner and a naval officer as observer – flew through cloud and icy conditions but, close to their limit at 24,000ft, found what they were looking for, a large contingent of the German navy, capital ships and destroyer escorts, in the Schillig Roads, steaming north from Wilhelmshaven towards Heligoland. Delighted with their success, the wireless op telegraphed the news on his Morse key but his equipment was frozen.

The wireless sets all the bombers had were difficult to tune, which had to be done manually, were not properly insulated against the cold, to which they were very susceptible, and communication between aircraft and base was often lost, especially at long distance. The message was not understood.

They landed home in the early afternoon and passed on the message the old-fashioned way. It was too late really to contemplate a mission with a healthy outcome but the orders were clear: three Hampdens of 49 Squadron and six of 83 (Scampton), and six Wellingtons of 37 (Feltwell) and three of 149 (Mildenhall) were to take off on 'armed reconnaissance'.

The Hampdens flew into appalling weather. The crews could see nothing, there was no chance of a successful attack, so they turned back. The Wellington crews found nothing either. From the enemy's point of view, the only sign of war so far had been a single scout flying too high to worry about.

Meanwhile, seven Whitleys of 58 Squadron and three of 51 set off for Germany from Linton-on-Ouse. They attacked in several different places with millions of weapons, doing no damage whatsoever. The weapons were leaflets telling the Germans to stop it while they still could. Three of the

Whitley crews could not find their way home before their petrol ran out and had to crash land in France.

There would be many such raids, by IX Squadron and others, having no discernible effect on their targets but causing losses to Bomber Command. The leaflets were called nickels, and the activity nickelling, but quite why is not known although there are several unsubstantiated theories.

To navigate, the tools were primitive. They had maps, of course, and time pieces. The compass was more or less reliable except in stormy weather, when lightning and static electricity affected it, but it was only useful if you knew where you were. As the Irishman said when asked directions, if I were you I wouldn't start from here.

The air speed indicator could freeze up. Home-based radio stations could sometimes get a fix on a lost aircraft, and that fix might be received if the wireless was working well. So, if a crew couldn't see anything to help, their dead reckoning relied on sources of information that could all be wrong – air speed, wind speed and direction, compass readings. Some crews carried a sextant, which could give general assistance in a cloudless sky. And when you did get back to base, your aerodrome and all the others nearby might be shrouded in fog.

ERKLÄRUNG CHURCHILLS

„Wir, die Vereinten Nationen, verlangen von den Nazis, den Faschisten und den japanischen Tyrannen bedingungslose Übergabe. Das heisst, dass ihre Widerstandskraft vollständig gebrochen werden muss, und dass sie sich rückhaltlos unserer Gerechtigkeit und Gnade anvertrauen müssen. Das heisst fernerhin, dass wir alle die weitschauenden Massnahmen treffen müssen, die nötig sind, um zu verhindern, dass die Welt aufs Neue durch ihre Intrigen und wilden Friedensbrüche in Jammer und Elend gestürzt wird.

Es heisst nicht, und es kann nimmermehr heissen, dass wir unsere siegreichen Waffen durch Unmenschlichkeit und Rachsucht beflecken werden. Wir planen eine Welt, in der alle Völker Glieder einer Familie sind, und allen der Weg offen steht zu Leben, Freiheit und Menschenglück."

Nickels, leaflets, were dropped by the million for much of the war. Nobody can quantify any real effect they had, although the hundreds of aircraft and crews lost on that job were real enough.

The last word about the first day is from *The Times*: 'Aircraft of the Royal Air Force carried out extensive reconnaissance over Northern and Western Germany. They were not engaged by enemy aircraft. More than 6,000,000 copies of a note to the German people were dropped over a wide area.'

CHAPTER 6

The Shadow of Death

First of 55,000 fatalities

According to *The Times*, London on this Monday morning, 4 September, showed 'quiet and resolute preparedness for whatever may come. Overhead were the innumerable barrage balloons, gleaming like beads of quicksilver, serene and beautiful, against a background of blue sky and cotton-wool clouds.'

The weather was not so good over northern Germany, which forced the crew of the 149 Squadron Blenheim, in a repeat of their first trip, to go in

Place.	Date.	Time.	Summary of Events.	References to Appendices.
			OPERATIONS RECORD BOOK	R.A.F. Form 540
			of (Unit or Formation) .... No. 9 SQUADRON.	No. of pages used for day...................
HONINGTON.	1/9/39		Squadron Mobilisation ordered. Aircraft despatched to Dispersal Points.	
HONINGTON.	2/9/39		Squadron standing by for orders. 4 G.R. Observers attached to Squadron for recognition of Ships. P/O. CHAMBERS, P/O. ARKELL, P/O. COOK, and SGT. GROSSEY, but P/O. COOK ordered to return. F/O. J.P.C. ROLT assumed the duties of Squadron Adjutant.	
HONINGTON.	3/9/39		State of War with Germany declared as from 11.00 hours.	
HONINGTON.	4/9/39		Sections 1 and 4 carried out a raid on 2 Battleships at BRUNSBUTTEL. Section No. 1. 1. S/LDR. LAMB, P/O. CHAMBERS, F/O. LEECH, SGT. BRYANT, SGT. SMITH and A.C. HAWKINS. 2. F/SGT. BORLEY, SGT. MILLER, CPL. PARK, L.A.C. WARE, and A.C. HENDERSON. 3. F/SGT. TURNER, SGT. JARVIS, SGT. WALTON, A.C. DAY, and A.C. BROCKING. Section No. 4. 1. F/LT. GRANT, P/O. LAMBERT, P/O. ARKELL, F/O. TURNER, CPL. KIRCHER, and A.C. GRIFFITHS. 2. SGT. PURDIE, F/B. THOMPSON, A.C. GIBSON, A.C. MUSHAM, and A.C. TAYLOR. 3. SGT. BOWEN, SGT. BALMER, A.C. NICHOLLS, A.C. LAMB, and A.C. WILKIN. Cont/P.T.O.	

very low to spot naval units anchored offshore near Brunsbüttel, a small harbour town of Schleswig-Holstein near the Danish border, population around 7,000, and at Wilhelmshaven, population 118,000. The populations were safe but Brunsbüttel was an important naval base on the Elbe estuary, the western terminus of the Kiel Canal and 60 miles downstream from Hamburg. Wilhelmshaven was the chief naval base for all the North Sea fleet, with ten harbour basins and six dry docks and, currently, the battleship *Admiral Scheer*, with destroyers and cruisers nearby including the training cruiser *Emden*.

Yet again, the wireless message was not understood and so orders to mount an attack were not issued until the middle of the day, after the Blenheim got back. The orders came from HQ of 2 Group of Bomber Command, for five Blenheims of each of 107, 110, and 139 Squadrons to fly

Wellingtons with No. IX's pre-war squadron letters, KA, which were changed to WS as the war began, are here practising over Stradishall for the Brussels air show, July 1939. L4275 KA-H, top of picture, was shot down at Brunsbüttel on 4 September 1939, captained by Flight Sergeant John Turner. Nearest, L4278 KA/ZA (two letters indicating a machine officially on the reserve) was section leader Flight Lieutenant Peter Grant's machine on that operation.

Also on the Brunsbüttel raid, pilot Sergeant Tom Purdy, here sitting with his back to the snooker table in the Sergeants' Mess, Honington, 1940. On the evening of 27 December 1941, on the way to Düsseldorf, Hauptman Werner Streib *would find and shoot down Wellington Z1907 of 57 Squadron. Its second-tour captain, Warrant Officer Thomas Purdy DFM, aged 28, husband of Ellen May, from South Shields would be killed with four of his crew.*

to Wilhelmshaven, and from 3 Group for six Wellingtons of IX Squadron and eight of 149 to fly to Brunsbüttel.

The briefings for all the squadrons were unusual enough, being the first of their kind any of the men, the briefers and the briefed, had ever been to, but with the addition of a message from King George VI:

> The Royal Air Force has behind it a tradition no less inspiring than those of the older Services, and in the campaign which we have now been compelled to undertake you will have to assume responsibilities far greater than those which your Service had to shoulder in the last war. I can assure all ranks of the air force of my supreme confidence in their skill and courage, and in their ability to meet whatever calls may be made upon them.

Whether or not they had much idea about the reality of the calls being made upon them, there can be no doubt that the King's message, welcomed though it must have been, was entirely unnecessary as motivation.

Squadron Leader Lennox Lamb, a New Zealander, would be leading the IX Squadron men. Of his briefing, he reported that 'I was ordered to carry out a bombing raid on warships inside Brunsbüttel harbour'. Squadron Leader Paul Harris was ordered to do the same job for 149 Squadron. After enduring a 24-hour stand-by, the take-off was frantic, more like a fighter-squadron scramble than a planned bombing raid.

The Wellingtons were away around 4pm, as were the Blenheims. Seven of the 149 Squadron Wellingtons turned back at various stages in foul weather and very poor visibility that ruined the formation. Squadron Leader Harris, with none of his guns working, pressed on but was hit by flak from a ship, jettisoned his bombs and gave up the mission. One of his wingmen, already going home, dropped his bombs on Denmark by mistake.

Number IX Squadron had proved its ability in formation flying while showing the wings over France and, despite the weather that had caused 149 so much trouble, found Brunsbüttel.

Wellingtons L4268 piloted by Flight Sergeant Ian Borley, and L4275 piloted by Flight Sergeant John Turner, were the wingmen in Squadron Leader Lamb's section of three. Flight Lieutenant Peter Grant led the other section with another Turner, Flying Officer Robert Turner beside him as second pilot. Sergeant Tom Purdy and Sergeant Charles Bowen were Grant's wingmen.

By the standards of Bomber Command later in the war, these pilots were old men. Until recently, they had been used to flying biplanes, Heyfords, and some of them Virginias before that, and to a settled, regular RAF life. They were mostly married. Sergeant Borley was 30 and had been a pilot on No. IX since 1933. Lamb was similar, 29, although some of the crews were not so venerable, especially the gunners. Despite the stratagem of self-defending aircraft, gunnery had yet to be regarded as a specialised single craft. Gunners who were just that, not wireless operators by first trade, were often ground-crew volunteers, keen young lads who were desperate to do their bit and go a-flying. Flight Sergeant Turner had AC2 Ken Day, aged 20. One of Borley's gunners, Leading Aircraftman Harry Dore, was 19.

The two section leaders, Lamb and Grant, carried the full crew of six that included the extra side and/or dustbin gunner. Their wingmen had the usual crew of five: pilot, second pilot, observer/navigator, WOP/AG, gunner, except either Borley or Flight Sergeant Turner also had an extra man, Sergeant Heslop, who is not mentioned in the ORB but is listed on the Runnymede Memorial.

Grant's section took off at 15.40. Less than 3 hours later they were in among it. This is his report:

The bombs were dropped at 18.12 hrs at a Battleship which was at a point about ⅞ of a mile due south of the entrance to Kiel. Height 6,000 feet. Immediately after the release we were forced to pull up into the cloud owing to the very high concentration of anti-aircraft fire and turned for home without waiting to see the results. The shore batteries had three or four guns which were firing with far less accuracy than the ships. Six or eight cruisers were firing at us as well as the battleship. We were hit three times. All three machines dropped their bombs at the same time.

As to battleships, the *Gneisenau* and the *Scharnhorst* were both there.

Lamb's section was up later, at 16.05. By the time they arrived at Brunsbüttel the local staffel of Messerschmidt 109s was ready and waiting. The best bomber the RAF had was about to meet the best fighter in the Luftwaffe – nine of them. Lamb's report showed the normal RAF-officer restraint while describing desperate measures:

Towards the end of a fighter attack carried out by nine German fighters at approx 18.35 I jettisoned my three bombs 'live and in stick' at 400 feet on the south side of the harbour. At the moment of bombing I felt sure there was no shipping in the vicinity but having pressed the bomb release I saw a merchant ship, approx 7,000 tons, athwartships. I climbed rapidly, still being attacked by fighters and succeeded in reaching cloud cover. It was necessary for the safety of my crew that these bombs were jettisoned as the decreased load enabled the machine to successfully evade the attack.

He hit the merchant ship and set it on fire, and his co-pilot, South African Flying Officer Peter Torkington-Leech, manning one of the gun positions presumably while the designated gunner was firing from the dustbin turret, claimed to have shot down one of the fighters. This claim was not substantiated, so probably there was non-fatal damage inflicted.

The worry expressed earlier, about how groups of bombers might stay together to defend themselves while under fire, was now well illustrated.

Lamb says he was at 400ft. German reports back this up although there is some confusion in aircraft identification. One fighter pilot said he saw three Wellingtons flying very low over the sea and came at them from above and behind. Two sheered off into the clouds. One, either Borley's or Flight Sergeant Turner's, flew on, we must assume because no crew member had seen the German, and was shot down in flames. Another pilot of the same Gruppe, II/JG77 (*Jagdgeschwader*, fighter wing) based at Nordholz, near Cuxhaven, stated that he saw another lone Wellington, so either Turner's or Borley's, and shot it down.

The *Luftwaffe War Diaries* have *Feldwebel* (Sergeant) Alfred Held taking 'the Wellington by surprise before its pilot could reach cloud cover', and *Feldwebel* Hans Troitsch soon afterwards bringing down a Blenheim.

No Blenheims fell to fighters that day. Troitsch's victory was the second Wellington – or the first, depending on which version of events is correct. Held was given the credit at the time as the first victor, although he attacked an aircraft on its own while Troitsch claimed to have seen three together, which must have been before they bombed. Regardless of the primacy claims of Troitsch and Held, there can be no doubt that, as the IX Squadron ORB reported, 'Nos 2 and 3 of No. 1 Section did not return to base'.

None of the bodies of Borley's crew were found, which suggests that his was the aircraft downed by Held out at sea rather than the one destroyed before the attack was made on the ships. Flight Sergeant Turner's body, and those of two of his crew, were found.

The scheme for the Blenheims was much the same as the one for the Hampdens the day before. The weather worsened as they flew over the sea, with mist, rain and low cloud, 'a solid wall of cloud from sea level to 17,000 feet', according to 110 Squadron's leader, acting Flight Lieutenant Ken Doran. The five Blenheims of 139 Squadron went badly off track, could not find the target, jettisoned their bombs and turned back. At least that meant the five of 110 Squadron had surprise on their side as they spotted the *Admiral Scheer* and went in, led by Doran. To find the battleship after flying almost blind was 'an incredible combination of luck and judgement' in Doran's opinion.

The sailors on the battleship were said to have 'looked up as if watching an airshow' while Doran's flight went in low to hit the *Admiral Scheer* with three or four bombs, one sticking, the others bouncing off, and one near-missing in the water next to the ship, but none of them exploded. Later at home, Doran would give an interview describing the raid in which he produced the line that made him famous: 'We could see a German warship taking on stores from two tenders at her stern. We could even see some washing hanging over the rails. Undaunted by the washing we proceeded to bomb the battleship.'

The tale of Doran's washing went round the RAF messes in short order, with various jokes attached about catching the Germans with their pants down, but there was a more serious side to the story. While one of the 110 five had strayed and couldn't find the target, with surprise gone the navy gunners set about the fourth to attack, captained by Flying Officer Henry Emden. It flipped sideways and crashed into the pilot's namesake, the training cruiser *Emden*, killing a number of sailors (said to be nine) and, with an extra man on board, all four air crew.

Now it was 107 Squadron's turn; one aircraft was not present, presumed off track somewhere. The German machine- and flak-gunners were highly accomplished at their trade and there were many of them, in ship and shore batteries. The Blenheims flew right into their fire.

Exactly what happened is not certain. One Blenheim went down in the harbour, one was blown up by its own bomb exploding as it hit a warship, another was shot down, another was forced to ditch.

Eleven men of IX Squadron, including the unlisted Sergeant Alexander Heslop, were dead at Brunsbüttel, and another fourteen of 107 and 110 at Wilhelmshaven. Two more were POWs. Of the twenty-nine aircraft setting out on this raid, fifteen never found the target, seven were shot down, leaving only seven that attacked and came home. If this was to be the pattern for Bomber Command, the life of air crew was likely to be very short.

The return on this investment was nine (probably) German sailors killed and presumably some injured; no damage to the target ships, some damage to the training cruiser *Emden*, possibly to another warship, and to a merchant ship; little damage to the Luftwaffe.

The Ministry of Information issued a communiqué that night:

A successful attack was carried out during this afternoon by units of the Royal Air Force on vessels of the German Fleet at Wilhelmshaven and at Brunsbüttel, at the entrance of the Kiel Canal.

Several direct hits with heavy bombs were registered on a German battleship in the Schilling [*sic*] Roads, off Wilhelmshaven, which resulted in severe damage.

At Brunsbüttel an attack was carried out on a battleship lying alongside the Mole, causing heavy damage. During the operation, which was carried out in very unfavourable weather conditions, our aircraft encountered air attack and anti-aircraft fire, resulting in some casualties.

The Danish government protested that a bomb or bombs had fallen on Esbjerg, causing damage to Danish lives and property. The British apologised, with profound regret for a most unfortunate incident.

The Ministry of Information later issued 'a fairly full account' of this, the first active operation of the RAF in the war.

> The attack was pressed home with the greatest vigour and daring. The fighting qualities displayed by RAF pilots were splendid. The results they achieved are of the highest importance. The navigation of the squadrons was accurate and as they approached the naval bases they flew low to make sure of hitting their targets.
>
> From the naval point of view their attack will have its effect upon the future course of the war at sea, as the ship hit was one of the most effective units of the German Navy.

German reports indicated that the ship in question was the *Gneisenau*, which had been bombed but not hit.

So sensational was the news about Brunsbüttel that King George VI wanted to hear the story for himself, and Squadron Leader Lamb was sent by royal command to Buckingham Palace to tell it, on 8 September, the date of the next Wellington fatality, and it was IX Squadron again, recorded thus: 'During air firing practice at Berners Heath an accident occurred to aircraft L4320. The following lost their lives: Pilot Officer Rosofsky, P/O Clifford-Jones, AC1 [Aircraftman First Class] McGreery, AC1 Purdie.'

Also killed but not mentioned in the ORB was 20-year-old AC2 William Hilsdon, on secondment from a training squadron, No. 215; and it was McGreevy, not McGreery. The accident seems to have been a case of pilot error, the aircraft flying into trees and crashing near Thetford.

The first week of the war had been, for the RAF, a shambles, characterised by bloody disasters at Brunsbüttel and Wilhelmshaven, fatal crashes in training and crews getting lost in the dark.

Arriving at IX Squadron, Honington, from 38 Squadron to take up one of the captain's positions in A Flight under Squadron Leader Lamb, made vacant after Brunsbüttel, was Frank Cyril Petts. He would finish the war as Flight Lieutenant DFC and Bar; in 1939 he was a sergeant pilot, but no ordinary one. On 38 Squadron, Petts had worked with the Air Fighting Development Establishment, and various techniques had been prescribed for dealing with fighter attacks. Petts: 'The official theory at that time was that fighters had such a small speed advantage over the modern bomber that any attack must become a stern chase and, since we mostly flew in sections of three in a Vic, of course the fighters would do likewise.' In a stern chase, a straightforward battle would develop between the fixed guns of the fighter, whose pilot had to fly along his own line of fire, and the more flexible options of the bombers' moveable, aimable guns in hydraulic turrets.

Should evasive action be required – bearing in mind the absolute necessity for the bombers to stick together – one technique was 'Rotate', in which the two wingmen of the section orbited the leader, clockwise or anticlockwise, depending. Another was 'Scissors', which began like 'Rotate' but fooled the attackers by reversing at halfway to original positions. The leader, neither scissoring nor rotating, would have to fend for himself. Not content with the orthodox, Squadron Leader Lamb devised his own defensive manoeuvre, which didn't have a name except when it was being discussed out of Lamb's hearing. Petts:

> The other sections wouldn't touch it but we had to, and we tried it first on 27 October 1939 with Spitfires from 66 Squadron pretending to be Germans. As they turned to attack, we changed from Vic to a vertical step formation, with me at the bottom. The Spits closed in. Our leader ordered a sudden throttling back, which can be sound practice for upsetting a fighter pilot but not in a close formation of Wellingtons stepped down vertically.

The reason it was a bad idea was that pilots B and C could not be sure of throttling back at exactly the same time and by exactly the same amount as pilot A.

The pilot in the number two aircraft, Flying Officer John Chandler, the other Brunsbüttel replacement, found himself in Lamb's slipstream and could not stop his aircraft going into a sudden descent. Petts, at number three below, saw him coming and threw his Wellington into such a steep dive that the man in his rear turret, Sergeant Robertson, knocked himself out on the roof of it.

To illustrate the somewhat makeshift nature of bomber crews at that time, Robertson flew mainly as the observer/navigator, manning the rear turret when required. Operating the beam guns, which fired through apertures in the fuselage side, and the under-gun in the dustbin turret, was the wireless operator. Petts had a full-time front gunner, and a second pilot who deputised as bomb aimer. Squadron Leader Lamb had the same crew make-up of five altogether. Chandler had his second pilot but then only two young AC2s, one 18 years old training as a wireless operator, the other 19, normally ground crew. Petts: 'Our number two, above me, dropped like a stone. I reacted by putting the nose down on full throttle, which bounced Sergeant Robertson around in his turret and KO'd him, and shot Aircraftman Kemp right out of his dustbin turret into the fuselage.'

According to Squadron Leader Lamb, there was nothing wrong with his idea. They just weren't doing it properly so they had to try again three days later. Petts's attention was frantically divided, between his air speed indicator and the aircraft above. 'We were at 800 feet, just below the cloud base and, as before, changed from Vic to vertical step and throttled sharply back.' Chandler, from being behind Lamb, was suddenly in front. Petts: 'I looked up and saw Chandler hit Lamb's starboard wing with his tailfin, just behind the engine.' This brought Chandler's nose up and a smash was inevitable. Petts stuck his own nose hard down and didn't pull out until he was level with the tree tops. Sergeant Robertson's voice came on the intercom: 'They've missed us'. He'd seen the two bombers fall past his turret, locked together, breaking up as they spun to oblivion. Petts:

> A group of us were in the Sergeants' Mess later, talking about what had happened. I took a draw on my very large brandy when I realised that Lamb's rear gunner, Sgt Smith, who was actually an observer like Robertson and had been with Lamb at Brunsbüttel, was sitting next to me. This I thought pretty odd as I'd seen him getting into the aircraft. 'How on earth did you get out of that?' I said. Smith replied that he'd been in his turret when F/O Torkington-Leech, second pilot as gunner, the first man to claim to have shot a German down, had said that he would occupy the turret in question, so Smith came back to the mess in a huff.

In the scramble to find and train air crew, more were being lost in accidents than on ops (the numbers for 1939 were seventy-eight aircraft lost on training flights, sixty-eight on operations). Squadron Leader Lamb, New Zealander, regal interviewee and one of the first notable flyers in these hostilities, and all his crew were dead, including Torkington-Leech and two more veterans of Brunsbüttel, Sergeant Cyril Bryant and Leading Aircraftman Stanley Hawkins. John Chandler and his three crew were dead too.

All the families were offered funerals with full RAF honours at All Saints Church, Honington. Some chose that; some preferred their own home churchyard.

The wreckage lay for weeks by the Rectory at Sapiston. While two other squadrons had crashed a Wellington each with only one air-crew death, IX Squadron had now lost five of these aircraft with twenty-four dead.

While some squadrons still had nothing to do except practise, others like No. IX made armed reconnaissances, which were sweep searches for hostile ships in the North Sea. If they saw anything at all, it was most likely a couple of fishing vessels off Yarmouth. From this time until the ban was lifted against bombing enemy territory, these sweeps would go on and on, each one usually about 5 hours, searching the grey ocean and almost always finding nothing. In between sweeps, there was training, of course, and many, many stand-bys at an hour's notice for sweeps that were then cancelled.

Everyone knew that the 'no civilians' stricture could not last and that both sides could be sure of being bombed at home eventually. In turn, the bombers would be allowed to do the job for which they were designed, but nothing was known about how best to set about the work.

Let us imagine that we have orders to bomb an important industrial target in a well-defended area of Germany. The view at the time was that four bombers to a target would be enough, but suppose we really wanted to make sure and hammer it. Suppose it was a big target, like the Krupp works at Essen, and we wanted to send a decent sort of force to it, say, twenty-four Wellingtons. What will be the briefing? Here's your target for tonight, chaps, off you go? Except it wasn't tonight. It was today. Wellingtons were day bombers.

Nobody had ever sent that many bombers to one land target so plans were drawn up to see how co-ordinated bombing might be done in a modern air raid.

Six Wellingtons each from Nos IX, 37, 38 and 115 Squadrons took off after breakfast on 28 November, and rendezvoused over Upper Heyford. Under the direction of Wing Commander R A A Cole of No. IX, they formed up in 5 minutes and set off for Rhyl, north Wales. The weather was unkind and the formation had to drop at times from 6,000ft to 2,000ft in rain and cloud over the Welsh hills, but they stayed together and arrived at Rhyl to find cloud down to 2,000ft, when the idea was to deliver a high-level attack, defined as 10,000ft, on targets of opportunity. The Wingco decided to stay up top and try to find targets through gaps in the cloud, while the specially assembled defences of Rhyl fired blanks at them. Here is the Wing Commander's report.

The exercise was most useful and many points of instructional value were learned:-

1. A force of 24 aircraft could put in a co-ordinated attack. First squadron to attack: 9 Squadron. Time over target 12.00 hours. Last squadron to attack: 115 Squadron. Time over target 12.15 hours. This time could be reduced under more favourable weather conditions.

On the night of 17/18 August 1943, three precision targets at Peenemünde would be bombed at night by 600 4-engined aircraft in 3 waves of 200, and each wave would bomb in 10 minutes. In November 1939, three months into the war, this exercise set out to prove that two-dozen Wellingtons could attack a target in daylight in a quarter of an hour. When orders were eventually given for the first night raids on Germany, 4 bombing hours would be allowed for 100 aircraft.

> 2. Rendezvous of squadrons can be carried out successfully provided care is taken in co-ordination prior to exercise and if squadrons are not rushed.

Memo to Air Officers Commanding, Royal Air Force, Second World War: do not ask your squadrons to rush.

> 3. Get away. It will appear at the moment that we shall have to accept the fact that a Wing is unable to form up again quickly after an attack. Flights of six will have to keep together for support after the attack. On completion of attack, No. 9 Squadron turned quickly off target and when clear of A-A fire reduced to 140mph and continued for 30 minutes at that speed but still remaining squadrons did not close up.

Before the year was over, German fighters would be closing up and demonstrating what they could do to flights of six Wellingtons trying to keep together for support in daylight.

> 4. The most difficult aspect of the whole exercise under trying weather conditions was the selecting of a target and passing the order to attack it to the Wing. Unless good weather conditions prevail one is on top of the target before any definite action can be taken, so the passing of an order selecting the target becomes a nearly impossible task.

So, a choice would have to be made, between bombing on clear, sunny days only or selecting the target in advance.

> 5. It is considered essential that good field or sea glasses should be provided for this type of commitment. No. 37 flew in pairs and the other squadrons in 'Vic'. It is considered that one type of formation should be adopted.

This was the state of the art of bombing in Britain. Crews of skill and limitless courage would fly in pairs or a V and look for their targets with binoculars.

Towards the end of November, No. IX was re-equipped with the Mark IA Wellington with hydraulic, rotating gun turrets made by Frazer Nash, armour protecting the starboard fuel tanks but, for some bizarre reason, not the port tanks and not yet with self-sealing tanks at all, or proper, efficient heating for the crew. Although the IA was better defensively than its predecessor, limitations in the firing arcs of the guns left it vulnerable to attacks from above and on the beam.

CHAPTER 7

The Battle of Heligoland

Tommies in sunshine

Air Vice Marshal John Baldwin, known as Jackie, had been called out of retirement to command 3 Group of Bomber Command. He was keen on another attack against warships, and his senior colleagues agreed. He called a meeting at Mildenhall on17 December, 19.00 hours, attended by squadron COs and flight commanders of IX, 37 and 149 Squadrons. Twenty-four Wellingtons were to look for warships in the Schillig Roads. If none were found, then they were to look at Wilhelmshaven where, it was believed, lay the battlecruisers *Scharnhorst* and *Gneisenau* and many other warships. Baldwin emphasised the vital importance of formation discipline.

They were to fly in a shape called a diamond. Up front would be two sections of three in vic, all 149 Squadron. Behind them, to the right and 500ft above, were two more sections also in vic, being three of 149 and three of IX. Similarly, but to the left and above, were six of IX arranged in the same way. Bringing up the rear, 1,000ft above in line astern and stepped down, were two rows of three, all of 37 Squadron.

There had been no time for the squadrons to practise this. On the Rhyl exercise, IX and 37 had flown together; they had also co-operated on one sea sweep, but 149 had not flown with either. In IX and 37, they were not all the same crews anyway. No. 37 had been on ops but had had no experience of meeting the enemy.

Baldwin added that, in the morning, they were to stand by at 2 hours' readiness from 07.30. If the attack went ahead, they were to ensure that none of their bombs fell on land or on merchant ships. Confirmation of the op would come after a recce flight to determine the weather over the target, in which case they would rendezvous over King's Lynn.

The weather report turned out to be favourable: patchy cloud. There was no intelligence report on the fighter strength around the target area, and there was a general feeling that the Germans were a bit leery anyway. In fact, nearby, were little short of a hundred Me109s and 110s that could be scrambled in minutes, flown by men who were very keen indeed to shoot down a Tommy or two.

At around 09.00, nine Wellingtons of IX Squadron took off from Honington. A few minutes later, the nine of 149 Squadron left Mildenhall, while the six of 37 Squadron were delayed, missed the RV over King's Lynn and had to motor to catch up. It happened to be an exceptionally cold day in an exceptionally cold winter. Inside a draughty Wellington, it seemed that there could be nowhere as cold as this.

The plan was to fly at 14,000ft, north east to latitude 55°, well to the north of the target area; turn right along the latitude line, then right again, south, towards their destination. The cloud hid them for much of the way but, some 2 hours into the journey, it began to thin. The front man of the second section of the leading group had engine trouble and could not keep station. He and another turned away for home.

The twenty-two flew on, not yet in sight of land, and the cloud vanished. Turning south in a clear blue sky that they seemed to have all to themselves, dustbin turrets were lowered and manned, just in case, although they expected their route, away from known positions of flak ships, to give them the advantage of surprise.

They knew nothing of enemy radar. On Heligoland a German navy operator, watching on his recently delivered Freya radar set, was near incredulous as his newfangled machine told him that a formation of aircraft was about 70 miles away. At the Luftwaffe experimental station on Wangerooge, the Freya operator saw the same thing and calculated the hostiles' distance as 113km, or 20 minutes' flying time.

They had to be hostiles. There were no German aircraft aloft in that region. The message from Heligoland went round the houses and back through naval exchanges before reaching Luftwaffe HQ 20 minutes later, where it was disregarded as duff gen from the incompetent sailor boys. The Wangerooge message went direct, but wasn't believed either. The new kit was showing seagulls. It was a beautiful, sunny day. The Tommies wouldn't come in this weather.

Observers on the ground with binoculars soon confirmed the radar reports – better than that, double confirmed them, sighting the bombers twice and making forty-four – and the fighters scrambled. First up was a night-fighter squadron, six Me109s of JG26 led by *Staffelkapitän* 'Macki' Steinhoff, who would become a formidable ace in the Battle of Britain.

Other future top scorers there that day were Gordon Gollob, who would retire from the air with 150 claimed kills, and Helmut Lent, destined to be one of the two most successful night-fighter pilots in the Luftwaffe. On this day Lent, with only one Polish victory to his credit so far, refuelling and impatient after returning from a patrol, famously took off with his armourer still on the wing changing an ammunition drum. The armourer, Paul Mahle, slid off and rolled to safety, which was one of the most unfortunate survivals of the war for Bomber Command. In 1943, Mahle would develop the upward-firing cannon system known as *Schrägermusik* (slanted music), which accounted for so many hundreds of Lancasters and Halifaxes and their crews. If only Lent had been a little more impatient.

The Germans faced an enemy who had bravery, instincts and common sense but no real notion of air fighting. The assumption was that the fighters would come in from behind; there had been no training in how a Wellington might deal with a smaller, faster, better armed and more acrobatic foe who did something unexpected.

The 110s had 20mm cannon, effective at 600yd, beyond the range of the Wellington's machine-gun turrets. The fighter pilots knew that if they dived in from the side, those machine guns couldn't get to them anyway, while nobody in the RAF – officially at least – had considered such beam attacks a serious possibility.

The Wellington pilots had no tactic other than sticking together in formation as recommended after the Rhyl exercise, and/or hiding in the clouds, but there were no clouds.

The formation flew on, searching for warships and finding only the forbidden merchantmen until Wilhelmshaven, where there were warships all right including *Scharnhorst* and *Gneisenau,* but they were forbidden too, tied up at the quay. Bombs dropped on them could easily hit on land, and that was strictly against orders. The ships had no restrictions on their own activities; the anti-aircraft barrage coming from them was thick and angry. With heavy flak exploding in black thunderballs all around, No. IX's Sergeant Frank Petts was finding life difficult.

> I was the outside-left of the whole team and in our wide turn over the water it was increasingly hard to keep up. Even at full throttle and full revs on the props I was lagging, then the flak stopped and there were the fighters, about forty of them. Hoping to gain some speed I dropped my bombs, which were four 500lb general purpose, quite unsuitable anyway for trying to sink battleships.

For everyone that day it was a new experience, the biggest, fiercest, most appallingly deadly rumble anybody had witnessed so far in this war. Petts:

> LAC Balch on the front guns got a fighter. It was a Me109, sweeping wide, possibly looking to come in on the leading aircraft. I saw Balch's first burst take off part of the cockpit and his second hit in the same area. The Messerschmitt went into a catastrophic dive pouring white smoke. By now I'd decided I'd never keep up and Ginger Heathcote [second pilot] said we could drop back and join the 37 Squadron six at the rear. Thank goodness I didn't.

The bombers tried to keep together for support but it proved impossible. The formation was now all over the place and, without the combined defences of the group, the fighters had it even easier.

The IX Squadron section of six had become detached from the rest. In came the 110s. Flying Officer John Challes's machine was shot to pieces in mid air; Flying Officer Douglas Allison was last seen heading for home with an engine in flames; Pilot Officer Eric Lines was not seen at all. Lamb's replacement, Squadron Leader Archibald Guthrie, went into the sea on fire but got a 110 which force-landed. Every man was killed in these four Wellington losses.

It so nearly could have been even worse. Petts: 'I turned about 40 degrees to starboard and headed full pelt for the waves. I was fairly well occupied with matters arising but I did notice the needle on my ASI reaching one o'clock second time around, which I later worked out meant 300 miles an hour.' The Pegasus engined Mark IA Wellington had a specified maximum speed of 265mph, and Petts was not the only one in that aircraft wondering how much faster they could go without something falling off. A fighter had attacked just before the dive, and there were more during the dive, and as Petts pulled out of it at sea level, three Me110s settled in behind him. This was a particularly exciting time for Bob Kemp in the dustbin turret. In full kit he was a tight fit in there, and if the Germans didn't get him he was liable to be knocked off the aircraft by a wave-top. Petts:

> We had an agreed drill for stern attacks. Robertson in the rear turret called it. 'Here's one coming in,' he'd say. 'He's coming . . . get ready, get ready . . . back! Back!' I'd slam the throttles shut and the pitch levers to full coarse. Our guns would be firing, there'd be enemy tracer past the windows and, with any luck, an enemy aircraft past us too.

'OK, he's gone,' somebody would say, and we'd be back to full speed ahead. My gunners claimed three 110s and two 109s that day. I could confirm with my own eyes Balch's 109 and a 110 he got. The others I couldn't say for sure. Robertson said he'd had a go at that 110 with no effect and one of its crew had made a rude gesture at him. As we throttled back, the 110 was suddenly in front and Balch gave him the full benefit.

By now two of Petts's gunners were wounded; Balch's was only a graze on his foot but Kemp had a very nasty thigh wound and was losing a lot of blood. Second pilot Heathcote managed to prise him out of his dustbin and treat him on the rest bed. The ammunition was gone anyway, the aircraft was full of holes and the starboard engine showed zero oil pressure. At least the fire in the starboard wing had gone out. Petts found he could climb gently to 1,000ft and set a course of 270°. With no clue where they were, he and Ginger Heathcote reasoned that if they went due west they should hit Britain somewhere.

Similar alarms, battles and mayhem were happening to the rest of the formation. One of 149's Wimpys went down in the fight and another ditched on the way back, with all crew killed. In the starboard six, Sergeant Jack Ramshaw's machine of No. IX was hit in the wings but claimed two Messerschmidts downed by w/opAG Leading Aircraftman Walter Lilley, a lad of 21 from Kippax in Yorkshire. AC1 Charles Driver, a member of the squadron's ground crew acting as temporary air gunner for the second time, was in the front turret. He watched in horror as half of it was shot away, his guns were rendered u/s and a fire broke out behind him. He beat the fire out and went to help his mate Walter at the back who was mortally wounded. Driver laid him on the aircraft floor and went to the skipper's aid. Petrol was leaking, the pumps weren't working properly and the second pilot, Sergeant Bob Hewitt had a wound in his right arm. Driver began pumping petrol by hand as Ramshaw headed for home. They lost height steadily and were almost in the sea by the time they saw the English coast. Driver kept pumping while the pilot ditched, as near as he could to a trawler he'd spotted.

Trawler skipper Sinclair took the observer Leading Aircraftman Conolly and Ramshaw aboard his vessel *Erillas* without difficulty. Bob Hewitt fell in the December waves, Driver pulled him out and they too boarded the trawler and set off for the shore and Grimsby Hospital. Leading Aircraftman Walter Lilley had fought his heart out and went down with his aircraft.

For the rest of IX Squadron, Flight Lieutenant Peter Grant and Sergeant

Tom Purdy, both veterans of the 4 September battle so long ago, were the only two pilots to land at Honington base. Four of the IX Squadron port formation of six had fallen. The other two staggered in to emergency landings. Sergeant Petts, starting from nowhere, heading due west and, spotting Butlin's camp at Skegness, came in at Sutton Bridge with two wounded crew, his starboard wing badly shot up and having been on fire, and the starboard side of the fuselage 'freely peppered', as they called it then.

Flying Officer Bill Macrae, who had been in the leading section of the port six, also couldn't make Honington and landed at North Coates Fitties, with patterns of holes in the wings and large parts of the tail section, plus a holed fuel tank and the fuselage peppered.

It was something of a miracle that Petts and Macrae got back, a miracle ascribable equally to crew and machine, and a double miracle that nobody in Macrae's ship was hit, so many were his bullet holes.

The six of 37 Squadron had emerged from the flak some way behind everyone else, still flying in their three pairs but in line astern, just as a flock of Me110s came hurtling in, led by Helmut Lent.

First to go down was the front man, raked by cannon fire from a Me110 and hitting the sea with wings on fire. His number two, Flying Officer Lemon, was alone and pursued by two Me109s. As they dived and raced at zero feet across the waves, the Wellington crew were rewarded with the sight of one of the fighters dipping his wing in the sea and disappearing in spectacular fashion. Lemon flew very low all the way home and waited for the others to come back. None of them did.

Of the twenty-two Wellingtons that reached the target, twelve were lost with fifty-eight crew dead and five POWs, while German air crew claimed thirty-four out of forty-four Wellingtons downed, later reduced to twenty-seven.

The ten returning Wellington crews claimed six 110s and six 109s. Actual score was no 110s although nine were damaged of which two force-landed, and two 109s shot down plus one force-landed. This was war as it had never been experienced before – terrifying, electrifying, shocking and, not surprisingly, liable to produce unreliable witnesses.

The newspapers were no more reliable.

Air Battle in Bight. 12 Enemy Craft Shot Down. The Air Ministry announced last night that a bomber formation of the R.A.F reconnoitred the Heligoland Bight area yesterday afternoon with the object of attacking any enemy warships found at sea.

No warships were encountered at sea, but the bombers met strong fighter forces.

Fierce fighting followed and 12 Messerschmitts were shot down. Seven of our bombers are at present unaccounted for.

The German news agency reported thirty-four 'of the most modern battle aeroplanes' shot down for the loss of two of their own. Two British crews were taken prisoner while the German pilots parachuted to safety and parts of the British planes were washed ashore.

Another report from the Fatherland gave fifty-two as the number of bombers engaged, with at least forty going down. *Oberstleutnant* Schumacher, the senior officer on the German side of the fight, gave a press conference in which he praised the British pilots as brave and enterprising, and the sound construction of the German aircraft, some of which had come home with thirty-five bullet holes, and some with one engine out of action. He confirmed that losses were two Me109s.

In his written report, he said that damage to his fighters was due to 'the tight formation and excellent rear-gunners', but that 'maintenance of formation and rigid adherence to course made them easy targets to find'.

Another commander, *Hauptman* Reinecke, wrote:

The Me110 is easily capable of catching and overtaking this English type even with the latter at full boost. This provides scope for multiple attacks from any quarter, including frontal beam. This attack can be very effective if the enemy aircraft is allowed to fly into the cone of fire. The Wellington is very inflammable and burns readily.

A reflective piece by *The Times* Aeronautical Correspondent asked if all this bomber activity was really worthwhile:

There have been since the outbreak of war a great many air operations the purpose of which is obscure. On all these occasions proof has been given of the fine fighting spirit of the Royal Air Force officers and men, and of the technical excellence of their equipment. But the question has been asked if an adequate return is being secured for the losses incurred.

The task of the bombers in seeking to obtain results (against warships rather than land targets) is multiplied in difficulty many times over, while the task of the defences which are set up against it is facilitated.

Petts was Mentioned in Despatches; his DFM would come later. Macrae had the DFC. Flight Lieutenant Grant and Leading Aircraftman Conolly were MiD. Jack Ramshaw had the DFM, as did his front gunner, the 18-year-old fitter/rigger seconded to the job, AC1 Charles Driver. He would stay as ground crew for another eighteen months before taking up gunning full time, and eventually would be commissioned. Some of the other survivors had medals too.

The men left from this calamity were interviewed by the RAF's Commander-in-Chief, Ludlow-Hewitt. Group Captain Hugh Pughe-Lloyd MC, DFC, OC IX Squadron at the start of the war, was now a 3 Group staff officer. He criticised the route taken to the target, running so far down the coast, 'giving the enemy all the warning he could get'.

Like the modern sports team defeated by a large margin, the senior commanders tried to take some positives out of the action.

The front runners, four of them as it panned out, had stuck together, lost only one and shot down many enemy, as then thought. The top brass still didn't know about the Freya radar. Had its operators been believed sooner, the

Air Vice Marshal J E A 'Jackie' Baldwin CB, DSO, OBE and MiD three times in the First World War, was AOC 3 Group at this time, 11 May 1940. He visited RAF Honington to present the DFM to Sergeant Jack Ramshaw.

AC1 Charles Driver was front gunner in Jack Ramshaw's Wellington at the Battle of Heligoland. After being fished out of the sea, 18-year-old Driver was awarded the DFM.

bombers who were first in and first out may not have been so unscathed.

The two that ditched would have had enough petrol to make it home if they had had self-sealing fuel tanks and armour in the port wing. Well, at least we can learn from that.

Baldwin was so sure that tight formation flying had saved the homecomers, that he blamed the losses on the dead commanders of IX and 37 Squadrons, Guthrie and Hue-Williams who, in his view, had shown poor leadership in flying too far ahead of their followers. Ludlow-Hewitt said this was a 'great and unforgivable crime', and that formations, unshaken under attack, were like the Thin Red Line of yore.

How many more Wellingtons would have to be shot down, and how many more men would have to die, before it was realised that Wellingtons in daylight were not a good idea?

Overheard in the IX Squadron Officers' Mess after the 18 December raid: 'The air was so thick with lead that I had to blind fly for ten minutes.'

CHAPTER 8

Germany?

Not yet

The old year went out in a flurry of snow and a lack of success. More losses to the German fighters finally convinced the senior commanders that Wellingtons could not defeat Me110s, no matter how close they kept formation. No more Wellingtons went in daylight to look for ships around Heligoland, and Ludlow-Hewitt was replaced as C-in-C by Charles Portal in April 1940.

In 1939, nobody had known how aerial warfare would work out. There were plenty of theories but the only way to prove any of them was to go and do it, and the only option was far away, a long journey that would test everything about the aircraft and the crew, to a place much more heavily defended than had been realised.

This was the first plain showing of the conundrum that Bomber Command would never solve. Experienced crews were much more likely to return, much less likely to be lost but – how do you get the experience? Frank Petts: '[after Wilhelmshaven] We had ten days' special leave and returned to find a new flight commander and a new squadron CO, Wing Commander 'Square' McKee. After Brunsbüttel and Wilhelmshaven there was a feeling, voiced mostly by the sergeant pilots, that we knew more about the war than either of these officers.' Not entirely fair, Frank. McKee had had the other great Heligoland experience, of 14 December with 99 Squadron, when they lost five Wellingtons, and was a leader from the front, an up-and-at-'em type. The flight commander, Squadron Leader L M E Jarman, later Air Commodore DFC and three times MiD, indeed had had no combat experience, but where was Petts going to find a flight commander who could say he had been shot at by Me110s? There were not so many around.

In March 1940, reconnaissance sorties brought home information about navy and troop build-ups in German ports and various sailings north to what looked like jumping-off points for an invasion of Norway. In response, twenty-four Wellingtons of IX and 115 Squadrons were moved to Lossiemouth, 2 April, to form a bomber wing under the orders of Coastal Command.

The brief seemed to reverse recent trends. Although sea sweeps had been fairly frequent, training had concentrated on night flying. Now it looked as if they were back to Wilhelmshaven-style daylights, trying to bomb shipping. Frank Petts:

> We were trained in night bombing of land targets; now we were being used in daylight against shipping. We'd been given postcard-size ship silhouettes with appropriate text, something like 'This is the Hood, one of ours', 'This is the Scharnhorst, much the same size, attack on sight'. Our means of attack was usually B bombs, which were like long, thin oil drums which weighed only 220lb and which, amazing to behold, floated.

Air Vice Marshall Sir Andrew McKee KCB, DSO, DFC, CBE, and CO of IX Squadron in 1940. From the moment he joined the RAF, in January 1927, he was known as 'Square' McKee, a simple reference to his personal geometry, his height of 5ft 5in being observed as equal to his width.

The idea was to fly just in front of the enemy warship at 10,000ft or lower, and drop the B bomb so that when it bobbed back up to the surface, said warship's thick armour plating would be obligingly steaming over it. Worried in case somebody more vulnerable might steam over, the bomb's designers had incorporated a humane self-sinking device. If the bomb for some hardly fathomable reason managed to miss the warship, the soap which held its nose-cone on would dissolve, the case would fill with water and down she would go. Frank Petts:

> One of our trips [7 April] was with six of 115 Squadron, to look for shipping off the Danish coast. We didn't find any but, on the way home, the 115 boys were jumped by a group of Me110s. It was over in an instant: two down. Balch saw one, from the rear turret. 'Fighters attacking

behind . . . they've got one of 115 . . . he's on fire . . . they're baling out
. . . they're shooting them up on the way down . . . they've gone.'

No bodies were found of the twelve men who died. Petts: 'Shooting trained aircrew meant they couldn't come back at you again, assuming they might have survived the Danish sea in April without a dinghy.'

Britain had been becoming increasingly furious with neutral Norway. Thousands of tons of (neutral) Swedish iron ore were being shipped from the Norwegian port of Narvik to Germany and thence down the ship-canal system to the industrial heartland, the Ruhr. The Royal Navy laid mines inside Norwegian territorial waters in an attempt to stop the traffic. The Norwegian government issued a heated protest, threatening to declare war on Britain. The Allies jointly issued a list of sea areas into which Norwegian ships would sail at their peril.

The Germans were outraged, naturally. This was the most flagrant violation of neutrality ever seen. Added to which, the Allies were obviously too cowardly and weak to fight Germany directly, and so conducted an underhand war using the neutral countries as pawns in the game.

As the newspapers published the Allies' list of forbidden sea areas on the morning of 9 April, Germany simultaneously invaded Norway and Denmark. Such action was deeply regretted by Germany, and it was only important military objectives that were the concern, and it was all done to secure Scandinavia against Allied aggression. Germany would respect the freedom and independence of the peoples of Denmark and Norway, and hoped very much that such respect would not be prejudiced by anything as silly as resistance, passive or active.

There was nothing the Allies could offer Denmark, but perhaps the Germans could be stopped in Norway. Bomber Command, without any fighter cover, was to slow the march of the invaders.

As the Aeronautical Correspondent of *The Times* put it, 'Command of the air over Norway will certainly have to be established before the Germans can be dislodged', but the Luftwaffe had every important airbase in Norway and Denmark from which to operate, while every op for the RAF bombers had a 300-mile sea flight on either end of it. They were taking off from the British mainland on the strength of scanty intelligence about a very fast-moving enemy who had caught everyone by surprise.

Orders were received at IX Squadron to attack enemy cruisers at anchor in Bergen harbour. They took off at 15.40 on 9 April. The targets were located and bombs were dropped. No hits were observed but Squadron Leader

Peacock did shoot down a Dornier Do18 flying boat. His immediate DFC was announced a few days later in the *London Gazette*: 'After the original attack by his formation he returned alone and repeated his run over the target in the face of heavy anti-aircraft fire. When on the return flight to his base he again turned back to attack a hostile flying-boat which was shot down into the sea.'

The German troopship *Levante* was the target on 11 April for No. IX. Frank Petts remembered the briefing:

Square McKee, our CO who was not coming on the op, asked us 'Have the captains worked out how you are going to attack any German aircraft you see?' It seemed to be the unique preserve of sergeant pilots to get up the CO's nose, and I did it again by saying 'Sir, we don't attack German aircraft. We run away from them'. There followed a mild explosion and a dissertation on how easily a Wellington could dispose of German fighters. 'Sir,' I said, 'how would you deal with one that sits back out of range of your guns and uses his cannon on you?' 'Nonsense,' said Square. 'They can't do that.'

Well, I told him I knew from personal experience that they could, and they could also sit on top of you, where you can't get them but they can get you. 'You're imagining things,' said McKee. I suggested he asked Sergeant Ramshaw about imagination but McKee had the last word. He told us we'd never win the war with spirit like that.

On the op our section split up, attacked by 110s. When we got back, the intelligence officers said there were no 110s so far north. I said my crew knew a 110 when they saw one, because we'd seen plenty at Wilhelmshaven.

The RAF was still not allowed to bomb Germany. All the ports where ships and troops had massed, and were still massing, could have been bombed but instead the bombers had to wait for the ships to set sail.

While trying to find two battle cruisers and a cruiser in ten tenths cloud down to 600ft, 12 April, horizontal visibility 1 mile in rain and sleet, Wellington P2520, captain Sergeant Charles Bowen, veteran of the squadron's first op, was lost with all hands. His was one of ten aircraft, Wellingtons and Hampdens, lost off the Norwegian coast that day, mostly to fighters.

The advanced bomber wing of IX and 115 Squadrons left Lossiemouth for their home bases on 14 April, No. IX being one short of their original twelve and 115 two down. The Germans had everything they wanted at very little expense. They were secure against attack through Scandinavia, they had ports like Bergen they could use for their U-boats against the American aid coming across the north Atlantic, they had fjords they could hide their battleships in, and they had their iron ore.

They had also humiliated the foe. They had invaded and taken two countries with the utmost speed and efficiency, meanwhile exposing the British and French as unable to do the slightest thing about it. There were hopeful articles in the press, and small victories trumpeted, and talk of a long campaign to reverse Hitler's great gamble, but the British and French governments were deeply shaken. If the Germans could conquer Poland, Norway and Denmark without any trouble at all, who was next?

An exception to the no-bombing-on-land rule was military targets in Norway occupied by the Germans. The prime one was Stavanger airfield. Six Wellingtons of IX Squadron went there on the night of 20/21 April. They met bad weather over the target area. Frank Petts:

> We tried from several directions but southwards stretched a solid sheet of low stratus. We could not find a break. Gilbert Heathcote [who would be killed in a Stirling at Brest in December 1941] had left my crew and was a skipper himself. He was coming back from this trip with not much idea of his position except it was over the sea somewhere, when the clouds suddenly broke and there were mountains smack in front. The crew never could agree afterwards on how much of a loop they did.

Three went to Stavanger again on the 30th on a joint raid with 99 Squadron. They had six bombs each, five of which were delayed action for up to 12 hours. ORB: 'Each captain claims to have actually hit the aerodrome with the one bomb which was seen to burst. It is assumed that the remaining delayed action bombs were dropped on the aerodrome.' Air crew might have believed they'd had a hit but really they were doing well to get anywhere near their aiming points. Bomb aiming was not a specialised trade. In the bigger machines, the Whitleys and Wellingtons, the observer did it, leaving his navigator's table as the target approached to clamber into the nose, or the second pilot did it.

Still the arguments went on about bombing targets that were not strictly military. The British position seemed to be that so long as the Germans didn't bomb British civilians, the RAF would not attack Germans. That the

Luftwaffe had already bombed Polish and Norwegian open cities did not come into the equation.

With the news that the Norwegian town of Kristiansund, 15,000 population, had been burned to the ground after five days of bombing, the British government reserved the right to withdraw orders prohibiting bombing civilian populations in the event of such bombing by the enemy.

They still didn't do it, though. It was more Norwegian airfields, more minelaying, small numbers of attackers, not much damage.

McKee, with Squadron Leader George Peacock DFC as second pilot, led six Wellingtons of IX Squadron for Rye aerodrome in central Denmark, about 60 miles inland from Arhus. ORB: 'The Danish coast was sighted at 21.15, approximately 5 miles south of Vorupor but an accurate pinpoint could not be made until Klitmonner was sighted [Klitmøller, 25 miles or so north]. From here a course was set direct to Rye.' This was a flight of about 230 miles, south-easterly, right across Jutland. 'The ETA at the target was 21.44 and although a search was made, Rye aerodrome could not be located.' Such an ETA would have been feasible if they'd had 500mph aircraft or Rye was not where it was.

There were five of them by now; one had gone home with u/s gun turrets. They set off for the east coast and made a pinpoint at 55.45°N 10.05°E (probably Ashoved peninsula).

> Here the formation separated, each aircraft setting a course from this point to Rye [now about 80 miles north-westerly]. Two aircraft found the target and carried out attacks. The remaining aircraft searched the area for approximately one hour, between 1,500 and 8,000 feet, but were unable to find the target and therefore returned to base with full bomb loads.

The weather over Denmark was 'clear but hazy'. There was no opposition. The wind was not as forecast but even so, that was a very poor display, and a half-hearted one from the higher command. Five Wellingtons on a 7½-hour trip, wandering around Denmark so that a few bombs could be dropped severally from 1,500ft and 10,000ft. What was the point of it?

Whatever had been the preoccupations of the RAF, the British government, the press and everyone else during the last month, Norway and Denmark would be almost entirely forgotten soon after dawn on 10 May.

Preparations had been made in Bomber Command in case of an attack by the Germans through the Netherlands, Belgium and Luxembourg, amid many arguments with the French. The British wanted to attack the Ruhr with the heavy bombers, flying from England across the Low Countries, in the expectation of destroying vital supplies of fuel and so on, which would greatly hinder the German advance.

The French didn't want that, as it would set the Luftwaffe free to bomb French cities and the British bombers' effects on the Ruhr would not be felt in the short term. They urged battle-support from the heavies, and from the France-based Blenheims and Battles. Air Marshal Portal, C-in-C of Bomber Command, was certain that fifty Blenheims and a hundred Battles would be able to do little to stop the Wehrmacht and would suffer huge losses in the process. Although it had been shown in several conflicts that bombers could be useful in support of an advancing army, there was no history of bombers stopping one.

Neville Chamberlain resigned as Prime Minister in favour of Winston Churchill on 10 May 1940. On the same day, Germany launched the Blitzkrieg against Holland and Belgium, British troops crossed the Belgian border from France to meet the Germans, and some Luftwaffe Heinkel He111s got lost on their way to a French target and bombed one of their own cities – Freiburg – by mistake, killing about sixty people. In the heat of all the Blitzkrieg success and excitement, as the German army and air force began its bash through Western Europe, Hitler still found time to charge the British with the inhuman cruelty of bombing the innocent citizens of Freiburg.

Surely, the bomber war was about to begin in earnest.

CHAPTER 9

Pilots

Tiny Cooling, Wellingtons, 1940
The phoney war was over and everywhere was
bustle and confusion. The spectre of 18 December
hovered over the airfield and for us freshmen,
thrown together with some experienced fellows and
told that we were now a crew, it was bewildering and
ominous. After a few false starts we eventually had
a briefing. We were to crater Waalhaven airfield and
soften up the German army there, in support of a
Dutch counter attack.

As we climbed above the shore, the setting sun
glinted on windows and narrow waterways, and up
ahead there was another set of lights, in a curtain,
rising from the ground with smoke behind. It was my
job to shut the wireless operator into the front turret,
then I was ordered into the astrodome to watch for
fighters although we weren't really expecting any. As
we went into our bombing run routine, the curtain of
lights was dead ahead, rising balls of pink, green,
white, slowly ascending towards us then hurtling
past. Then three things happened at once. The flak
curtain seemed to part and let us through, there was
the bucking bronco effect of dropping our bombs, and
I heard a smacking sound like hands clapping. I
looked, and we had a hole in our wing.

*Rupert Cooling, called Tiny
because he was 6ft 7in, was
the tallest man on a squadron
led by one of the shortest.
When Square McKee came to
offer Tiny a captaincy, he had
to stand on a box to do it.
Cooling's first op was on
10 May 1940, as a second
pilot aged 20.*

'Pilot from second pilot,' I said. 'We've been hit outboard of the starboard
engine.' I was quite surprised to hear myself on the intercom. I sounded rather
nonchalant.

PILOTS

I flew the aircraft over the sea while Sergeant Douglas [captain] checked the damage – the damage that he could see, that was. He took over for the landing, and we were down, and then we tugged viciously to the right and ended up square across the flarepath. The flak had punctured our starboard tyre, we had a self-sealing fuel tank bulging out like a huge haemorrhoid dripping and ready to burst, and we had holes punctured all over the starboard engine. After the interrogation, where they gave you sweet milky tea and as many cigarettes as you could smoke, Douglas bought me a pint. So, that was it. My first trip. It was good to be home. And I'd learned that it was possible to go out and come back.

We got to the Ruhr all right [15 May]. God knows if we got to Bottrop. We saw St Elmo's Fire for the first time, which turned the props into blue disks and there was a flickering lilac rainbow arc between the two front guns. Our wireless had gone for a loop and Dougie said the compass was drifting idly around and around, and we flew along with absolutely no idea where we were or where we might be going. It was a kind of limbo, eerie really, and then somebody said 'Maybe we're over England', so we came down through the cloud and saw we were over land but we didn't know which land. We signalled SOS with the downward recognition light and a flarepath lit up. Of course, the Germans knew SOS as well as we did, and I was standing by with the Very pistol ready to fire the aircraft. But it was the strip of a private aero club at Shoreham-by-Sea which, like a lot of south coast landing fields, had been alerted because of the expected escape of the Belgian royal family, following the Dutch a few days before. We weren't quite that important so we were offered sofas and chairs to kip down on in the flying club.

I don't know if our w/op Sergeant Oliver had been practising his French in Morse or if he was perfecting his knowledge of Q codes. Maybe nobody had told him that we were landing. Anyway, he hadn't wound in his trailing aerial and we lost it on the roof of Lancing College. They rang up next day and said they'd got 60ft of copper wire with some lead balls on the end and did it belong to us? So Oliver was in for a half-crown fine for losing his aerial.

It was that peculiar time in the war [20 May] when nobody was sure about what to do. We've got this force, we'd better use it, but how? As a force we were grotesquely under trained, but so were the Germans. They didn't know what to do about it either. We were showing the flag more than anything, roaming the countryside in the moonlight.

As we crossed the Suffolk coast near Southwold [3 June] we could see two sunsets. One was the fires at Dunkirk. There were several other

Wellingtons near us and it was one of the times I really felt I was doing something. Dougie had put me as first pilot on this sortie and I joined in a small formation with some other aircraft. Each was flying along, rising up and down on its own individual air currents, and I felt quite a surge of emotion.

Night of 5/6 June 1940 and the squadron was at full strength. Cooling as second pilot with Sergeant Douglas, plus Kirby-Green, Smalley, Purdy, Bull, Canton with Pilot Officer Walsh and five others went to the Somme to attack roads and railways. All complained about being hindered from doing their job properly by 'the intensity of the searchlight activities'. Smalley and three more captains switched to secondary targets. The picture shows Smalley's attack, at Rosières-en-Santerre; the objects in the squarish yard to the right of the bomb bursts are German guns.

Air crew sergeants lounging in the Honington sunshine, 1940. The one in the chair reading the paper is part of a May intake crew, Pilot Officer McDiarmid's wireless operator, Sergeant Jerry Hoey, from the Republic of Ireland.

The Wimpys went their separate ways and when we got to Dunkirk we made our approach high and to the south, avoiding the Royal Navy whose aircraft recognition wasn't so hot at that time. The sea was like a new sheet of beaten copper, with movement frozen by our height and the thousands of waves reflecting the glow of the blaze all about. We had sixteen two-fifty bombs which we dropped one at a time, hoping that we'd keep a few German heads down so that another boatload of our boys could get away.

Frank Butler's navigator, Charlie Naylor, was a very unusual chap for air crew. He didn't drink except in extreme moderation, he didn't smoke, he didn't chase women and he didn't swear. He was like the son of the manse. Unnatural, almost. Yet everybody liked him. He played chess all the time with a sergeant from the ack-ack unit. Anyway, he roomed over the corridor from me. We had our own rooms in the Mess in those early days. One morning [14 June] he knocked on my door and woke me up. We'd come back in the early hours from another raid on northern France, La Capelle, near the Belgian border. He came in with this anguished look on his face. 'Bob Hewitt's missing,' he said. 'His wife's expecting a baby.' He stood still in his shock. He was a big pal of Hewitt's. Then he collapsed onto his knees and buried his face in my bedding. He was sobbing his heart out, distraught, like a little girl. I was very embarrassed and had no idea what to say or do. Eventually he stopped. 'Sorry,' he said, 'I had to talk to someone.' I mumbled a few comforting words and put my arm around his shoulder. He just said thanks and went.

Another time, I'd had a couple of hours' sleep after ops when I was woken with the news that I was a captain today. Frank Butler was missing. Take off at 09.30 to help in the search. We began our sweeps 50 miles out, halfway to Holland. While the gunners searched the sea for a little yellow dot of a dinghy, and the sky for a little black dot of a fighter, I flew at 600ft in ever increasing rectangles, making 90° turns and lengthening the line each time until we'd drawn a straight-sided Catherine wheel and were 20 miles off the enemy coast. Then I flew to another starting point and did it over again.

If we found them, we'd have to circle over them with the telegraph key pressed down, so the rescue people could get a good bearing. This would alert the Germans too and we could expect interference from them by sea and air. But, we didn't find anything. We got excited about a yellow oil drum, but that's all it was. Nobody found anything. They were down there on the sea bottom, Butler and his men, and the son of the manse Charlie Naylor.

One afternoon the CO, Square McKee, came bouncing up to me and did his usual trick of backing up to the briefing table where there was a block the navigators used to stand on so they could lean over and peer at their maps. He stood on this block, which brought him somewhere near level with me.

'Can you be a captain?' he said. I said I thought so, but he wasn't interested in what I thought. 'Can you, or can't you, damn it?' was his attitude, so I said I could, and Square told me to pick up with the next new crew that came in.

New skippers had to practise night flying. You'd do three circuits and landings, with a minimum crew on board which was you, the second pilot and the w/op. I was made up to captain at the same time as Pilot Officer Wanklyn and we were on for our practice on the same night. Wanklyn said he was going to something in the Mess, would I take first turn, so I did, and finished about half-past nine. Wanklyn was in the crew room. He said 'Aircraft all right?' and I said it was fine as far as I was concerned. He took off and I was making my way back when there was a god almighty thump, the typical ball of flame that you learned to recognise with the black smoke, and it was Wanklyn going in. He might have been on the downwind part of his circuit, I don't know, but pilot error I would say. When I walked into the Mess some of my crew were there looking like ghosts. 'Thank Christ,' they said. 'We thought that was you.'

We were having lunch in the Sergeants' Mess [19 August]. We heard the whistle of a stick of bombs coming down and immediately the dining room took on the look of the *Marie Celeste*. Plates of food steamed gently and not a soul in sight. We were under the tables. One bomb hit the parade ground

In July, a month of German ops with no losses, there were some important arrivals, including a new CO, Wingco Tim Healy taking over from Square McKee who was bound for higher things, and a shiny new Wellington for Tiny Cooling, T2468 WS/Y-Yorker.

and killed a number of airmen and WAAFs in the lunch queue, about a dozen. Another hit the barrack block and blew it to bits. When the racket died down, most of us sat back at the table and finished our lunch. We would find out what happened later.

Six of us were set for Hamm at 19.30. We took off, reached the coast, and there was something seriously wrong with the aircraft although we couldn't tell what. We couldn't get her above what felt like about 85 knots, although we couldn't tell that either because the airspeed indicator was u/s. So I turned round and came back, with a full fuel load and a full bomb load. We came in to land grossly overweight, with the airspeed showing as zero and the crew showing every sign of full confidence in me, such as tightly clenched arse cheeks and badly bitten lips. Anyway, we got down somehow by the seat of my pants, transferred to the standby aircraft WS/W and took off again.

My last one was an odd one. The Royal Navy was going to send fire ships into Boulogne while the RAF bombed the docks, and Tom Purdy was without a second pilot. I said I'd go. It was a highly specialised raid and desperately secret. We were to say nothing about it, even if it was scrubbed. I went over to East Wretham (Honington satellite drome) to collect a few spares from 311 Squadron. They were the Czechs who had been fighting in France, now flying all our old Wellington 1As. I had no worries about going anywhere with Tom Purdy. He was one of the very best and Boulogne was a great trip, good results, lots of flak, late back, bed 06.20. And then they decided I was to be screened [tour completed], along with a tremendous lot of others. They

Some of the Czech air crew have a beer with Tom Purdy, sitting on the right.

Jimmy James, sitting centre with some of his colleagues at OTU in April 1940, flew his first op to Duisburg, 18 May, as second pilot to Squadron Leader Peacock.

shifted out the old lags and brought in a lot of new boys. It wasn't 200 hours or a number of ops; they just decided, and that was that. I'd done twenty-seven ops, actually, and they sent me a short while later to Training Command.

Bertram 'Jimmy' James, Wellingtons, 1940

At Duisburg on my first, we circled the area for at least 15 minutes, at 10,000ft in bright moonlight. Never a shot was fired although a searchlight turned on to us. Bill [Webster, 36-year-old American volunteer gunner] fired down the beam and it went out.

Then we were bombing and machine-gunning German transport, roads and railways. It was armed reconnaissance basically, at low level. We had the Group Navigation Officer with us one time, Squadron Leader Graham, and he got us lost for a while. Somebody was chased by a fighter but we didn't see one. Two nights later we went with one other Wimpy from the squadron to a river bridge at Namur [River Meuse, near Charleroi, Belgium]. We had a very hot reception from light flak. George [Peacock] set us up at about 2,000ft then went into a shallow dive, the flak whizzing past us. On these low-level jobs we'd bomb at about 500ft, when George would pull us up and we'd get a 500ft boost when our bombs exploded, and we'd come home with a lot of holes from the flak.

My last was Duisburg again [5 June]. Square McKee always went to the control tower to say a last word to the crews flying on operations. We took off and Square came over on the radio, saying 'Good luck' as ever. George Peacock's normal reply was 'So long, sir' but tonight he said 'Goodbye'. McKee said 'Come off it, George. We never say goodbye,' but George said nothing more.

An hour later, crossing the Dutch coast, we were caught in searchlights at 10,000ft. Four flak batteries opened up on us and the port engine caught fire. The skipper gave the order to bale out. Three of us left by the front hatch but Ronnie Hargrave's parachute caught fire and he fell all the way and was killed [Sergeant R C Hargrave DFM, w/opAG]. Another left from the centre, and Bill Webster from the rear turret. We saw our aircraft blow up and go in. The skipper had no chance to get out himself.

I sprained my ankle in landing but managed to walk towards the coast for two nights and a day. I had some very good help from the locals but was eventually taken up by the Dutch police and handed over to the Germans. Later, at prison camp, I was delighted to meet up with Bill again and hear his story about his parachute jump.

His way out had been on the port side, where all the flames were. He hesitated, hanging half out of the turret, with his leg caught in his guns. The aircraft went into a steep dive, his chest-mounted parachute pack whipped up past his head in the wind, and the chute opened with a crack. The sudden force of it hauled Webster clear, leaving only a little skin, blood and RAF cloth behind when he might have left a whole limb.

About a year after our capture we were in Stalag Luft I, Barth, and Bill Webster was in the top bunk above me. One night, everybody in the hut was woken by a noise, and somebody got up and put the light on. There was Bill, lying on the floor groaning but not too badly hurt, and he said 'I was dreaming. I thought I'd bailed out of a Wimpy'. [See also Escapes, Evasions and Captures, p. 223.]

Alan Mackay, Wellingtons, 1940–1

An ancient custom was with the non-return from an operation of a friend or roommate, and we were all one or the other. A share-out would be made of the best of his uniform and whatever was left of parcels from home. We did it in an atmosphere of 'it might be me next'. Gordon Heaysman, Hemmings's second pilot, who was a fresher like me, was reported shot down as was another Wellington that night, with all lost. Next day we heard Heaysman and crew were all right so there was a mad scurry to return those things which had been reallocated. To the eternal credit of their friends, whom they may have otherwise thought a right bunch of gannets, it all went back apart from the Christmas cake Heaysman's mother had made him.

I was joined up as second pilot with Batchelor, who had come from towing drogues in Fairey Battles. I think I had more hours on Wellingtons than he had but he was a squadron leader and a regular officer so he was the boss. He did the take-off and landing. I did some in the middle and searched through the astrodome, so that was my first sight of searchlights and so on, through the astrodome. And frightening it was. You saw the lines of tracer snaking up, waving, trying to seek you out.

As well as our bombs we often had leaflets, called nickels for some reason, in largish bundles. We were supposed to undo the bundles and shove them down the flare chute. Sometimes, especially if the Germans were firing at us, we said to hell with it and let them go tied up in their bundles, hoping they might hit somebody.

My first as captain was Wilhelmshaven. Nobody had told us about area bombing. It was still a gentleman's war as far as we knew and we were told to bomb shipping only and to keep well away from the houses. We had a shock when we were boxed in. You had a line of searchlights either side then they closed the box with more searchlights fore and aft. You were trapped and they threw everything into the box. The dodge was to change the pitch of the propellors and put the engines out of synch. The difference in the sound gave the impression you were diving and the searchlights dipped to follow while you flew straight on and got away. That was the idea anyway. When we got there, we bombed and reported that ours had fallen half a mile north of the target, although how we calculated that I've no idea.

There was no planning at all. You chose your own height. We generally flew at 12,000ft where you didn't need oxygen all the time. You could struggle up to 18,000 in a Wellington but it took a long time getting there when you could have been on your way to the target. You chose your own directions too, according to the skills of your navigator and, if several squadrons were attacking, anything could happen. Occasionally you'd see something flash past your window, and it was a load of bombs. Haphazard, that's what it was, a bit of a shambles, and we knew it.

The worst job was if you were tail-end Charlie, the crew with the camera. At the briefing they would say 'Tonight, it's you' and you were given the company camera, which meant being last man in and flying straight and level until our navigator as bomb aimer, George McRiner, said he'd got a good shot.

There was a very heavy fall of snow one day [10 February] so we all thought, good-oh, a night out in Bury St Edmunds, but the CO said no, you're flying tonight, and he had all the erks and WAAFs in lines, twelve abreast, walking up and down the grass all day, stamping the snow down with their feet.

It was Hannover we were going to, and we bombed a flak emplacement. On the way back, as was our routine, we came down to a thousand feet as we crossed the coast, the argument being that we were less likely to be spotted by a night-fighter and, flying flat out, or as flat out as a Wellington could go, we offered less opportunity for the flak outposts to get us lined up. It was a full moon as well, so that didn't help matters.

Anyway, we were going fine when Bill Ainsworth in the front turret chirped up, Suffolk coast ahead, 5 minutes. George [McRiner] said that was impossible. We were 30 miles away. Bill gave his considered opinion that the navigator was off his chump because he could see searchlights and gun flashes. The coast was being attacked. As this discussion was becoming animated we reached this coast and saw that it was a convoy, one of ours, being attacked by a couple of German aircraft. As soon as the ships saw us they banged away at us also, so Milly [Millington, second pilot] fired off the colours of the day. The ships just carried on firing while the Germans saw our flare and turned on us too.

We were being hit all over the place, and they knocked out the starboard engine and damaged the port one. We staggered along but we were dropping lower and lower and, as we crossed the coast at last, it was obvious we weren't going to make it home. We also realised we'd been flying very low over the sea and we'd forgotten to inflate our Mae West jackets. Must remember next time, we said. It was black-out of course, deep, deep darkness, and we looked for somewhere to lob down. It was flat country and there were some decent patches of different coloured black that looked as if they might be good fields so I put the undercart down and had a go. We hit something, a tree, or a pole put in the field to stop people landing in it, and spun around. Milly hurt his knee but that was the only injury.

We all clambered out and had a look around. There was a house. We could see it against the sky. It was after one o'clock in the morning but there was somebody out walking who just said goodnight as if he met a bomber crew every evening around there. We marched up to the farmhouse and knocked on the door, and an old boy leaned out of an upstairs window with a shotgun and told us to bugger off. He let us in eventually but we had to remove our flying boots in case we dirtied his carpet. We found out that we'd crashed between Martlesham and Woodbridge, 20 miles or so from Honington but, more important for us, a mile or two inland.

They'd been appealing for volunteers to go to the North African theatre and we thought that sounded a lot warmer than Suffolk in winter. George didn't want to go so Alan Butler came with us, who'd been observer with Flying Officer McIntosh DFC. We set off [9 March] with a load of mail for the soldiers in Africa, petrol and miscellaneous supplies, intending to stop off in Malta, but we were hardly a hundred feet up when the airspeed indicator packed in.

Our wireless and R/T were fitted up for the Middle East so we had no communication with the ground and they'd doused the flarepath lights. We fired off all our Very cartridges, got nothing and lost sight of the aerodrome. Our new observer said where he thought it should be so I did a quick turn and we saw the church, so I told the crew to prepare for a crash landing and be ready to get out fast as we had over a thousand gallons of petrol on board. Landing without your ASI in daylight is bad enough, when at least you can see roughly how fast you're going, but this was night, pitch black.

We were just over the perimeter hedge when the flarepath came on. We hopped over a cement mixer and got down. It was a very close thing, landing

Wireless operator Sergeant Jim House receives bread, coffee and no sympathy from the captors of Mackay and crew. The skip himself looks on grimly.

on estimated speed with a lot of petrol swishing about. We only just made it, so we expressed our relief by going on a bender. We were all fully recovered by the time we set off again next night, except Milly who was feeling a bit rough.

They told us Malta was no good anymore, so we would go to Benina, near Benghazi, 1,920 miles and 12 hours away, which was the limit for a Wimpy. I think it was the first time anybody had tried it non-stop. In any case, we had no margin for error. Twelve hours was a long time in a Wellington and, for me, it was largely without the help of the second pilot who was laid out on the cot saying he would never go drinking with us again. Little did we know what a prophet he was.

We crossed the Tunisian coast on ETA with 10/10 cloud below. We were pointed more or less due east when the sun rose and we were duly impressed

Before the war Sergeant Alan Mackay had been a sub-editor at D C Thompson, the Dundee publisher of the Beano *and* Dandy. *In prison camp, Stalag Luft III, Mackay promoted himself to editor and produced the 'Daily Recco', a remarkable camp newspaper, at first hand-written and pinned up on the noticeboard every day. In its later, typewritten format, much and often censored, it had to report such news as was available of the massacre after the 'Great Escape'.*

with the speed it came up in southern parts. One of our wing tanks didn't empty so we were flying heavy on one side for a lot of the way and no matter what I did with the trim I still had to make constant and continuous corrections and physically hold the kite level. It was very tiring and Milly was u/s with a self-inflicted alcoholic wound. Jim [House, w/op] wasn't having any joy with contacting Benina so we had to go down below the cloud to see exactly where we were. We broke out at a thousand feet, over the sea. Jim got a bearing from Malta but thought it was a bit fishy, possibly a German signal to mislead us.

At any rate, we hit the Bay of Sirte [Khalij Surt, Libya] at a spot which, when we'd left England, had been occupied by the Eighth Army. They'd been doing a rapid retreat while we'd been airborne but nobody had told us. We came in at a thousand feet and the Germans were very welcoming. They shot the aircraft full of holes from the ground and a Me110 added some more from the air with Steve Bevan, our rear gunner trying to make some holes in return. Amazingly they missed all of us crew and there was just about enough Wellington left to land so we came in on the beach, got out, shot some Very cartridges into the remains to finish her off and waited. What seemed like the entire Afrika Korps came at us. They were in a great semi-circle, infantry, tanks, motor bikes, armoured cars, the lot. They obviously expected six British airmen to cause a lot of trouble. The senior officer came up to me and actually said, like they do in the films, 'For you ze var is over'.

Warren Ramey, Wellingtons, 1941–2
Pearl Harbor was attacked on 7 December 1941, when there were some 6,000 Americans in the RCAF, including about 4,000 air crew at some point in their training and 800 operational air crew in Britain with Fighter, Bomber and Coastal Commands. One such was Sergeant Warren Thompson Ramey of Whitefish Bay, Milwaukee, Wisconsin, and IX Squadron, Honington, writing here to an old school pal in 1942.

I can tell you I'm with one of the best bomber squadrons in England. It is one of the [censored] and has a shining reputation of marvellous deeds. If there is any special task to be done, we get it! Can't tell you the type of plane, but I can tell you it is as big as a house, goes like the very Devil himself is after it, carries tons and tons of bombs, has guns covering every available angle of attack and is as powerful as a fleet of trucks.

They are really swell to fly. I'm glad I decided to be a bomber pilot instead of sticking to the single engine ships. I'm kinda proud of myself for being able to fly these big ships. They run about a mile down the field before taking off. You can fly around for [censored] hours without landing if you wish. I'm getting all sorts of flying in – day, mist, fog, night, beam flying, low flying and just plain flying. My hours are piling up daily.

I've been all over Germany, France, Holland, Belgium and England by air. Have visited all the important places in this country and met people from every country in the world. New Zealand, Newfoundland, Iceland, France, Czecho-Slovakia, Russia, Poland, Belgium, Holland, Italy, Spain, South Africa, Australia, Rhodesia and plenty of others. I've bombed every city in the countries I've been over that has anything of value in it. I've been shot at by every anti-aircraft gun in Germany, been hit by a couple, flown a burning plane across the Channel and bailed out by parachute just half an hour's swim from the shore [England's shore, Herne Bay].

Perhaps you would like to go with me on a raid to, say, Hamburg? Okay, here we go. In the morning you go over your plane, from nose to tail, from aerial mast to tires, everything must be perfect. You don't get a second chance in this game. Then you air test it, which consists of flying it around to see that everything is in order. If not, you tell the ground crew when you land and they fix it immediately. The gunners check, double check and triple check their guns, turrets and sights. Guns must be in perfect harmonization and working order. Wireless operator checks all his equipment. He has a radio station of no small power to look after. His equipment may be the difference between arriving safely home through heavy fog, or not.

The morning is gone – dinner – then to the briefing to learn the target for tonight and each aircraft's duty. Can't tell you much about that or what follows but – we are on the line ready to take off – we get the signal and away we go down the runway, [censored] horsepower roaring out their challenge to the cold night air. Finally you are in the air – wheels up, everything set, you set course for your target.

It may take three and one half hours to get there or only one or two. Your crew are at their posts doing their special tasks. Gunners swinging turrets around looking for enemy aircraft, observer checking the course by star sights or ground fixes, wireless operator listening for signals of various natures, second pilot back in the fuselage checking oxygen delivery, oil consumption, petrol consumption and just generally keeping busy – pilot at the controls of [censored] tons of aircraft with its big load of bombs, keeping on the course given by the observer navigator, climbing, ever climbing into the cold night skies.

The temperature steadily drops, 10, 15, 20, 25, 30 below zero (Fahrenheit). Now you are over enemy territory, searchlights probe the skies for the plane. Huge cones are formed and must be avoided, the flak begins to burst in the sky about you, you 'jink' away, diving a bit when the shells are on your level, turning left or right or climbing, but always on toward your target. Finally you near it – Hamburg – way down there [censored] below, sirens are sounding, people are rushing to their shelters, gun and searchlight crews are rushing to their posts. Puzzling dummies are lit to

116

mislead you, searchlights spring into brilliancy from all over. Flak begins to blot the sky with fiery patches of flame. You see your target – let's say, a railway yard.

The observer is at his bomb aimer's position, his bombsight set, his finger on the bomb release – you are getting near the target – the ground defenses realize you are there, they multiply the shells by tens, the sky is filled with flying steel, stench of burned cordite and multicolored flashes. 'Left, left, left,' says the bomb aimer. 'Bomb doors open,' you say.

In the spacious belly of your plane is cradled a load of high-explosive bombs, the doors swing open, the target passes across the sight. 'Bombs gone,' says the observer and the plane leaps into renewed vitality as thousands of pounds of its weight screams downwards toward the target. A few seconds later the whole world seems lit up by the blast as your bombs hit the earth – what happens on the ground we don't see – we close the doors and head for home.

The gunners below won't give up and the shells scream through the air all about you, causing you to do things with the huge plane that people who have never been over wouldn't believe can be done. Then the long trek home – gradually descending – the sea – then the English coast and silently everyone breathes a sigh of relief – back to the field and down on good old terra firma. Gee, how good it is to be back.

There. You now have one operation under your belt. We have hundreds – really it isn't so bad – the shells lose their terror and the dodging becomes natural after a few trips. Don't know how much of that the censor will let through but can't see what I've given away so I figure all will get through. Hope so at least.

I reckon that's about enough for one letter. I'm well and fairly happy – I'll be happier when all this is over.

It was all over for Ramey on 22 April 1942 after Cologne, a small, experimental raid testing the new navaid, the Gee box, as a blind-bombing tool in cloud. Eight IX Squadron Wellingtons went. One fell at the target, another was brought down by flak over Holland, and Ramey's was very badly damaged. Outstanding pilot that he was, Ray Ramey struggled back to within sight of the home flarepath. With less than a mile to go and his emergency landing lined up, the aircraft gave up on her crew and they went in near Sapiston with only the rear gunner surviving. Warren Ramey's wife, Dolores, received the dreaded telegram from the RCAF Chief of Air Staff only an hour after the postman had brought her a new photograph of her husband, with a cheerful note hoping that she and the son he never saw, Steven, were well. A week later, the 700 pupils of Whitefish Bay high school held a memorial service and sang 'The Star Spangled Banner'.

SECRET No. 9 Squadron Combat Report

Date: 14th/15th June 1943. Pos. Oberhausen. Lancaster 'A'. Captain F/O Van Note.

Our aircraft was intercepted by a T/E E/A [twin-engined enemy aircraft] on the return journey from the target at 01.54 hours in bright moonlight at Soesterburg, 23,000 feet, rectified airspeed 165mph. The Boozer had shown Yellow and the pilot had been doing a moderate weave for about ten minutes when the rear gunner [Sergeant Dale] reported E/A 500 yards astern flying the same course. On instruction from the rear gunner the pilot made a diving turn to port and the E/A

An American pilot, Flying Officer Bob Van Note, from Boulder, Colorado, had a quite remarkable career. During a time when there were losses on virtually every German raid by Bomber Command – forty-five Lancs went down on his last three raids alone – Van Note suffered hardly a scratch worth reporting. The combat report is from his last, his thirtieth trip, thus completing his tour, twenty of them in his faithful ED493 WS/A-Apple. Van Note transferred to the USAAF after that. Here he is in captain's uniform with Mrs Van Note outside Buckingham Palace with his DFC.

Bombers were on their own once anything happened not covered by the orders and each crew felt themselves to be an independent team, alone in a hostile world. Over Cologne, 4/5 July, this was Bunker's view after bombs gone. Reggio nell' Emilia, 15 July: Flight Lieutenant Dicky Bunker was about halfway when his starboard inner went u/s. He wove his way through the Alps in the dark on three engines or, as he put it, the Alps 'were negotiated below safety height. Centre of Genoa bombed from 6000 feet at 04.03'. Bunker landed in Algeria after a 10-hour trip. Wing Commander Richard Henry Bunker DSO, DFC and Bar, was killed taking off in a faulty Stirling, 20 April 1945.

followed the bomber down. At 400 yards both the rear and mid-upper gunners fired bursts which appeared to enter the fuselage of the E/A. The pilot then started a barrel corkscrew and the E/A broke away starboard quarter from which direction it made another attack firing short bursts with cannon and machine guns, the tracer of which was observed to pass well above the bomber. Rear and mid-upper gunners fired long bursts and the tracer was seen to enter the E/A which broke away in a dive and was not seen again. No damage was sustained by the bomber. The E/A is claimed as damaged. No ground co-operation of any kind was observed and no unusual phenomena.

Mid-upper turret 250 rounds, no stoppages.

Rear turret 1200 rounds, no stoppages.

SECRET No. 9 Squadron Combat Report
22/23rd October 1943, Kassel. F/O Manning. Lancaster WS/B.
MU and RG both sighted a Dornier 217, 300 yards starboard quarter
up. RG ordered corkscrew starboard. Both gunners and E/A opened
fire. As the E/A's fire passed above our A/C, the navigator, standing
in the astrodome, sighted a second E/A port quarter up at 400 yards.
As he warned the gunners the E/A opened fire and hit the Lanc all
along the port side, killing the MU [Sergeant Provis], wounding and

*Flying Officer Albert Manning and crew, home from Stettin, 5 January 1944, in
the squadron's longevity record holder, W4964 WS/J-Johnny Walker. From the
left: navigator Flying Officer James Hearn, Manning, rear gunner Flight
Sergeant 'Pinky' Hayler, mid-upper Sergeant John Zammit, flight engineer
Sergeant Bill Burkitt, wireless leader Flight Lieutenant A G Newbound (standing
in for the regular man Flight Sergeant Caines). The bomb aimer, Flight Sergeant
Peter Warywoda, is standing behind Manning. Hearn, Burkitt and Warywoda
were crew originals; they and their skipper, and Zammit who replaced Provis,
were killed near the end of their tours, at Frankfurt, on 22 March.*

Bardney – note the tiny dots of Lancasters parked at their dispersals.

disabling the RG [Sergeant Birkinshaw] and slightly injuring the navigator [Flying Officer Hearn]. As those two E/As broke away, the navigator saw two Ju88s closing in, one on either beam down. They fired but missed. Pilot continued to corkscrew throughout these attacks which happened almost simultaneously. Hydraulic pipes below pilot's seat severed. Visibility hampered by reflection of searchlights on perspex.

Robert Lasham, Lancasters 1943–4
I did my early training in Florida – I was in Miami the day the Japanese attacked Pearl Harbor – came back to England, flew Ansons full of trainee w/ops, went to night-fighter school and eventually completed as a Lancaster pilot with several hundred flying hours more than most, including a lot of night experience. My second Dicky (work experience trip as second pilot) was with Flight Lieutenant Mitchell in O-Orange, quite a famous aircraft (ED700 WS/O). I stood behind the pilot's seat all the way to Berlin and back. He didn't say much and I couldn't see much. It was a quiet night for us, ten

tenths cloud, although the squadron lost two. It's not a good observation point, behind the seat.

My first as captain, Berlin again [2 December] seemed like routine until we were nearly home. Our fuel gauges were registering almost empty when we reached Bardney and there was a queue waiting to land so we were peeled off to Fiskerton. In fact there was plenty of petrol; it was just the gauges that were wrong. Fiskerton was only a few miles from Bardney so they put us in a car and whisked us back home for the interrogation, and we went to bed.

I hadn't heard much on the trip from my rear gunner, Eddie Clark, who was older than the rest of us. We were late teens and early twenties but he was in his thirties. Anyway, after we landed we found out why he'd been

This was Bob Lasham's bombing photo from his first trip as skipper, 2/3 December 1943, flying through the flak – 'routine until we were nearly home'.

quiet. His oxygen supply had partially failed and one of his heated shoes had packed up completely and his foot was frozen. He had to have some toes amputated and we never saw him again. If this had happened later in my experience I might have investigated more and come down lower, but my orders were to stay at that height and, being new, that's what I did.

There was a fortnight off for the moon, then it was Berlin [16 December]. On the return, our Gee box was u/s and the navigator got completely lost. I put out a Darky call [emergency distress codeword; Darky calls were made on a special radio-telephone channel under the control of the pilot]. After a quarter hour of this there was an answer, 'Churchyard', and a searchlight to show us the way to what turned out to be a tiny grass airfield almost on the beach at Donna Nook (Coastal Command Beaufighter station between Mablethorpe and Cleethorpes). After we got down, my first job was to telephone Bardney to tell them where we were. One of the Donna Nook people asked me if I'd missed my own base before. Oh yes, I said, on purpose and by mistake. Four times altogether. So how many ops have you done, he asked. I looked at my crew all standing round me with stupid grins on their faces, trying not very hard not to laugh. Four, I said.

We were up to six by Christmas, with Frankfurt and another Berlin. We reckoned if you got through six you'd probably got the hang of things and the crew would be operating and co-operating well, and you might even think you'd get to the end of it. My navigator Joey Bosley had arranged to get married on Christmas Day so they had to give us all leave. Excellent piece of navigation, we thought.

SECRET No. 9 Squadron Combat Report
Date: 14 January 1944. Time: 19.30 hrs. Height: 23,000 ft. Target: Brunswick.
Lancaster: 'O'. Captain: P/O Lasham.
The Lancaster was doing a banking search to starboard when it was struck by a burst of cannon and machine gun fire from the port bow down which damaged the rear of the fuselage and the rear turret. The pilot immediately commenced to corkscrew and while climbing starboard was hit again on the port wing.

Sergeant Swindlehurst was our rear gunner for the first time, which made him a regular, and we had two more first-time strangers in the crew who must have thought they'd joined the circus. A fighter had a go at us and did manage to wreck the rear turret and generally shoot us up but otherwise we seemed

CHRISTMAS 1943
IX Squadron Bomber Command
R.A.F. Bardney Lincolnshire

Composed in the IX Squadron Sergeants' Mess, Bardney, Christmas 1943. Sung to the tune of 'Bless 'em all':

They say there's a Lancaster out on the field, waiting to go on a flight
With hydraulics leaking and engine revs down, but hoping to get there all right.
There's one or two cylinders running a temp, one rudder adrift from its fin,
But with good navigation and much concentration we're hoping to get to Berlin.

We know that the Hun has some very fine kites, of this we're no longer in doubt.
When ever a Focke-Wulf gets up on our tail, this is the way we get out.
We go into a corkscrew, we dive and we weave, we don't give the kraut time to think.
We show no repentence, just pass the death sentence and shoot him right down in the drink.

When over the target our bombs hurtle down, as soon as we press on the tit.

124

There's searchlights upon us, there's fighters around, two engines have gone for a shit.
The crew's in a panic, they want to bale out, all into the searchlights and flak.
There's no jubilation, complete consternation, we know that we'll never get back.

The end of our story sees us at The Gates, where Peter imparts all the gen.
It seems they've no room for a whole bomber crew, no billets for our type of men.
So that's it, we've had it, we won't get our harps, we won't get our issue of wings.
Too late for repentence, there's no bloody entrance, so join in the chorus and sing.
Bless 'em all, bless 'em all, the long and the short and the tall.
Bless the air gunners, the wireless op too, bless the bomb aimer, the pilot and crew
'Cos we're saying goodbye to them all, as into their aircraft they crawl.
They're off on an op and they may get the chop,
So cheer up, my lads, bless 'em all.

to be all right. I did my check around the crew. Everybody answered except Singleburst, as we called him. Doug [Nicholls, w/op] took the portable oxygen to see what was up but no reply came back. I sent Bill [Yates, engineer] who set off with the fire axe. Same result, nothing. I didn't know if they were falling out of a hole in the back end or what but I thought I had better get lower, below oxygen height, before I sent anybody else to see what was happening.

I only had one of my own crew left, Harry Wilson the bomb aimer, so I sent him. He found two men unconscious through lack of oxygen, including Singleburst with a slight wound from a cannon shell, and Bill just coming round from his no-oxygen black-out. Bill decided we had landed in Germany and Harry was the enemy, so he attacked him with the fire axe. No harm done in the end.

We were coming home one time and a coolant tank burst and, as it would, set the starboard outer on fire. The coolant was glycol based and burned with a brilliant light, which made you feel very exposed like you were walking down Piccadilly without your trousers. Following procedure, I said 'Fire drill, starboard outer. Prepare to abandon aircraft,' expecting the flight engineer to feather the propellor and work the extinguisher. Bill [Yates, engineer] moved rapidly to feather the wrong engine, the starboard inner, and dived for the escape hatch with his parachute. His second mistake of the night was to pull the rip cord there and then, so silk streamed out behind him as he headed for the door. I'd have liked to have seen the expression on his face but I was too busy feathering the burning engine and restarting the good one. We got back a bit late but I still couldn't sleep. Next day we were on again and, on the way to the briefing, Sergeant Powell, our mid upper, told Bill Yates that the CO had issued special instructions that we were to take off 30 minutes before everybody else. Why, says Bill. To practise feathering, says Powell.

We were sometimes scrubbed when were in the aircraft, ready to start the engines. It was never explained why, or how we were supposed to wind down. Our answer was simple. Officially we weren't allowed off the station until told so, but we knew where to go and what to do. It was down to the Jolly Sailor to see Mr and Mrs Turner. Harry [Wilson, bomb aimer] was very friendly with them and we used to stop behind after time to help them wash up and so on. This was entirely out of the goodness of our hearts and nothing at all to do with the great rashers of gammon with eggs and chips that came out afterwards for our supper.

We thought of Mrs Turner as quite an old lady. She was probably mid-forties, which seemed old to us, and she used to put up aircrew wives sometimes in her letting room, but she stopped it. She had too many grieving widows to deal with when husbands failed to return. She couldn't stand it anymore. I was in the flight offices one day when a gunner came in asking if he could have the morning off later in the week to get married. He was given a seventy-two (hour pass), came back, and was killed on his next op, so he had a three-day honeymoon and a three-day married life. Such things were everyday, commonplace. It happened all the time.

At this time of the war, we were virtual certainties for a second tour if we got through our first. I suggested we transfer to pathfinders. Some of the boys were reluctant, thinking that they might not get caught for a second, but I was sure of it. A second tour with Pathfinders was only fifteen ops, we could stay together as a crew, we could get it over with, and we all got promotion by one rank. Seemed like a good idea at the time, so we went to 97 Squadron.

Bob Lasham DFC and Bar finished with over fifty ops, having insisted on keeping going until all his crew had their forty-five.

SECRET No. 9 Squadron Combat Report
Date: 24th March 1944. Time: 00.47. Height: 24,000 ft. Target:
Berlin.
Lancaster: LL845 WS/L. Captain: Flight Sergeant W R Horne

On leaving the target the Navigator was using broadcast winds which
took the aircraft 60–70 miles off track, which eventually brought our
aircraft into the Ruhr. Ten minutes previous to striking the Ruhr the
Rear Gunner had gone unconscious due to lack of oxygen, cause
unknown. The rear turret was unserviceable also, possibly due to
frozen hydraulics.

On entering the Ruhr, a master beam picked us up and the aircraft
was immediately coned by approx 30 searchlights and fired on by very
accurate heavy flak for 40 minutes, which holed the starboard
mainplane, bomb aimer's position, pilot's windscreen, port mainplane,
bomb doors and port fin. During all this period the Pilot was wounded
and blind, the Bomb Aimer had flak in his leg and the Rear Gunner
was unconscious on the rest bed. Through alteration of course and
height and diving turns, our aircraft escaped the searchlights and flak.

The Mid Upper Gunner and Engineer were searching and our
aircraft was almost at once attacked from the port beam at a range of
approx 200 yards by an unidentified enemy aircraft which fired a two
or three second burst and broke away starboard quarter down, where
we lost him. The burst damaged the MU perspex. MU Gunner did not
see him on account of his searching the starboard beam. RG Sergeant
Parkes fired 0 rounds. MU Sergeant Morton fired 300 rounds.

Russ Gradwell, Lancasters, 1944
When we were on those 5 Group ops, with Cheshire marking, he went in
very low and so was especially vulnerable to the heavy machine guns and
light flak. The idea came up that a pair of Lancasters would go in first, before
Cheshire, and drop containers of 24-ounce anti-personnel mines to silence
the machine guns. They picked me and Phil Plowright to do it, because of
our excellent navigators, the navigators said. Good-oh, we thought, and we'll
have to go round and come over again to bomb with the rest.

No one told us how we should do it, so our two crews sat down in the
Jolly Sailor at Bardney and talked it through. I'd been on very good terms
with the owners of the pub ever since my first night on squadron, which was
February, when I went there and asked for a slice off the ham hanging behind

the bar instead of my change. Anyway, we decided that whoever was in front when we reached the target would act as marker and put his navigation lights on, so the other could see him and concentrate on dropping the mines accurately. As the Germans could see him also, it would be expected that the second Lanc wouldn't take too long about it before he took his turn as lit-up decoy for his pal.

We did this a few times and, one night after debriefing, Cheshire came over on the scrambler telephone to thank the boys for completely silencing the guns and making his job of dropping the markers so much easier. Phil Plowright replied that it should be the bombers thanking the wing commander, who was so accurate with his marking that it made our ops worthwhile. I said that I didn't believe the wingco dropped his markers at all, but simply leaned over the side and placed them on the ground. Cheshire was highly amused but pointed out, in that rather posh sort of haw-haw voice of his, that if Flying Officer Gradwell had ever flown a Mosquito he would know that the wings got in the way of such a procedure.

We flew op after op and got to the end, except it wasn't counted as the end because some of the French trips in the spring had been demoted to one third of an op, as being only a third as dangerous as going to Germany. The big thing in July was the doodlebugs, the V weapons, and we were off to some caves at a place called St Leu d'Esserant, where they were assembling these buzz bombs, which were coming into London at more than 100 a day, and several thousand people had been killed.

So, this was my thirty-third, my crew's thirty-second, although officially we were on twenty-nine. We'd been together for six months on ops and a lot more in training. I'd met my rear gunner, Les Sutton, on the way to a training unit. Pete Lynch, my flight engineer, had been an apprentice at A V Roe, building Lancasters, which seemed like an excellent qualification. We used to say that if all the bits were heaped in a corner of a hangar, give Pete a day or two and a Lanc would roll out.

So, we crossed the French coast and straight away saw dogfights all around, and aircraft going down. There was nothing we could do except plough on and, about halfway between the coast and the target, it came to our turn. We were flying south east, into the moon. Anyone behind us would have seen the unmistakeable shape of a four-engined bomber against the circle of light.

Les Sutton had been a gamekeeper in civilian life. He had exceptional night vision; that was his official RAF category, exceptional. The rest of us were marked above average but Les was even better. Suddenly he screeched out 'Corkscrew port, go!'.

In all our time together, I'd never heard him say it like this, because we'd never been attacked by a fighter before. In fighter affiliation, the practice was 'Rear gunner to pilot.' 'Yes, rear gunner.' 'Prepare to corkscrew. Corkscrew to port, go'.

We could smell cordite. It was extremely tense inside that Lanc, with the only sound being my commentary to the gunners – diving port, rolling, climbing starboard, rolling. Then I thought I heard someone laugh. It sounded very like one of my own crew laughing on the intercom and when I heard it again I interrupted my commentary to ask who the bloody hell it was. Bill Best, the Canadian mid-upper, owned up. His reason was that his hydraulics had been shot away and he was slowly spinning around and around in his turret, out of control. You had to be there; it seemed funny at the time.

'Not to worry, skip,' he said. 'Every time the bastard goes past, I'll give him a burst.'

'Level out,' shouted Les Sutton in the rear turret. 'Level out, skip.'

We had complete trust in each other, I had complete trust in Les, so I obeyed his curious order. The reward was the sight of the fighter passing underneath us with the pilot apparently slumped at the controls. It looked like the gunners must have got him. His aircraft had automatically reverted to flying straight and level and would do that until it ran out of fuel, so it was goodbye to him.

We were flying straight and level too, nobody was injured, so I decided to go on to the target on the grounds that I would rather be one of 200 in a bomber stream than on my own flying home. Atch Atkinson, the bomb aimer, called up to say he'd got the markers so I replied, as always, 'OK, over to you,' and took my last look around outside before concentrating on the instruments.

I saw a small fire on the port wing. Let's be rid of the bombs, I thought, and we'll deal with the fire later. Pete Lynch feathered both port engines and switched all the fuel off on that side, but nothing happened. The fire was inside the mainplane, inside the middle of the wing. The fighter must have shot a hole in a tank and a spark from an engine or ack-ack from the ground had set it alight.

While I strained to keep us straight on just the two starboard engines, the little flame moved slowly but certainly back across the width of the wing, like an oxy-acetylene torch cutting through sheet metal.

Pete said 'I think we've had it, skip'. He knew every component and he could visualise what was happening inside the wing. The flame was getting near the main spar. If it cut through that, we would be in a one-winged aircraft, so I gave the order to bale out. Pete Lynch went to pick up three parachutes and gave one each to second Dicky Oldacre and to me. Atch unshipped the escape hatch and dived out, followed by Oldacre, Pete and Tommy. Bill Best was still going round and round in his turret although not laughing so much by this time. He reached down to grab the stirrup he used to haul himself in and out of his position and jammed it into the turret mechanism.

With that stopped he dropped down into the fuselage, missing by the very narrowest squeak dropping a great deal further, through the hole in the floor that none of us had realised was part of our damage, and he hadn't got his parachute on yet. Jim [Price, w/op] called me to say that he and the gunners were going, which left me.

I had to use full right rudder and full stick to keep her in line against the pulling power of the two starboard engines. George the autopilot wouldn't have been any use. He wasn't strong enough to do this job, so I had to climb down from my platform onto the cockpit floor, standing on one leg, keeping one hand on the stick and one foot up on the rudder bar. I knew what would happen when I let go. The aircraft would take a huge diving turn to port and on into a spinning power dive and I would be stuck in the cockpit, pinned to the wall by centrifugal force.

I would have to let go of the controls with my hand and foot and at the same instant dive from the cockpit down through the bomb aimer's hatch. I thought, I'm not really cut out to be a circus act or a Hollywood stunt man but there was no point in messing about. Do it.

Next thing I knew, I was swinging from my parachute, descending on a glorious moonlit night towards a forest. And, like so many bomber crew whose first parachute jump was their only parachute jump, I couldn't remember pulling the rip cord. I had no real idea how I came to be there, swinging gently in the French July air, and I had no idea how I could avoid being speared and slashed by the trees I was going to hit, or how I would reach the forest floor if I became suspended by chute and ropes in the tree tops. I needn't have worried. I landed in a heap on the ground, stowed away my chute and Mae West, realised I was in enemy territory on my own and began imagining a German soldier behind every tree.

For the rest of the story, see p. 236.

Pilots of 'B' Flight pose in the summer of 1944. From the left, back row: Ray Harris, Jack Sheppard, Harry Pooley (flight commander), Roy 'Puddle' Lake, Bill Begg (killed at Münster aqueduct, 23 September 1944), Les Keeley; front row: Ron Adams, Doug Tweddle.

Ray Harris, Lancasters, 1944–5

I left school in Eastbourne at 14, and messed about at this and that until I was 16 and a bit. I went to the RAF recruiting office in Brighton and told them I was 17¼ and wanted to be a pilot. They believed me but said my maths wasn't good enough, so I went back to my old teacher and sat in his room for a few weeks. The teacher told the RAF when he thought I was up to the mark, and that was that.

When it came to crewing up, I was worried. The other learner skippers were all older than me. I wondered if I was military enough, then I found my first crewman at a railway station on a bleak November night. There was quite a crowd of airmen, standing around in overcoats. I said aloud, but to myself, 'Nobody will fly with me,' and a boy turned to me and said 'I will'. The boy became our rear gunner, Sandy Sanders.

It was May when we reached IX Squadron, and they seemed to be losing a crew on every op. I went second Dicky

Flight Lieutenant Ray Harris after the war, with DFC ribbon.

131

to the railway yards at Nantes with Harry Forrest, who had been there since February, so that made him an old hand, and our first as a crew was Cherbourg, which was the German guns on the coast at St Martin-de-Varreville. D-Day was coming up, not that we knew it, and we were bombing all along there so the Germans couldn't guess where the landings would be.

We did all sorts of French trips, supporting the army and hitting the V weapon sites, before we switched to Germany and then back to France again. Our old Lanc, W, was shot down with another crew in it. By the end of July we'd done fifteen ops but the squadron had lost quite a few (twenty since the beginning of May). I did my eighteenth on my twentieth birthday.

[On the way to Russia, 11 September, first *Tirpitz* raid] When dead reckoning said we were over Archangel we went down low and saw the ships, the harbour and the town. The problem now was to find the airfield. We stooged

There was a mass daylight attack on night-fighter bases in the Low Countries on 15 August 1944 as a prelude to the renewal of raids on Germany. Ray Harris was first to bomb the base at Gilze Rijen: 'Bombs seen to hit runway'. After the rest of the squadron had finished with it, there was nothing left of the base.

around and were delighted to see an airfield with aircraft, including a Lancaster, which must have been the right airfield because we hadn't been told about any others around there.

We followed another Lanc in and there was very little room to stop on the grass [of Kegostrov, not Yagodnik]. I got the aircraft down almost to walking pace when we hit an invisible ditch. It was the slowest prang on record. The weight of the bomb [Tallboy] gave us too much momentum, and we buried our nose in slow motion into the soft soil of the local garrison's rows of potatoes, with our tail sticking up in the air.

We missed the actual raid, but there seemed to be no end to the supply of free vodka so we wondered how we might get some of it home. The word was that a supply of condoms had been thoughtfully brought to Russia by the medical officer, in case we boys should find ourselves unable to resist the seductive charms of the local talent. We made some discrete enquiries which resulted in the condoms being requisitioned for vital military purposes. We filled them with the free vodka ready to fly them back to Bardney, hoping that variations in air pressure would not strain the rubber unduly.

Fighter escorts as seen by Punch.

" *I think it's wonderful how the little ones manage to keep up with the big ones.*"

[U-boat pens, Bergen, 12 January 1945] I'd caught a glimpse of them [Polish Mustang fighter escorts] about half an hour before on the flight over but I hadn't seen a sign of them since. We were designated wind-finder, so I flew in a wide triangle while Doc [Young, navigator] calculated the wind speed and direction and Bill Brownlie transmitted the data to the rest of IX Squadron so they could set up their bomb sights. As the others began arriving, a few little clouds were starting to drift across, 18,000ft below, and there was some haze but the bombing conditions were good. I was early so I asked Fauquier [617 Squadron, master bomber that day] for permission to bomb. Jimmy [Parsons, bomb aimer] stood out for his single-minded approach to his work, even among that good company, and he began calling the run which was perfect.

Our ritual on Willing Winnie [PD198 WS/W-William], as soon as we turned for home, was for Doc to break out the Woodbines. As we did that, at last the Poles appeared. I had two exceptional gunners with me that day, the squadron Gunnery Leader Bill Gabriel and his deputy Mac Williams, and we had cause to be grateful for that. 'Four Mustangs approaching, skip, starboard bow,' came from Bill Gabriel in the rear turret, on the intercom. I thought, what's the use of a fighter escort now? We'd bombed, we were leaving the coast behind. They would surely have been better employed protecting our aircraft which were still going round and round over the U-boat pens.

I'd almost finished my Woodbine and, as always, I was scanning the sky. I couldn't see the Mustangs. I thought they must have swung round from the bow and be coming up behind. And they were, except they were Focke-Wulf 190s.

Both gunners shouted 'Corkscrew starboard,' just as a salvo of cannon shells crashed into us, so that's what I did.

Like all the others in the Lanc and in any other aircraft that ever was attacked, I was terrified. No matter how well trained we were, no matter how battle hardened, being shot at was the most frightening thing. They'd said at the briefing there'd be no enemy fighters.

'Corkscrew port, port, go!' Mac was screaming into the intercom while he fired off four or five short bursts. I did as bidden, and with rather more effect and urgency than I ever had in fighter affiliation, but we took another lot of cannon shells. Mac came on to say he couldn't rotate his turret. The hydraulics had gone. 'What about you, Bill?' I said. But he didn't reply.

Corkscrew port! Corkscrew starboard! The shouts were still coming from the mid-upper turret and the occasional shot was still being fired off from the Brownings. This was a grossly one-sided contest. I reckoned we'd been hit by ten, a dozen, maybe more of those bursts of cannon shells when Bill came on at last. 'Hello, skip,' he said. 'Rear gunner here. Sorry about that. Buggers cut my oxygen supply. Got the pearly grey mists for a bit there.'

So, that was all right, then his voice changed. 'Bloody hell,' he said, 'here they come again. Corkscrew starboard. Go!' We tried, but Winnie was handling badly. The trim tabs on the ailerons had gone. Well, they were still there, some of them, but I couldn't move them. Neither the hand trims nor the servo trims would work.

Things went quiet for a bit, and would you believe it, a FW190 come up on our port wingtip. I could see the pilot clearly. Up yours, mate, I said to him, and I slid open my side window and fired my service revolver as he peeled away. I knew it wouldn't do any good but I thought it might make me feel better.

'Here they come, skip,' said Mac. I thought Winnie was so badly shot about that we'd probably fall out of the sky anyway, without more encouragement from the Luftwaffe. Nothing else to do so I pushed the stick forward. Maurice Mellors, the flight engineer, was standing behind me, gripping the back of my seat as we dived straight for the sea. There we were, breaking the downhill speed record, and Mac came on the intercom.

'They're going,' he said. I thought he meant some more component parts were about to fall off the aircraft. 'What's going?' I said, a bit sharp. 'The one nineties,' he said. 'They're in line formation. Heading for home. Thank Christ for that.' Well, we could only assume they'd run out of shells. Four of them. They'd used the bloody lot up, shooting at us, and we were still flying. Or they could have been up to their fuel limit. Who cared why? We were just delighted they'd gone, after fifteen attacks altogether.

We were still heading straight for the briny and, without the trim tabs, I didn't have the physical strength to pull her up alone. 'For Christ's sake, Maurice,' I said. He was a big Manchester copper who reckoned he could handle most things but it took all he had, combined with all I had, to pull Winnie's nose up. We levelled off at 1,000ft. We'd lost 11,000ft since we were first attacked. Time to review the situation, but Bill Gabriel suddenly spoke up. 'Skip, if you can, I could do with some help,' was what he said, and he hadn't said anything for quite a while. I sent Jimmy to see what was what.

Bill had been hit in the head and leg. There was blood everywhere. Jimmy somehow got him onto the rest bed where he could give him morphine and try and do something about the bleeding.

The good news was that we still had three-and-a-half engines. Only the port outer was struggling, but all the other damage meant that the best we could do was level flight at a thousand feet. By trial and error, we worked out that our stalling speed was 160mph instead of the usual 95mph. So, we had a flight plan of sorts. Level at a thousand, and one sixty or faster. Anything else and we'd be in the drink.

What about landing, at maybe 60mph quicker than usual? And what about the undercarriage with the hydraulics not working? I'd never done it on the compressed-air bottle. So, where was the nearest, widest and longest runway? RAF Carnaby, near Bridlington on the Yorkshire coast, was the nearest emergency place. Doc, I said, we want to go to Carnaby. Is it left, right or straight on from here?

We got there, goodness knows how, and I went on the VHF. 'Hello Carnaby, hello Carnaby, this is Rosen William. I have wounded on board and am coming in to land. I regret this may cause damage to your runway as I don't think the undercart is going to work and I can't drop below one sixty without stalling.'

We could see the fire engines and ambulances rushing about, and I told Maurice to blow the undercarriage down. We could hardly believe it but we heard and felt it operate with a gratifying, solid clunk. Two green lights came on. We had wheels. I gave the order. Safety positions.

It was a pretty good landing. I remember the time, 16.04, well in time for tea, and nobody else felt the tyres touch the tarmac. It's all right, Doc, I said. You can stop calling the airspeed. We're down.

Bill Gabriel was taken to hospital at Driffield where his shrapnel was removed and his wounds repaired by, of all people, a German prisoner-of-war doctor. We had debated about (a) whether to go with our old mate Bill in the ambulance, or (b) whether to go to a public house in order to drink large quantities of beer. It must have been the shortest debate in history. A WAAF happened to mention that there was a really good little pub in the village of Lissett, 5 or 6 miles away. She would take us, and pick us up at closing time, that is, if we wanted.

We'd lost Ernie Redfern on that op, on his fortieth, and when I got back to Bardney from Carnaby, the first person I saw was Frances Redfern, arriving at the aerodrome, looking for her husband who had just been awarded the DFC.

Both of Harris's gunners received the DFC for the Bergen trip. Harris had been awarded his DFC a few weeks before and was recommended for a DSO for Bergen, but never got it. There were 1,200 holes in Lancaster WS/W, Willing Winnie.

CHAPTER 10

Observers/Navigators

H R 'Sam' Hall, Wellingtons, 1940
I was the first officer observer on the squadron, which I didn't know of course, and from New Zealand. When I arrived, I found a much older chap in the Mess hallway, waiting for me. This was Squadron Leader Pretty, pilot from the Great War, who was President of the Mess Committee. 'You're rather late,' he said. 'Sorry, sir, the train was . . .'. 'Never mind that,' he replied. 'I mean you're late for lunch and there isn't much left. Will a little cold pheasant do you?'

I was crewed with Pilot Officer Bertie Barnard. We went to Calais for the barges and I got down into the bomb aimer's spot, issuing instructions to the pilot who took no notice at all and veered away to starboard. I said 'There's the target, away to the left, can't you see it?' Bertie, who usually stuttered, said very firmly 'Are you flying this aircraft or am I?' He waited until another Wimpy was coned by the searchlights then turned in and followed my directions while the enemy was otherwise engaged.

I had my own room in the Mess and, for the first few weeks anyway, exclusive use of a batman. He was a rare example of the right man for the job, having left service as a butler to the managing director of Henly's Motors. He was only an AC2 but he was efficiency personified, and a brilliant therapist. He'd prompt me into telling him about last night's raid and I'd get all the stress and emotion off my chest while he said 'No, goodness me, sir, really, oh, too bad, sir,' and then he would come up with tea and toast at the moment he judged to be the right one.

The C-in-C of Bomber Command came to inspect us, Air Marshal Sir Richard Pierse. Our CO then was Tim Healy.

Wingco Healy: 'This is Pilot Officer Hall, sir.'

C-in-C: 'Ah, Hall, and when did you last operate?'

Hall: 'Last night, sir.'

C-in-C: 'Ah, good, good. And where did you go?'

Hall (thinks, doesn't he know? He sent me): 'Berlin, sir.'

C-in-C: 'Good, good. What did you think of it?'

Hall (thinks, not the right time to say I was scared out of my wits): 'Very interesting, sir.'

C-in-C: 'Good, good, and how may trips have you done?'

Hall (with pride): 'Four, sir.'

C-in-C (turns on heel, speaks to Wingco): 'And now I'd like to talk to someone with experience.'

We had quite a few intruder attacks and on one such the enemy was shot down right in front of a hangar. Apparently, as the aircraft started the bombing run, an airman manning a Lewis gun had jerked the barrel to vertical and, without waiting for orders, opened fire. The German flew right through the stream of bullets and went straight in. We looked at the crashed aircraft and the dead bodies and thought, there but for the grace of God.

It was still the practice for navigators to decide on the route. Some captains wanted to know, some left it to the experts. Bertie left it to me but I had some trouble with the pronunciation of English place names. At one briefing, Wingco Healy said we should avoid Harwich because there was now a balloon barrage there. I wrote this down as Harridge and never did find it on the map. I wasn't too bothered. I had my route worked out.

The balloons used to give out a warning from radio transmitters, called squeakers, which the pilots could hear in their headphones, and on our way home across the sea Bertie said 'I think I can hear squeakers. Are we on track?' Definitely, I said. I got a good pinpoint on the enemy coast. 'They're getting louder,' he said. 'Make another check'. So I did, and we were right on track. 'Well, they're getting worse. Where are you heading for, anyway?' Harr-Witch, I said, whereupon the aircraft was stood on one wingtip and flown swiftly in the opposite direction. I had to give him a new course for Honington and then endure a continuous diatribe of incisive remarks connected with the inadvisability of being navigated by ill-educated, dim-witted, obscurely bred specimens of subhuman from the colonies.

The main thing in Bertie's life seemed to be the gathering around the Mess room fire with drinks, in his case pints of Guinness. If the chat and the beer were flowing he wouldn't bother about the regular dinner and would end up scrounging around the kitchen. One night, all he could find was a loaf of bread. There was a slicer there so he decided to operate it but was careless with the positioning of his left hand. The slicer took off the top joints of two fingers.

'C-c-c-c-christ!' he bellowed. 'I've c-c-c-cut my b-b-b-bloody f-f-f-fingers off!' We ran to the kitchen to find him ferreting through the slices of bread. 'I've f-f-f-found them,' he said, holding up two little red things with white breadcrumbs sticking to them. He rinsed them under the cold tap and set off for Squadron Leader McCarty's quarters. Aiden McCarty was the MO and greatly admired by all of us. He sewed the bits back on and Bertie was excused duties for three weeks.

We were long before the days of 'Bomb gone, camera gone'. We'd only recently got one camera between us, and I had it at Cologne [27 November], and I was convinced we were on target. There was very little on my picture. They identified some woods which made us 7 miles away from where we should have been. Next time out I produced a photograph only 2,000yd from the aiming point, which was regarded as an outstanding result.

Aiden McCarty, although highly respected and well liked, had a reputation for being somewhat irascible, believing that no illness or injury should interfere with the peaceful, orderly life of a Medical Officer such as he. A phrase he used to greet each of his morning queue of patients passed into squadron lore and became its second motto: 'There's always bloody something'.

George McRiner, Wellingtons, 1940–1
I was this young Scots laddie [18, from Biggar], and they put me with an old hand, Pilot Officer Berry. My first was only a short one, to Antwerp, not hard for me, but Berry had just about had it by then. He had a very bad case of The Twitch. Not so inspiring for your first trip. There was another pilot, Morgan, later on, who was near the end of his tour, and it showed. Thoroughly decent chap but ops had got to him, and I flew with him three times in four days. We younger ones were always astonished to find out that these old men, these ancient warriors who'd flown a tour, were only those few months older than us.

Coming back from Düsseldorf with Berry, he made a complete hash of the landing. We spun off the flare path and caught fire. You had to get out quick because the Wellington's fabric went up in almost instant flames. We did all get out and I thought that was enough for Berry but it wasn't. He never said a word about that landing and I was off with him again, to Gelsenkirchen [11 November] and a few days later I was with him to Berlin, which was the kind of place that imprinted itself on your mind. That was a long trip too, 8 hours and more, and navigating was hard. It was all dead reckoning, from height and speed, wind speed, and the best assessment you could make of your ground speed, backed up by sightings of features on the ground. We often flew in very good weather. On those nights we could see Germany and the Germans could see us.

By the May of '41, I was a senior man, along with another sergeant observer, Copson, who'd flown as captain rather than the pilot. In the Polish airforce, the navigators were the captains. I'd had a lot of experience with quite a few different pilots and then suddenly they gave me this chap Green who was, to be frank, green in more than name. So, I wasn't the first navigator to feel that, as I was running the show, I should be captain. The CO was in agreement and Green was quite relaxed about it, perfectly amenable. We navigators used to refer to the pilots as drivers, airframe. We saw ourselves as the brains behind it. We gave the directions and the drivers turned left or right accordingly. Of course, they might have argued that we didn't say much when evasive action was required.

My first as skipper was Boulogne [15 May], shipping, not too bad, then it was Kiel [18 May]. That was a dicey one. We had to drop our bombs from 200ft, which is well below where they can hit you with heavy flak but they made up for it with everything else, and as bomb aimer the captain/navigator sees everything at close quarters.

Squadron Leader Wasse that was, now Wing Commander and our CO, was one of the old school, a military man as well as a flying one. There was a scruffy little sergeant pilot, I'd never seen anyone so scruffy, and he

The Short Stirling, the RAF's first four-engined bomber, was relegated to training duties after many losses had proved it to be too vulnerable to German defences.

did something to upset Michael Wasse who called him into his office. Whatever was said it infuriated Wasse even more and he pulled out a revolver. He didn't shoot the scruffy sergeant. He only put a bullet through the ceiling.

Cologne was my last with IX Squadron [11/12 December]. By now I was Flight Lieutenant DFC, with thirty-four trips, 202 hours 26 minutes of operational flying. Michael Wasse signed me off as 'above the average'. I don't know what happened to my desk job, because the following month I was with 149 Squadron on Stirlings. A disappointing aircraft, the Stirling. It was poor on height and there was always the likelihood of something going wrong with the undercarriage. You always felt very nervous when landing in one.

Graham Welsh, Wellingtons, 1941–2

I was new in the crew, and we were over the sea on the way home [Kiel, 23 October 1941]. I was taking astro sightings to confirm our position and saw the second pilot going back to the rest area. We were just flying along so I thought I'd go up to his seat and get his view of things, and I'd not been there long when Tommy [Wilmot, pilot] signalled for me to take over. I did have some experience flying twin-engined aircraft but I had no idea Tommy knew about it. Anyway, I climbed up and carried on flying. He went back to the rest area too, and after a while suggested to the fellow there that he might get on with his navigating. It gradually dawned on the two pilots that it was the new observer driving and their feet didn't touch the floor or the sides of the aircraft as they did the length of a Wellington in point one of a second.

Our CO Michael Wasse was popular with all and a real inspiration. His successor [Wing Commander Inness] was very different. He could be described as dour and distant, especially towards non-officer aircrew. He was an old India hand, flying Hawker biplanes against marauding Afghan tribesmen.

The Gee box came in, supposedly a blind-bombing aid but mainly a getting-home aid. I used it all the time and had no problems with the equipment itself. The difficulties came with things like power failures in the aircraft, and the weather could always interfere, with we Gee-men marking the target on time for the main force following through. Also, for distant places like Kiel, the angles between the transmitters back home became narrower the further you went and so the more fuzzy your readings became. Over England I could navigate with Gee to within 200yd.

It was basically a 12-hour shift, from briefing to post-op interrogation, with an early breakfast after and straight to bed. It was difficult to sleep in the daytime, particularly if you knew the squadron was operating again that night. We were slated for another op to make it ten in April and I was apprehensive. When we reached the aircraft I realised Ian (Pearson) was drowsy, Webborn (gunner), now well into his second tour, was almost in tears and Howarth (w/op) was in a poor way. I had a strong premonition that if we flew we would not return and so I did the unthinkable. I ran back to the CO and told him that the pilot, the rear gunner and wireless operator were unfit to fly. I half expected Inness to promise me a court martial but he sent the three to the MO who confirmed my opinion and we all were given a week's leave.

I had three to do to finish my tour, and I was with Sergeant Langton, a relative new boy. We were on our way home [Cologne, 30 May] when there was a big explosion on the port wing. On one engine we lost a lot of height and Langton for some reason insisted on flying as slowly as he could, fractionally above stalling speed, which meant we were ever mushing towards the ground. I was observer acting second pilot and really the senior man, and I kept warning him. When we dropped below a thousand I ordered everything loose to be thrown out but it didn't help much and soon we were level with the squirrels. I think Langton had frozen.

We were going straight for a farmhouse and he didn't see it. I was standing beside him. I saw it all right and shouted, and he pulled up on the stick and the wing dropped and bang, we were down in the farmyard. We were in Belgium, not far from Antwerp. Langton was badly hurt and the rear gunner Sergeant Pexman was killed. Front gunner Johnson was uninjured, I'd taken a blow on the ankle and Howarth the w/op had a badly lacerated hand. We three spent almost a week evading capture but they took us when we were looking for a doctor for Howarth.

See also Stalag Luft III, p. 234.

Ken Chamberlain, Wellingtons and Lancasters, 1942–3

I don't know how I ever got to the squadron, really, never mind do a tour. I was 19, near the end of my training, on a cross-country. Rowland Hill was the pilot, great-great something or other of the penny post man, who was 19 as well, and he didn't like the temperature and pressure readings on the port engine. Our rear gunner [Frank Crook], an old man of 24, was an engineer in civilian life so Roly called him on the intercom for advice. 'I would say your port engine's about to catch fire,' said Frank. 'Oh, do you really think so?' said Roly. 'Look,' said the gunner. 'There's a perfectly good airfield down there, let's land and have it looked at.'

I don't think Roly felt comfortable about landing at a strange airfield and asking about his engine so no, he'd throttle it back and it would be fine. I gave him the course for the next leg of the cross country and, as forecast, the engine caught fire. From my seat on the port side, I had a good view.

The flames were leaping past my window. The altimeter started to unwind and the airspeed built up. We were obviously in deep trouble and Eric Shipley in the front turret said 'Roly, do you think I might come out?' Roly said 'Well, if you want to,' and he came and sat on half of my seat. Roly said 'It's all right Ken, I can see an airfield,' and I said 'Roly, there are no airfields around here.' 'I can see a flarepath.' 'Roly, there are no airfields.'

The next I knew, there was an almighty crash and I came to, lying in a field with the aircraft burning steadily beside me. Roly had mistaken the railway yard at Spalding for an airfield and tried to land on that. To his eternal credit, once he realised, he did manage to get the aircraft over the last houses in Spalding before we went down in an orchard, but he was still killed, as were all the rest. The Wellington had broken its back and thrown me out but kept all the others inside.

I was given a month's sick leave after that, and when I got back I was crewed up with a new lot. We took off for our first night flight and the aircraft in front of us went straight in, bang, and we flew through the flames. I went to the MO next morning and said enough was enough. Certainly ninety-nine out of a hundred doctors would have classified me as LMF, Lacking Moral Fibre, and ninety-nine out of a hundred station commanders would have agreed and thrown me out. I just happened to have the one doctor who took an interest and the one station commander who was willing to take the time and persevere. They left me in the navigation section and told me to fly when I was ready. Maybe they were short of navigators.

I got to Honington in June of '42 and was crewed up with a very tall, very pleasant American skipper called Storey, who'd volunteered for our war. He didn't seem to be the best of pilots and he went back to being a second pilot for a time, while we swapped over to an experienced captain called Stubbs. Well, we soon found out what kind of a fellow he was.

We were slated for Bremen, the last of the three 'Thousand Plan' raids [25 June], and it was announced that the squadron, being an aircraft short, had borrowed a Wellington from the OTU up the road. We all knew what that meant. Instructor pilots, showing off to their sprog pupils, had been

Wing Commander Leslie Vidal James DFC had done his first tour with No. 149, and many of the ops had been in his Wellington 'The Ozard of Whiz'. He arrived as the new IX Squadron CO in May 1942 and went on his first with them, Emden, 20 June. He and crew all died in a crash in Holland, shot down by Oberleutnant Egmont Prinz zur Lippe Weissenfeld, *who scored three that night.*

throwing this thing all over the sky and it was not in tip-top, over-Germany condition. Worse, it was the early Pegasus-engined version (2 x 1000hp), not the much better Hercules-engined version we were used to (2 x 1675hp).

The proposal was to draw lots for it but Dick Stubbs said there was no need. He'd have it. Over the target we were hit by flak and the port engine stopped, often a disaster in the Pegasus Wimpy, being so underpowered. Stubbs told us not to worry. He would get us home, and he did, and a few nights later we were off to Bremen again [2 July]. We were coned by searchlights and hit by flak again and Sergeant Newby, our bomb aimer, was wounded very badly. So that was life with Dick Stubbs.

We did a few more trips in Wellingtons then the squadron changed over to Lancasters and moved to Waddington. Our first was to Essen [16 September] and we didn't get very far in a brand new aircraft. In Lancs, we had a new crew member, the flight engineer. Ours was Tom Parrington, and one of his jobs was to watch the four red lights which indicated flow of fuel to the

Bomb damage to Bremen, photographed after VE Day.

engines. If a light came on, something was wrong with the system, that engine was being starved and Tom had to switch it to a reserve tank. As we took off across married quarters with a 4,000-pounder on board, all four red lights came on. It was a toss-up who was coughing and spluttering the most, Tom or the engines. Anyway, he got them all switched to the little 100-gallon wingtip tanks and we flew out to the Wash to jettison the bombs, but the engines kept cutting out two at a time and the lights kept coming on. We flew home with all four engines running off one wingtip tank and landed on the last smell of petrol. Next morning I was due to be interviewed by Wingco Southwell for my promotion. 'What do you think of the Lancaster?' he said. 'Well,' I said, 'I don't think much of the fuel system.' 'Ah,' says he, 'you'll be in Dick Stubbs's crew.'

145

New-looking Lancasters line up for a photocall at Waddington.

We'd been doing a lot of formation training in daylight, flying wingtip to wingtip at low level, then when we set off on the raid, which was the Schneider factory at Le Creusot [17 October 1942], we were in thick fog over the Channel at nought feet and couldn't see anything. Just as we came out of it, near the French coast, another Lanc swerved right across us. The slipstream forced our aircraft into an instant half roll. She went through 90 degrees in less than the wink of an eye and everyone swore that the downward wingtip was in the water. Stubbs got her back, brilliant flyer that he was, and resumed formation as if nothing had happened. We'd just settled ourselves and our nerves from that, when there was a terrific bang, the front Perspex had a great hole in it and Tom Parrington was covered in blood. It wasn't flak, though. It was our first and only experience of being hit by heavy seagull.

When you had an engine failure or other problem that brought you home early, that was DNCO, Duty Not Carried Out. It counted as a trip for the aircraft but not for us, so I had to set off thirty-four times to get to thirty completed. Less than two weeks later I was a Gee instructor at 14 OTU.

Henry 'Tug' Wilson, Lancasters 1944–5
Tug Wilson was shot down over Denmark on his sixth op with 61 Squadron. He evaded capture – see p. 240, and joined IX Squadron in November 1944.

I was Pilot Officer Wilson now, very knowledgeable about Denmark but not much more than a sprog navigator, so they put me with a tour completed crew whose navigator had elected not to continue – Squadron Leader Melrose's outfit. Doug Melrose used to take quite a bit of stick in the Mess because he was a little short chap who insisted on growing this huge, droopy, bushy

146

moustache which was a bit out of RAF fashion by then. They used to call him the man with the rug in his mouth. He was a bloody good pilot, whatever.

When we were attacked by a fighter and Ernie [Stalley, rear gunner] shouted corkscrew, Doug would throw the ship about and get us out of it and then come over on the intercom, all calm, and say 'What course, Tug?' What course? He'd just had us all over the sky and my instruments were all over the floor and he's asking what course. I'd say just keep going where you're going and when I've found my stuff in every corner of this bloody aircraft I'll try and work something out.

Flying Officer Alf Jeffs and all his crew, including Sergeant Clarence Higgins and Warrant Officer Second Class 2 Hugh Fisher, were killed on 7 April 1945 after an op to Molbis. Blown off course by strong winds, their new Lancaster on her first trip burst into flames in mid-air near Wantage.

Jeffs had taken W4964 on her last op, counted then as 106 with Tirpitz as the 100th. This is J with 104 up, waiting for her 105th painted bomb and Flying Officer Jeffs to take her to Bremen.

I took a few extra trips, with Keeley, Jeffs and Waters. There was one to a railway bridge at Bad Oeynhausen [23 March 1945]. We were in N and the flak got us three times on our Tallboy run, and twice again while we were diving away. I was sitting with my feet in the hole ready to bale out and I said to Waters, is this where I get a bar on my caterpillar? I was a member of the Caterpillar Club for my parachute jump in Denmark and I thought I was going to have to do it all over again. Waters just said, hold on a minute Tug.

We were hit in both main tanks, the port inner was u/s, the bomb aimer's panel was smashed and neither gun turret was working. So I climbed back to my desk and navigated us to Seething. It was an American base and the Yanks were deeply impressed with our aircraft. They couldn't believe such an old wreck could fly.

I'd had a letter forwarded to me by the Air Ministry, which was from my helpers in Denmark giving an address I could write to. They obviously wanted to know if I'd got home all right. I worded the letter very carefully so it would look real enough to any censor but didn't actually say anything. The simple fact of it was the message. Next thing, I had notice that on 10 April 1945 I was to be court martialed for 'attempting to communicate with countries under enemy control'. They must have run my letter through the Enigma machine and found an uncrackable code. It was a sensation at Bardney. I was stopped from going on ops, presumably in case I baled out to give a hand to the German war effort, and all sorts of learned friends came up from London to see if I should be sent to The Tower. An officer from Waddington defended me and common sense prevailed. I was found not guilty, allowed to go back on ops, but the £10 I'd had from the British consul in Malmö was docked off my wages.

CHAPTER 11

Wireless Operators

Joseph Anderson, Wellingtons, 1940–1

We [Pilot Officer Hemmings and crew] went to Hamburg [16 November 1940] and circled the target for half an hour trying to see through cloud. There was very heavy flak, flares, flaming onions and batteries of searchlights. No results observed. We got lost over England with the wireless u/s and no QDMs or fixes, and when I got it repaired after cruising around at 500ft for an hour, we found ourselves over Gloucester. Needless to say we were the last ones home.

After dirty weather over the sea, there was clear moonlight over the target [Düsseldorf, 7 December] but we ran into electrical storms coming back and our starboard engine almost froze up, and there was an eighth of an inch of frost all over the inside of the turrets, the guns and the heated suits. A flare went off in the chute and the second pilot got frostbite in his hand putting out the fire. These trips could be very cold. There was one to Bremen when the temperature was off the clock, minus 35 °C, and three of us had frostbite because the heating system froze up.

Hemmings had to force-land at Bexhill, coming back from Venice [21 December] because we were out of petrol. We'd had headwinds all the way there and came straight back over the Alps with no oxygen. Dawn broke, we were over Germany, and then 200 miles from the French coast with only 40 gallons of petrol left. We were ready to bale out but somehow the engines kept going, over the French coast, and we prepared for ditching. We saw a Spitfire, then the English coast, and the engines cut. After force-landing at a small village near Hastings we were given hot tea, breakfast at an hotel, then train to London. I went home for the night and met the crew again at Liverpool Street next morning, and we all arrived at Honington at about half-past one to find the windows of the Mess filled with smiling faces. [See also Alan Mackay, p. 110.)

149

Berlin was a long trip [23 March, Pilot Officer Sharp] so we had to conserve oxygen. I could not find any beacons that worked, only German ones that I didn't know the position of. Unable to get a fix on way back, I tried Hull, Tangmere and Pulham. Dawson got lost and was sending P-priority, short of petrol. Morgan got lost and was sending SOS. Nothing was heard from Wasse for three hours. I eventually got a bearing from Hull and we landed at Feltwell, as did Wasse. Everybody did reach home in the end, although Stark flew back from Hannover on one engine.

Sergeant Joseph Anderson flew four more operations with Pilot Officer George Sharp. They were shot down – Berlin on 9/10 April – with all crew killed. Joe Anderson was 21. His previous skipper, Pilot Officer Hemmings, finished his tour with No. IX but, as Squadron Leader Garrard Hemmings DFC, Lancaster pilot with 156 Squadron, was killed with all his crew at Russelsheim on 13 August 1944.

Robert Woolf, Lancasters, 1944–5

In training, we were returning from a cross-country one dark early morning when a Stirling, right behind ours but slightly higher, met another one head on. The sky filled with the red and yellow light of the massive explosion. It was a fireball, a huge fireball. There were pieces of blazing aircraft thrown in every direction. As if that wasn't enough of a shock, we had some garbled comments on the intercom when Dougie [Melrose] and Ted [Selfe, engineer], and Ernie in the rear turret, by the light of the fire saw another Stirling pass directly underneath us, no more than 30yd away. Our skipper was able to make a decent landing shortly afterwards, which was a tribute to him and his skill and discipline, but he was one silent and shaken captain, and so were we all as we handed in our parachutes and waited to find out which of our friends had perished in those flames.

[At IX Squadron, Bardney] When the Battle Order was posted up on the notice board, all those listed for the trip felt the tension, and this would continue to build up right through the briefing, the preparation for the flight and the pre-flight meal. Sometimes the reaction would be instant. Suddenly some fellows would need to go to the toilet in great haste. Others would try to show a forced kind of levity, cracking jokes and laughing too easily. Others would become quiet and withdrawn. Nobody wanted to reveal the fear they felt inside but it was deep in our souls and I know that I always gave a thought to whether this trip would be the one from which there would be no return.

*Jimmy Moore, navigator,
joined fellow Aussie Bob
Woolf in Doug Melrose's
crew. Moore was in his
thirties and so much
older than the rest.*

By the time we were taken out to dispersals the tension had reached a high peak and in the buses there was quite an amount of heavy humour and repartee between crews. Those young WAAFs who drove us out to our aircraft were so considerate and friendly, and they did much to soften the emotional stress of the occasion. So, we clambered aboard and set about checking our equipment once more, leaving nothing to chance. This busy activity was good for our nerves and the familiarity of it was reassuring as we waited for the word Go.

As it happened, on our first op [Duisburg, 21 May 1944] we needed some of our spare hour. I was doing my tests and found that one of the two generators wasn't working. Well, that didn't matter in theory. The Lanc only needed one generator and had the second as back-up. Still, it wasn't the best thing to happen on your first operation. The skipper spoke to the control tower and the Chiefy of the electrical section came out. He checked the instruments and concluded that, yes, it was indeed the case that we only had one generator. The point was, should we go? Dougie asked me what I thought.

We both asked Chiefy what he thought. He assured us that a second generator failure was most unlikely. It was decided. We would go. We would carry our 4000lb cookie and our load of incendiaries to Duisburg. Doug signed Form 700, to certify that the aircraft had passed into his command in a serviceable condition and Chiefy went his way.

When the Go signal was received, engines began to fill the air with their crackling roar and our Lancaster became alive and vibrated with power as the revs were run up and we rolled onto the perimeter track to join the long line of aircraft moving towards the runway.

As far into the formula as this, there was still the possibility of a scrub, an immediate cancellation of the whole op by Bomber Command, usually indicated by yellow Very lights from the control tower.

For me and plenty of others, the mixed feelings of relief and disappointment [at a

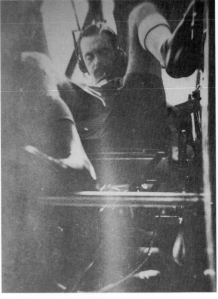

Doug Melrose always alarmed his crew by dropping off for half a minute immediately after take-off. Flight engineers, beware.

scrub] and the sudden escape of pressure had one result only: an irresistible urge to remove to the Mess as fast as possible and get thoroughly hammered. It was generally the sort of carry on where you'd expect to get footprints on the ceiling. Leaping about like wild monkeys, getting thoroughly sloshed and singing extremely rude songs late into the night had not yet been classified by doctors of the mind but it clearly was an effective therapy. It came naturally and it worked.

We'd found out during training that our skipper had a very bad habit. No sooner were we off the ground and climbing than he would fall asleep for about half a minute, but we rather hoped he wouldn't do it on ops. Luckily, Ted was on the ball and kept us going upwards while our captain took his nap. Doug would never believe he did this until one day Sammy [Morris, bomb aimer] broke all the rules and took a camera with us and got a photo of Doug in the land of nod while at the controls of the King's Lancaster WS/J-Johnny Walker.

We functioned well on our first trip. We did our various jobs by the book as the skipper liked but, with ten tenths cloud over the target, there was not much to see in the way of results. I somehow managed to fulfil all my wireless-operating tasks while keeping half my attention on the remaining generator ammeter and the other half on Monica, which was our fighter-warning device. We didn't know then that the Germans used it to home in on us.

There was heavy flak over the target but we weren't hit. We had no idea who was hit, or if anybody was, alone in our cramped, vulnerable, black metal tube in the black sky. A Lancaster and her crew made an independent fighting unit, operating under a mixture of general guidelines and strict instructions but, when it came to it, we were alone, depending only on ourselves and our aircraft.

Looking for V1 sites and expecting a hot reception, we did ten ops in about three weeks, then we switched back to Germany [Scholven-Buer, 21 June] and the flak was very evident, very heavy, very solid, and we all had a few holes. There was no warning before a sudden burst in fiery red and the rattling sound of shrapnel against the sides of the aircraft. The night-fighters were having a go as well. Over a well-defended target there was no

Ray Cornelius and crew were killed after three weeks on squadron, 21 May 1944, Duisburg, Bob Woolfe's first op. Back row from left: Fred Violett, engineer, Alex Porter, bomb aimer, Jim Gledhill, navigator, Ralph Hawksworth, mid-upper; front: Les Chappell, w/op, Ray Cornelius, pilot, Joe Marshall, rear gunner. Ralph Hawksworth was 19 years old, as was Fred Violett. Joe Marshall was the oldest at 24, and married. None of the bodies were found.

let-up of the continual flashes in the bomber stream, producing the inevitable bright cascade of colours when an aircraft was fatally hit and blossomed into a huge ball of flame, gradually falling earthward like some giant firework.

We lost one over the target and another which was hit by flak and dived thousands of feet upside down. The pilot ordered the bomb aimer and second Dicky out but couldn't go himself as some of his crew were wounded. He got home on two.

SECRET No. 9 Squadron Combat Report
Date: 21st June 1944. Time: 01.30. Height: 17,750ft. Target: Scholven-Buer
Lancaster: LM548 WS/C. Captain: Pilot Officer W R Horne

Hit by heavy flak and/or cannon fire from fighter. Considerable damage caused, starboard inner engine caught fire. Both gunners were wounded. Aircraft went into steep dive with flames coming from rear turret. Crew ordered to prepare to jump. Air bomber and 2nd pilot then left aircraft. Remainder of crew unable to leave. Captain finally managed to pull aircraft out of dive at 2,000ft and flew back to England, making landing at Wittering. [Flying Officer Alfred Kidd, bomb aimer, was killed in his parachute jump.]

Night-fighters were deadly sinister because we never knew where they were until they moved into Monica range or were spotted by eye. We sometimes saw them flash past in the opposite direction or right across our bows, pursuing somebody else. If they did see us, we had to hope the encounter would be a momentary thing and that the darkness would give us a chance of escape, because they outgunned us by so much with those cannons.

French railways, trying to stop German reinforcements, 12 July. Coming home we were diverted to Balderton, near Newark, an American glider base. It was always a delight to be diverted to American aerodromes because the breakfast we received was so much richer and more selective than anything the RAF could provide. Imagine, as many eggs as we could wish for, and a variety of food that otherwise we could only dream about. This was all served up with a warm welcome from the American personnel who always showed a great interest in us fellows and our Lancaster. When we landed and Doug opened the bomb doors, one Yank looked up in awe and shouted 'Goddam, it's a flying bomb bay!'.

Back to Germany, Kiel, 23 July. We'd dropped our bombs when suddenly we flipped upside down, and J-Johnny fell in a long spiral, and we remembered something similar happening to Horne at Scholven-Buer. We all thought we were goners, of course, except we had Doug and Ted, and they likewise managed to pull us out of it somehow and we levelled out flying low over Germany. Just where in Germany we didn't know, and the boys to tell us were somewhat hampered by an accident to a tin can that we used to save us from venturing all the way to the Elsan at the back of the aircraft. The fluid in the can had spilled during our rapid descent and saturated our Gee box and radio, so they were no help. The front half of J-Johnny was filled with Window (anti-radar chaff) flying about, and Jimmy Moore had lost his navigation chart.

The regulation was that you had to empty your pockets of all private stuff before a flight,

**AVIATEURS ANGLAIS
31 JUILLET 1944**

LE 31 JUILLET 1944, UN VIOLENT BOMBARDE-MENT A ÉTÉ EFFECTUÉ SUR LE TUNNEL DE RILLY-LA-MONTAGNE, OÙ SE TROUVAIT LE MONTAGE DES "V1" ALLEMANDS.
PENDANT L'ATTAQUE, UN "LANCASTER" A ÉTÉ TOUCHÉ PAR LA D.C.A. ENNEMIE.
L'APPAREIL, QUI PERDAIT DES MORCEAUX DE SA CARLINGUE, SE DIRIGEAIT TOUT DROIT SUR LA COMMUNE DE PUISIEULX.
A UNE TRÈS FAIBLE ALTITUDE ET A L'ENTRÉE DU VILLAGE, L'AVION VIRA SUR SA GAUCHE POUR ALLER EXPLOSER DANS LES CHAMPS.
N'OUBLIONS PAS CES 7 AVIATEURS ANGLAIS CITÉS CI-DESSOUS, QUI,SACHANT LEURS DERNIERS MOMENTS VENUS, ONT SAUVÉ, PAR LEUR GESTE, UNE PARTIE DE LA POPULATION.

C.E.M. WORNER
W.E. MOSELEY
T.J. PEACORE
R.T. MC KIDNEY
W.D. PHILLIPS
J.S. ANDERSON
J. KERFOOT

Bombing a V1 site at Rilly-la-Montaigne, on 31 July 1944, Flying Officer Charles Worner and crew were all killed. The local French saw the doomed machine hurtling towards their village of Piusieulx in a curving dive. As the plaque explains, they also saw it being dragged around at the last moment to crash into open fields, where it disintegrated entirely.

but Jimmy had a three-page letter, from his family in Australia, in his battledress pocket. He stuck these pages to his table with drawing pins and, from memory, sketched out the area of Europe we were in and the various appropriate latitudes and longitudes, as far as he could. From this he worked out an approximate direction for home and, pointed in the general direction, we reached the English coast. At Bardney, in interrogation, the Intelligence Officer said 'Where's your chart, Moore?', and none of us would ever forget the look on that officer's face as Jim sheepishly presented him with a three page letter from Australia with Schleswig-Holstein drawn on the back. And we never did find that chart and never knew how it escaped from our aircraft.

When Lieutenant Shuff of the USAAF landed his B17 Flying Fortress at Bardney on the morning of the 29th, we got quite excited. We were off for a couple of days' holiday, that is, a General Liaison Visit, to an American bombardment group. We spent a very interesting two days, escorted by American aircrew throughout, being shown the whole routine and

Liaison, American style. From the left: Ted Selfe, flight engineer, Bert Hoyle, mid-upper gunner, Doug Melrose, pilot, Bob Woolf, w/op, Sammy Morris, bomb aimer, Ernie Stalley, rear gunner, Jimmy Moore, navigator.

Trossy, 3 August – V-weapon raid, with flak very accurate but not too thick. Melrose, Woolf and co. bombed from 17,500ft and saw one kite go down, hit by falling bombs. The view was that formations should be staggered more, when hundreds of Lancs were attacking a precision target. This is Flying Officer Tweddle's shot of Trossy.

exchanging information on equipment, bombing techniques and crew functions. We went to their briefing for a mission and saw all the procedures. Quite a contrast to what we were used to. We went to a concert at night by Captain Glenn Miller's army band and enjoyed stuffing ourselves with American grub – they seemed to have more of everything than us – and they even made going home a bit special. The pilot of our Fortress took us down to zero feet and buzzed our aerodrome, very thrilling, but when we headed straight for the control tower we could see the occupants making for the door, and there was a lot of fuss afterwards about 'those crazy Yanks'.

[5 August, Saturday] Much to our pleasure we had successful results with our attack [on the Étaples bridge]. Having flown in conjunction with 617 Squadron, the Dambusters, who missed the target, we are feeling rather full of ourselves at present. There wasn't much opposition, peculiarly enough,

(Left) The railway bridge at Étaples was missed first time around, by IX and 617 Squadrons. Next day (right), 5 August, No. IX went alone and breached it in several places.

and only our squadron on it. Up to today, this squadron has operated on fifteen days out of seventeen. Some of the chaps, armourers and so on, haven't been to bed for three days. Ground crew never receive the recognition they deserve.

9 August, Wednesday. Arose at 01.00. Take off scrubbed, back to bed. Up again, mad rush to take off at 07.00. Target was La Pallice on west coast of

BARD 5.8.44// 8" 10.000 → 341° 1201
ETAPLES.X. 14x1000. C.27.5s. F/O ADAMS X.9

France. Trip went OK, not too much flak, over 6 hours in the air. Signals were a shambles due to badly planned briefing but no damage done. This was another joint op with 617 who attacked the U-boat pens with Tallboys while IX Squadron hit the oil storage with conventional bombs.

10 August, Thursday. Our a/c J-Johnny became serviceable today and we went up for an air test. J has been repaired after some clot took her on ops and nearly blew her out of the sky. He had to jettison his bombs which he did from a ridiculously low height and the shrapnel nearly wrecked our beloved plane coming very close to 100 trips.

Melrose and co.'s photograph of Brest, attacking ships that the Germans intended to use to block the harbour.

Bombing [14 August, Brest] was not as accurate as yesterday's. Don't know how 617 got on. I think Group is pitting 617 against IX to see who is best. There was a rhyme often quoted at Bardney. 'Six one seven shoot the line, Got their gen from Number Nine'. Flak was worse today and just as precise. We all had holes in our aircraft. Attacking in daylight at moderate height with a clear sky allows the German gunners to plot the bombing run – height, speed, direction – so they can put up a box barrage that we have to fly through.

(Left) *U-boat pens at La Pallice, 16 August 1944.* (Above) *Doug Melrose looks out from J-Johnny after that raid.*

[On the way to the first *Tirpitz* raid, 11 September] We encountered extremely bad weather on route and for the last hour of the flight cloud was down to 300ft combined with rain. None of the promised radio aids were available and the navigating was done by means of dead reckoning and map reading. Jimmy [Moore, navigator] and Sammy [Morris, bomb aimer] did a wonderful job and Doug flew so well considering the poor weather. We ultimately landed at Yagodnik after 10.25 hours in the air. A very exhausting time in a tin tube.

Doug was 'A' Flight commander, and so we led to aqueducts on the Dortmund–Ems Canal [Münster, 23 September]. It would be the last time that all the original crew flew together and the last time we flew in J-Johnny. It was throwing it down as we took off and things got worse over the Channel as we saw two kites go down together. They must have collided. We saw the

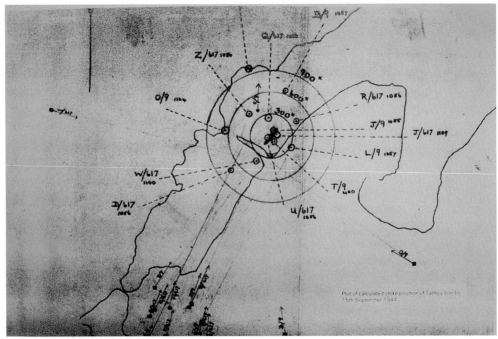

The official 'Plot of Calculated Strike Positions' of Tallboy bombs dropped on the first Tirpitz raid. Melrose in W4964 WS/J – shown as J/9 on the chart – was first to drop, followed by Tweddle, five of 617 Squadron (Tait, Howard, Kell, IX Squadron old boy Stout, and Pryor), then Harry Pooley in Lonesome Lola. Intelligence confirmed one hit and three near misses. The diagram shows Pryor (U/617) near-missing with his Tallboy dropped at 10.56. The single hit smashed through the foredeck, dropped at 10.55 by Flight Lieutenant Dougie Melrose, bomb aimer Flying Officer Sammy Morris. They didn't sink the Tirpitz, but so disabled her that there was now no need. Not realising this, IX and 617 Squadrons were sent on two more raids before the totemic ship was finally sent below.

yellow ball of flame slowly falling, leaving a streak of fire hundreds of feet long, before being scattered in a bright glow along the coastline.

So, everybody's tour was complete. We were all of four months older than when we started. Time for merriment and a good stretch of leave.

One night we were coming back from the pub, very pleased with ourselves, walking along the concrete path to our hut. The squadron had come home from an op around midnight or a bit later but soon after the last aircraft landed a group of Ju88 intruders attacked. One roared directly overhead, very low and clearly defined against the light night sky. Full of Dutch courage, we shook our fists at the beast and gave him the full benefit of our extensive knowledge of different ways of saying go away, you nasty person. To our horror and astonishment, he did a split-arse turn and seemed to come straight back at us. We did our own version of the manoeuvre and dashed into the nearest shelter, which was the toilet block. A Lancaster crew all trying to get through the door at once created the kind of comic log-jam you see in the films, and we were still in it after our adversary had whizzed past without bothering to stop, whereupon we bravely came out again.

They bombed and strafed most of the nearby 'dromes including Waddington and it was uncanny to see them silhouetted against the moonlit cloud base and sometimes in the moonlight itself, diving and climbing. Each dive was split by the yellow-white streaks of cannon fire or ended with the sharp crump of a medium bomb. The wireless said that there were sixty bandits over our region that night. They eventually came back and attacked us too at Bardney but no defence was put up against them by our side.

Intruders were a menace to our bombers returning from ops. They would hope to arrive at a 'drome when the aircraft were in their landing pattern. When a crew was absorbed in making a safe landing, tired after a long flight, a big Lanc was an easy target for a short burst of cannon fire. The word was on that particular night that eight of the raiders had been shot down, including 'ours', but that we'd lost fifteen plus the damage on the ground.

This was Unternehmen Gisela, *a kind of last hurrah by the Luftwaffe, a maximum effort of 200 night-fighters along the eastern side of England. Once their presence was known, incoming aircraft were warned and diverted to aerodromes hopefully beyond the threat. Nevertheless, at least seventeen home-coming bombers were shot down, plus two on 12 Squadron training flights, plus five from heavy bomber conversion units. The Luftwaffe lost twenty-five machines, all Ju88s.*

I wanted to try flying with other crews, to see how the experience compared with what I'd known all my operational life, but the CO, Jimmy Bazin, or Dougie always seemed to find a reason why I couldn't go. I finally got away with Flight Lieutenant Ray Harris [warships at Sassnitz, 6 March] and the first thing was how strange to hear different voices over the intercom, something I hadn't experienced since my days in Hampdens in Canada. We flew across Sweden whose neutrality allowed us to look down on fully illuminated cities and towns, so colourful, so brilliant, like diamonds on velvet.

The Swedes obligingly fired off a fair amount of light flak to show their neutrality but aimed it at 9,000ft, well below our height. There was a lot of light flak over the target too, and not much heavy stuff, but the bomber stream was very dense and we had two near misses with other Lancasters. One was a Lanc losing height right above us. I was in the astrodome and saw him, with no time to do anything except shout 'Dive, Ray, dive!'. His response was so immediate we dropped like a stone and I was thrown upwards, bashing my head on the dome which added greatly to the star count.

Just to finish off a rather special night, we had a chase by a FW190 which Ray lost in the clouds. His reflexes are superb and he is a very good pilot indeed and his crew work well together. It was a privilege to be with them and nice to find out there are teams as good as us.

[Back with Melrose, Essen, 11 March] The sky seemed filled with aircraft. Dense cloud covered the target so we bombed on PFF sky markers. Packed in close formation, Ernie [Stalley, rear gunner] watched in appalled disgust as a batch of bright yellow 1,000-pounders flashed past our starboard tailfin. Such a disturbing sight, so obvious in daylight, made us all wonder how often this must have happened on night ops, and how often that was the explanation for the red balls of fire in the darkness that meant another bomber going down.

[On the last day of the air war in Europe, 25 April 1945, a force including some 360 Lancs attacked Hitler's holiday cottage at Berchtesgaden] It was a fine day and the stream of bombers seemed to stretch from one horizon to

All the originals of the Melrose crew pose with J-Johnny at the end of their time together. Of the aircraft's 107 ops, Melrose skippered on 23 and was thus J-Johnny champion.

the other. We had a clear sight of the target and the military establishment at the foot of the mountains but seeing it and hitting it were two different things. We went on our bombing run with 617 above us. One of their aircraft was directly on us, on top of us, and Doug asked me to watch him from the astrodome. Sammy was calling his bombing instructions, we were moments from release time, and I saw the 617 aircraft had his bomb doors open. I watched in utter horror as the bomb was released and began its curving flight. It was heading absolutely straight for us. I had no alternative, even though we were on our run. 'Starboard, skip, a touch starboard,' I shouted. The bomb missed our port wingtip by nothing at all. I could read the word Torpex on it as it went past, the name for the explosive inside it. Well, the run up was spoiled and we couldn't make another, so we brought our Tallboy home for the last time.

George Thompson, Lancasters, 1944–5

The night of 31 December 1944 and 1 January 1945 was one of a series of cold ones, and it was perishing, frosty and black dark as the crews were taken to their dispersals at around 06.45. It was still dark when Flying Officer Harry Denton, a New Zealander, captain of U-Uncle, was first up at 07.44. At 07.47, Cliff Newton surged down the runway in R-Robert and took off. Immediately filling his place at the end of the runway was Flying Officer Buckley in A-Able. Both these two crashed on take-off [see p. 198]; six more of the squadron got away later, of which one failed to return [see p. 180]. Denton and crew flew on alone, to Ladbergen.

The crew included Sergeants Potts and Price in the turrets and a gentle giant of a Scotsman as wireless operator, Flight Sergeant George Thompson. This op was his fifth, with the same crew but they'd never had the same aircraft twice. They'd been attacked by a fighter on their first trip, to Heilbronn, but the others had been reasonably routine.

Flying through curtains of ack-ack, Denton made his run. Bombs gone, job done, then bang, bang, bang. One shell hit them amidships, ripped a great hole in the fuselage, set the aircraft on fire and filled it with smoke. Another hit the starboard inner engine and set it on fire too. Yet another hit the front turret and smashed its way through the cockpit canopy – or, maybe, it was more than three shells. Denton had no idea how many. All he knew was that the intercom was u/s and the freezing wind, blowing a double gale through the newly disappeared nose of the aircraft, had cleared the smoke, revealed the horrendous damage and was fanning the flames into fury.

The bomb aimer, Flying Officer Ron Goebel, thought he was quite lucky.

He hadn't had time to get from his bomb-release position to his front turret, where he would have been killed. Denton now thought they were being attacked by fighters. His gunners were firing back. If they were ordering a corkscrew he couldn't hear them, not that he would have had much hope of corkscrewing or completing any other violent manoeuvre. They were sinking, slowly but surely, towards the ground.

Two parachutes had been shot and torn open so that removed the choice of abandoning the aircraft. The best thing he and his engineer, Wilf Hartshorn, could do was to concentrate simply on keeping U-Uncle flying for as long as possible, at least until they were away from enemy territory. Navigator Ted Kneebone would need his most precise calculations to tell them when that was.

George Thompson knew that they were not being attacked by fighters. The gunfire Denton could hear was his own ammunition going off in the heat of the fire. Bullets were exploding everywhere and Ernie Potts lay dead or unconscious in his mid-upper turret. Thompson didn't know about the other crew members' parachutes being destroyed so, in his mind, leaving his post meant he would not be able to hear any order to jump. Despite that, he got up and, hunched over, headed back down the fuselage and climbed over the main spar, into the flames.

It was difficult enough crawling around a Lancaster when it was stationary. There were obstacles everywhere and no movement was exactly free. It was ten times worse when your space, already confined and awkward, was lit by fire, ventilated by a freezing hurricane and set with traps like exploding machine-gun bullets and a gaping hole big enough to drop through. Thompson struggled his way around the hole – it would be much harder coming back, carrying somebody – and reached the mid-upper turret and the lifeless dummy that was Potts. The gunner was spark out but not dead.

George Thompson, the big Jock, ploughman's son from Glencraig in the Kingdom of Fife, used to all weathers although not used to being freeze-dried while being roasted alive, pulled the gunner out of his blazing turret and, against the force of the wind, threaded him past the great hole to the rest bed, a spot where there was solidity and no fire – at least, no fire in the aircraft. There was fire in Potts's clothes.

Thompson was already badly burned. His face and legs were giving him hell, much of his flying gear had been scorched away but Potts's personal fire had to be put out. Lancasters had blankets as standard equipment but U-Uncle's blankets were burning worse than Potts's uniform. Thompson had nothing to use except his hands, so he used them.

Denton and the others were not aware of any of this. Everybody was concentrating on trying to keep the aircraft where it was meant to be: in the air, so long as they were behind enemy lines.

Looking up from his task, now completed as far as it could be, George Thompson saw that the rear turret was aflame too. The gunner, Sergeant Price, was lying helpless, overcome by flames and fumes, unable to do anything for himself about his inevitable and unbearably painful death by burning. Thompson's own pain would have been unbearable to almost all men but it didn't stop him making his way aft for a second time, forcing himself to slide down the ramp into the rear turret and, for a second time, dragging a heavy, smouldering, semi-conscious man, in effect a dead body, from his battle position to some sort of relative comfort and, for the second time, with hands already burned beyond repair, beating out the fires in the man's clothes.

That done, Thompson's military training told him that the skipper must be informed. The skipper must know that he had no mid-upper or rear gunner to defend them. Gripping the sides of the fuselage and various pieces of equipment to get past the holes, Thompson was putting burned flesh onto searingly hot metal but he had to get forward. He must make a report to the captain and not only about the gunners. The captain had no wireless operator either. There was no possibility of those burned hands working a wireless set. Unknown to George Thompson, some of the burning wasn't from the flames. Incredibly, inside that fiery furnace, the wind was giving him frostbite as he staggered and groped his way to the cockpit.

Denton, his friend Denton, the New Zealand country boy who had been to the Thompson family home a number of times, did not recognise him. The aircraft was a burned black wreck and so was this man, swaying behind the pilot, trying to say something above the wind and the engines. When a few words did get through, Denton realised who it was. The accent could not be mistaken. This was George Thompson. This filthy, frayed, blackened being who looked like he'd been tied up with Joan of Arc at the stake, was his pal George.

Denton took in the news about the gunners without emotion. It was one disaster on top of another, and the sight of all those German fighters flying past the other way didn't help matters. They took no notice of the doomed Lanc. It wasn't worth bothering with. They had no shells left anyway, after strafing some invading Allies' positions. In pursuit of the Germans came Spitfires. They felt obliged to lend a hand to their comrades and tried to guide Denton towards the nearest airfield. No airfield, though, could be near enough. Now, after three quarters of an hour of flying what seemed like half an aircraft, with three engines and more hole than skin, Denton knew they'd had it with proper landings. He felt he'd about had it too, with the frostbite he'd suffered.

The attitude of the aircraft was all wrong. She was tail down. She had virtually no Perspex in her front and the inrushing wind was causing enormous drag. She was flying along as if permanently about to stall and the pilot was having trouble seeing anything other than sky. Never mind airfields, anywhere would have to do and it would have to do this instant. Kneebone had told him they had crossed the Rhine at 4,000ft and now, at almost zero feet, they were over friendly country. This part of Holland was held by the Allies and very pleasant it looked, with its villages and flat fields.

George Thompson VC was one of only three Lancaster air crew other than pilots to be awarded the highest honour in the Second World War.

Denton was about to choose a field when a Spitfire flashed across his nose. He looked and saw the power cables the Spit pilot was warning him about. In among his efforts to climb over, the aircraft really did stall and she flopped down outside the village of Heesch, not far from Nijmegen. Denton disembarked using the quickest route, straight through the front where his Perspex should have been.

U-Uncle, god, what a mess she looked. How she'd stayed up in the air for 5 minutes, let alone 45, he could not imagine. Thompson got out, too, to congratulate his skipper on a good landing. Unusually for a pilot with so few ops clocked up, Denton's landing and his flying would earn him the DFC.

Help arrived. Ron Goebel, with nothing worse than frostbite, was sent back to Blighty and the rest were taken to hospital in Eindhoven. Sergeant Potts never recovered consciousness and died of his dreadful burns. Sergeant Price made a good recovery from his ordeal and owed his life to George Thompson. The doctors wanted to fly Thompson home to a specialised burns unit but the weather was too bad, so he stayed at a military hospital in Brussels, caught pneumonia and there, three weeks later, far from home, he died.

The award of the Victoria Cross calls for the highest standard of personal bravery. The many brave deeds of recipients of this coveted award during this and other wars are faithfully recorded and I consider the actions of Flight Sergeant Thompson on the 1st January 1945 fully merit the inclusion of his name among this illustrious and distinguished company.

Flight Sergeant Thompson in this instance acted in excess of the normal demands of duty and quite beyond that which any individual might expect of another. He has set an example of which the Service, his parents and his comrades may all be justly proud. I do therefore most strongly recommend the posthumous award of the Victoria Cross. [signed] A Hesketh, Air Commodore, AOC No. 51 Base, Waddington.

CHAPTER 12

Gunners

Dennis 'Micky' Mason, Wellingtons and Lancasters, 1942
After a tour with 149 Squadron in Wellingtons, I began with IX Squadron on the Cologne 'Thousand Plan', 30 May, and Squadron Leader Turner, an experienced operational pilot [this was Bob Turner, Heyford pilot 1938, veteran of Brunsbüttel, back with his old squadron as a flight commander]. He promptly took his new crew up on an air test. He made a bad landing and tipped the aircraft on its nose. I was high in the sky in the tail when the aircraft began to settle and then dropped like a stone, hitting the ground with a tremendous bang. The tail wheel came up through the floor and one new aircraft was definitely u/s. I had a few bruises but was fit to fly to Cologne with the same crew in R-Robert.

We were fitted with the new Gee box so we were among the first over the target, dropping incendiaries to light up the area for the bombers that followed. We were greeted by heavy flak and many searchlights. One aircraft flying alongside us took a direct hit, exploded and crashed in pieces, out of view but not out of our thoughts.

We set off to bomb Essen [1 June] but the oxygen supply failed so we couldn't fly at the necessary height. Rather than go home we bombed an aerodrome in Holland and got involved with a few enemy fighters. Our skipper was an aggressive flyer and we chased a Me110, much to everyone's amusement as he was much faster than us.

I crewed up with another flight commander, second-tour man Squadron Leader Clyde-Smith. We flew at low level over France [26 June] and dropped our mines in the estuary at St Nazaire. We were only a few feet above the sea when we were coned by eight searchlights and the guns were firing on us at point blank range. I was on the front gun and Chris Howe was in the tail. We both opened up trying to shoot out searchlights and the A-A. I blasted a gun crew off the top of a building but we were hit many times, including petrol tanks and hydraulics, and one engine failed but we were still in the air and we were not on fire. Wellingtons were potential torches, covered in doped fabric.

At any rate, we struggled over the water and were in sight of Abingdon aerodrome when our other engine packed up. No landing lights were on, we had no undercart, no flaps that worked, and in we came. I was standing next to the squadron leader when we hit the top of a building and scraped off our underside, leaving me hanging from the cockpit roof and the pilot half blinded. We skidded and slewed about for 200yd and ended up with our port wing between the wheels of another aircraft.

The squadron made several raids to Italian targets in the autumn of 1942, long journeys all, across the Alps. A daylight to Milan caught the attention of the press – Squadron Leader 'Tubby' Fry and crew make the top picture, and Fry with pipe can be spotted in the lower one. Dennis Mason and Harry Irons must be in there too.

THESE MEN WENT TO MILAN AND MADE THE JACKAL HOWL!

Some of the "Lancaster Lads" who carried out the devastating daylight raid on Milan, one of Mussolini's war productions centres thus creating a Second Front for the gallant Eighth Army now battling in Egypt.

We all managed to get out, with various minor injuries. They X-rayed us at the Radcliffe, strapped us up and sent us back to Honington, and we returned to work [Bremen, 2 July], where the flak was heavy and well aimed but we left the target blazing. Thinking we were home, flying at 50ft over the sea, we ran into a convoy of balloons. Goodness knows how but we managed not to touch any of them.

With the change to the Lancaster, I retrained as a bomb aimer. I flew in Oxfords dropping practice bombs and map reading and then I had my first flight in a Lanc. It was a disaster. The pilot overshot on his first landing approach, with me watching in the front turret. He called me back and we made another five attempts to land including one where we caught the undercart on the boundary fence. At last we crash landed on the grass and I jumped out from the astrodome, carrying my parachute. I should have had it open, with the difference in height between jumping from a Wellington and a Lanc.

Once a gunner, always a gunner, and on ops I spent most of the time in the front turret except when there was aiming to be done, but on air tests I'd be lying on my front looking down. Our skipper [Clyde-Smith] took a delight in dropping the nose of the aircraft so that I would lift from the floor. He'd keep me suspended as long as possible, then pull the stick back to drop me with a thump back on my padded couch.

Harry Irons, Lancasters, 1942–3

I came straight from gunnery school, without going through an OTU, and joined up with Dick Stubbs [August 1942] as his mid-upper on 8s a day. The crews converting to the Lancaster were teaching themselves, really. There didn't seem to be any organised instruction. Stubbs was the most experienced bloke on the squadron, halfway through his second tour. Our flight commander was Cowan and he'd never flown a Lancaster either. I was just the office boy so they put me in the mid-upper turret.

Stubbs was a strange character. Didn't drink, didn't smoke, didn't chase women, didn't swear. But when he was in the air he changed completely. From the time we took off until the time we landed, his language was unbelievable. So off we went to Düsseldorf [10 September] and I'd never been so frightened in my life. I didn't know what was going on. Never been to OTU and Stubbs said 'You'll learn as you go along', so that was the extent of my operational education. I couldn't credit the flak and the searchlights and all the aircraft blowing up. I had the best view from my turret. We were hit by flak and on top of that we had a lot of engine trouble with the Lanc.

There were immersion pumps in the fuel supply and they were not reliable. I was in a daze when we got back. But Stubbs was right. You did get used to it.

SECRET No. 9 Squadron Combat Report
Date: 20th September 1942. Target: Munich. Pos. 40 miles SE of Rheims. Lancaster: W4157 WS/V Captain: F/Lt Stubbs.

Ju88 attacked from port quarter up. First seen at 150 yards. Rear gunner fired two short bursts. Ju88 broke away to port beam. Evasive action slight turn to port. Ju88 fired machine guns and cannon which passed over port wing. Mid-upper gunner fired burst as Ju88 crossed under to starboard beam. Ju88 attacked from starboard to port underneath, using free gun. Evasive action turn starboard. Ju88 recrossed underneath from port to starboard and finally disappeared.

We were in ten tenths cloud, all the way there and most of the way back, then we broke into clear weather. And there was a fighter, a Ju88, 30yd away, maybe nearer. Me and Brian opened fire at the same moment. The Junkers had his nose slightly up and was too close, really, so his cannon shells went over us. We both belted away at him and he dropped away to port and he stayed there for a few minutes, then he dived and went right across us underneath, and I had about twenty bullet holes just miss my arse. Stubbs corkscrewed all over the sky and we got rid, and we landed full of holes, but we had holes in the aircraft anyway, from the flak. You always came back with holes in.

The flak was very bad [at Wismar, 23 September] and we got some more holes, but we definitely got a direct hit on the [Dornier] factory on our first run, which was good because Stubbs wouldn't go home until he was sure he'd got a hit. We saw one

The accolade for hitting the aiming point, as Harry Irons says, was a piece of paper. This one was earned by Squadron Leader Clyde-Smith, Dennis Mason and crew at Düsseldorf.

of our squadron shot down on the way in [Pilot Officer C J McKeen, R5907 WS/M]. We were in ten tenths cloud going back, absolutely nothing to see, and the Gee box was no use this far out. Ken [Chamberlain] got us home. Brilliant navigator. And then we got a piece of paper from the Group commander because we'd hit the aiming point. That's what they gave you, a sheet of paper with a drawing on it.

They used to give you a mining trip for a bit of a breather, a piece of cake, but they were very dodgy. You'd go out into the Baltic or somewhere and there'd be these flak ships waiting for you. And you had to fly low to drop the mines, so you didn't damage them, which gave the flak ships the piece of cake. Us.

Stubbs and his men from the Wellington days were getting near the end of their tours now. I still had a lot of trips to do but we all could look around and see the same thing. You saw the whole operational squadron when you were waiting to be taken out to dispersal. You'd sit there, having a smoke, knowing that a crew or two wouldn't be coming back. You'd wonder who all these new faces were and if you'd ever get to know who they were.

We were doing a lot of close-formation training [for Le Creusot], and we mid-upper gunners were like eggs in an egg cup, waiting for our tops to be sliced off. One day, there were ninety of us, flying in a gaggle at about 20ft over The Wash, and these Spitfires came at us. They came in from behind in a mock attack and we were too low to take evasive action. As the Spits tried to break away they hit the slipstream of ninety Lancs. If we'd been at a 100ft they'd have been all right. As it was, some of them just flipped over and went straight into the deck.

On the way, we were in a loose gaggle about a mile wide, easy meat for any fighters but we never saw any and it was crystal clear weather. We could see for miles and miles. We never saw our escorts either; we were supposed to have a couple of hundred Spitfires but they didn't turn up. The Lancs were still flying at nought feet and French people waved cheerily. The squadron were in and out of the target in 2 minutes. We were given 4,500ft as our height. The highest was 5,000 and the lowest 2,500, but one Lanc went in really low [Squadron Leader Corr DFC, 61 Squadron]. I don't know if it was his own bombs or somebody else's, but he blew up and went into the houses.

The official report said that almost all bombs fell across the works, creating tremendous damage. There was tremendous damage all right, but quite a few of the bombs fell short, onto the housing estate which was at one end of the factory. There were plenty of civilian properties destroyed as well as the target.

The Saturday after Le Creusot we went to Milan, travelling more or less the same route, eighty-eight of us this time, all Lancs, carrying the same load, six 1,000-pounders. They were so surprised in Milan they didn't even sound the air raid sirens. We did see some fighters, Italian air force, but they stood off and didn't interfere.

The press were all around us when we got back and they published a picture of our crew and Squadron Leader Tubby Fry and his crew in the *Express* and various national papers on the Monday. Later in the week the Italian papers had the same picture but they'd changed the headline to 'English Gangsters', and they put that in the *Daily Sketch* as well. I think that raid really shook the Italians. Ninety Lancs hitting a fairly compact town, coming all the way from England and wrecking the industry in broad daylight, well, I think they lost a lot of their appetite for the war.

Sometimes we would be diverted to another aerodrome and very occasionally it would be an American base. The Yanks were coming over in numbers now, with their four-engined bombers that could only carry a half or a third of a Lancaster load. Still, we liked landing at their bases. We loved telling them we could carry up to sixteen-thousand pounds, and we loved the ice cream they had.

Something else completely different was what they called a moling trip. These were against targets not normally in the firing line. It was low level, moonlight, no cloud, and we had twelve 1,000-pounders [17 December]. The flak on the Dutch coast was murderous, light flak from hundreds of guns. From a distance it looked like twenty firework nights all at once, purples, blues, yellows, all different colours. We were each given a village, and we went in at 200ft and there was a train puffing in the station and we machine-gunned that and caught it afire, and we dropped our bombs right along the high street. They told us that the German factory workers were being transported to these dormitory villages so they could get a good night's kip.

We discovered later that nine out of twenty-seven Lancs had been lost, and they sent the clever chaps to investigate. Stubbs said it was quite simple. If you had a good navigator you got there and came back. If you didn't, you didn't.

Those that didn't had strayed alone into heavily defended regions and got the chop. Another thing was that the briefing had said to fly the route at 10,000ft, assuming cloud. The cloud wasn't there, so the experienced skippers either went much higher or much lower. The others stayed at the given height, clearly visible and easy targets for the flak gunners.

One night [20 December, Duisburg], we were circling to gain height when there was a collision. We were right above it. Tremendous explosion, full petrol loads, full bomb loads, and they went into each other head on. [IX Squadron, Sergeant Hazell and crew, 44 Squadron Flight Sergeant Elger and crew, all killed] We were more than close. I don't know how we got away with it, and the funny thing was, with an incident like that, you still carried on with the op.

No question about Stubbs carrying on. Stubbs had the two necessary ingredients for a successful Lancaster pilot. He had reactions like lightning, so when we saw a fighter he was into his evasive action before we'd got half the order out. And, he had ice instead of blood. We were running into Germany one night with a full bomb load and all four engines cut out at once. Stubbs said that's a nuisance, four engines gone, or words to that effect. We dropped like a stone and I think Tom [Parrington, engineer] must have blanked out because he didn't do anything. So Stubbs said, very calmly and quietly, how about changing the fuel tanks over, which Tom did. The engines

Harry Irons's new unit: pilot Sergeant Doolan stands centre. Harry is third from the left.

all started up again and we carried on as if nothing had happened. Stubbs was only three or four years older than me but he seemed more, a lot more, like he'd had ten years' experience of this terrible job.

He was killed a few months later on a training flight, and Brian [Moorhead, rear gunner] and Bill [Colson, bomb aimer], they didn't last it out either.

One of the squadron rear gunners was killed, Reggie Robinson, called Robbie. He was a bit older than me, he'd be 20 or 21, from Brixton. They brought him back but there was nothing left of him apart from some of his upper body. We gunners knew each other. We went to his funeral. His skipper was Sergeant Doolan, who we'd taken as a second Dicky. He was famous as a pilot who couldn't land. Aircrew considered landing an important skill and weren't keen on flying with him. So he came in the Mess and said they'd put a nice new turret on his Lanc and would I like to get in it. Some of my pals said, you're not going with him, are you? I said there wasn't anybody else.

Hamburg [30 January 1943] was a nightmare. Half the squadron came home early because of the weather. We were almost there, we were there, but not over the target. We could feel the aircraft getting more and more sluggish, then we reached that point where the weight became too much and we dropped like an express lift. We could see Hamburg coming up fast underneath us. We dumped our bombs, the ice fell off, and we came home. It was DNCO, duty not carried out. I thought, if I have to do as many trips that don't count with Doolan as I did with Stubbs, I'll never get to the end of it.

Kiel [4 April] made my thirty. Including the DNCOs it was more like thirty-six. I said goodbye to my skipper and told him he never would learn to land an aircraft, and I went as a gunnery instructor, then I was on pulling drogues for the artillery to shoot at, which was my most dangerous posting of all. We pulled this long streamer about 200yd behind us, at 3–4,000ft, and the artillery aimed at the streamer. We lost quite a few shot down – aircraft that was, not streamers. Anyway, I survived again and went on to a second tour on Halifaxes.

Norman Wells, Lancasters, 1943–4

When we [crew of Sergeant Phil Plowright] went into the briefing room and saw we'd got Berlin for our first [2 December 1943], we thought Christ Almighty and yet, at the same time, it was something good. We were going to Berlin. That was the heart of the war. But when we got there, god, it was horrendous. We all thought, we can't get through this. It was a mass of

This was the sight greeting Norman Wells as he came into the Mess as a new boy. This photograph was taken around October 1943.

The date says 1943 but this photograph was taken in early March 1944. WS/J-Johnny has done over forty ops, which makes Plowright and crew about a third of the way through their tours.

LANCASTER W4964 WS-J IX SQDN BARDNEY 1943

CREW L TO R
P.E. PLOWRIGHT. R.P. ALLEN. F. CORR. N.H. B. LUCAS. N.F. WELLS.
FRONT
W.C. LEWIS. H. HANNAH

searchlights, and with the flak and the photoflashes going off and the bombs exploding, it was as bright as day. Nothing hit us but we could see plenty of other aircraft going down, plenty. I wasn't expecting fighters over the target, not with so much flak, so I could rotate my turret and I could look kind of forward, past the wingtip. Of course, I didn't do that for long, and soon we were on our way out of all the light and mayhem and we crossed some sort of invisible line and there we were, instantly, in black darkness, where we knew the fighters were waiting for us, and I realised that in all the light over the target I'd lost my night vision. Pretty scary, that first one. When we got back and walked down those steps and stood on the ground, we felt elated. We felt, thank God for that. Then we said, wouldn't have missed that one for the world. Well, we could say that, couldn't we? We were home.

It seemed to be Berlin every op, all the way through that winter. One time [15 February, largest of the Berlin raids, 891 bombers], we were hit on our way in by flak on the starboard inner and it was u/s. Sticky [Lewis, engineer] went to feather it but it wouldn't feather, so the prop was being pushed round and round by air pressure, which caused a lot of drag on us, but we bombed and came home. It was bloody hard work, that sort of trip. Phil would be rocking the aircraft most of the time, side to side, so we could see underneath, and you did nothing for hours except stare and stare into the darkness, knowing that all the others in the crew, doing their various jobs, relied on the gunners to spot the enemy. You couldn't relax. Even when you saw the sea on the way home and you felt you'd made it again, the fighters could still be following you. Our own navy shot at us once when we were coming up to the English coast.

I don't know what made a brilliant pilot. We thought Phil Plowright was brilliant. Possibly they all were, or most of them, but most of them weren't lucky. When we were in L, our own aircraft, we were hit and came home on three, then we went on leave and she went down with another crew. We went to Marseille in B, got a shell in the tail, came home, gave her back to her former owner, very experienced pilot [Flying Officer Manning] and down he went with the Group Captain on board, and we were there on the same op, just like them, in among it.

We were nominated PFF [Pathfinder Force] Supporter for Stuttgart, which is muggins who flies in front of the pathfinders to draw the fire so they can drop their TIs undisturbed. After doing that, you have to go around and come in again to bomb. We were in J-Johnny, never got a mark on that one, yet Backwell-Smith, a squadron leader, top man, FTR.

Nürnburg, that dreadful, dreadful night, we never got shot at but we damned nearly got rammed by another Lanc heading for the same cloud as we were. He was so close we could hear his engines as well as our own. I went to Berlin seven times, Frankfurt three times. Goodness knows how many went down on those trips. [Frankfurt – 53 Lancasters lost on those 3 ops; Berlin – 243 on those 7].

Another time, we were flying almost wingtip to wingtip with this Lanc, straight and level on our bombing runs, and he had a flak shell burst behind him at the perfect height, then another in front, and the third hit him right amidships and he just went up in a cloud of bits. You were not supposed to deviate from your run in any circumstance. If you did, it would show on your photograph, it would be at a funny angle, and the skipper would be up before the CO. So that chap didn't deviate and they got the chop.

There were French attacks with German ones in between. Mailly-le-Camp [Panzer base, 3 May] was a disaster. The markers had to be put down at 2 minutes past midnight, because the soldiers in the barracks would all be in bed by then. The time came and went and we saw no markers. Nobody knows quite what happened. There were stories about Cheshire arriving too soon, flying over and coming back late, and more about radios not working. We smashed up the barracks all right and left the town unharmed even though it was right there next door. I heard that the only French civilians killed were by a Lanc which crashed into their house [42 out of 346 Lancasters were lost on this raid].

Our last op [21 May] was back to Germany, Duisburg, so we couldn't help but feel a few butterflies. There were no easy ones but after all those Berlin trips and Stuttgart and Essen and whatnot, you'd pick France if you had a choice, which we hadn't, of course.

We were determined to be first back and when it was time to call base, Phil dispensed with the usual routine. Instead of the Rosen Johnny over business, he just said 'Johnny Walker, still going strong. Get some in!'. We were first back, at 03.09. We beat Redfern by 1 minute.

We had a few drinks, and later on our flight commander signed my log book, that was Flight Lieutenant Mathers, and the CO, Wingco Porter, he signed it and wrote 'First operational tour completed: twenty-nine and a third sorties'. A third? I don't know which one they were counting as a third.

Vincent Peace, Lancasters, 1944–5

The whole area [Heilbronn, 4 December 1944] was already well ablaze but before we [Flying Officer Peter Reakes and crew] could set ourselves for our bombing run, the Master Bomber ordered a rerun on a different marker and at a lower altitude, which let loose several minutes of complete mayhem. There were Lancasters flying in all directions, clearly visible in the bright glow from the fires below. We seemed to be not much above the roof tops. If I'd fired my guns downwards, quite a lot of firemen would have fallen off their ladders. We dropped our bombs and climbed with all speed out of the blazing, flak-infested area, when another Lancaster passed a few feet above us, almost on the same heading. If I could have stood up in my turret and reached out, I could have touched his tail wheel.

We also encountered *Schrägemusik* for the first time and didn't know what it was. Only a few seconds had gone by after this very near miss when I reported to the skipper that there was a string of multi-coloured balls arcing over us, coming from starboard down and looping up and across to port. A few more moments went by after this excitement when I lost all power to my turret. Nothing would work. The guns wouldn't fire and my heated jacket stopped heating. It was minus 30 °C outside and soon it was about that inside as well. I was still frozen at the interrogation, when they told us that the pretty coloured balls were from a night-fighter with an upward firing gun.

Our bomb aimer was Warrant Officer the Honourable Edward Percy Bates, son of Sir Percy Bates of Neston, fourth baronet and Chairman of the Cunard shipping line. We called him The Master. He played chess all the time instead of going to the pub, and he had a famous car, a huge American one like you saw in the gangster films. Wing Commander Bazin had to ask him not to park it in front of the station main office building because it was embarrassing for the Wingco when he rode up on his bicycle.

By the New Year, we'd been on squadron coming up for three months, and we'd done eight ops. We were late taking off on our ninth [Ladbergen, 1 January 1945] and flew a more direct route to catch up with the other bombers over the target. We started our run and behind us, just at our height, three bursts of flak exploded. I saw it from my turret and so did Geoff [Bamforth, rear gunner] and we told the skipper but he refused to do anything. To dive or climb was the obvious move, but no.

Percy Bates called 'Bombs gone', there was a bang and a flash in the front of the aircraft and a loud scream from the pilot. He managed to cry 'Bale out' before we went into a steep dive. Percy, Tom [Scott, engineer], Stan [Currigan, w/op] and the skipper were all killed. Frank [Alton, navigator] was doing a rock-climb up a vertical aircraft and Geoff was almost falling down it.

We three jumped into the German morning. It was around 11.15 and I had no idea what to expect. Possibly the Germans would shoot us on the way down. Possibly we would be treated according to the Geneva Convention, like we'd been told we would be. Possibly the German civilians might not accord with Geneva. In any case, I knew the rest of the boys had not survived because I watched our Lancaster go past me in flames and smash into the ground.

I didn't land all that well and I was sitting in the snow with a sprained ankle, beside a field gate, smoking a cigarette, when a Luftwaffe corporal turned up on a bicycle. 'You all right?'' he said, in perfect English. I said I'd never felt better, so he said to come along with him. He helped me fold up my parachute, put it on his cycle pannier and, as I hobbled along, told me about the marvellous time he'd had while he was a student at the University of Hull. We walked past several anti-aircraft emplacements whose gunners waved a cheery greeting, and we came to a hut where I was interviewed by a junior army officer. When I gave my name, rank and number, as per instructions, the German smiled. 'Peace?' he said. 'We have been waiting a long time for you.'

CHAPTER 13

Bomb Aimers

Ken Dagnall, Lancasters, 1943

I was just over 18. Jim [McCubbin, pilot] would be 22, a little older than most. We'd done OTU and instead of sending us to Lancaster finishing school they sent us to fly in Whitleys looking for submarines [October 1942]. That was a shocking aircraft, shocking. And to think people used to fly over Germany in them.

[After surviving a ditching and four days in a dinghy] We came to IX Squadron in March 1943, with three ops counted in our log books. They'd counted the one with four days in the sea as a double, even though it hadn't been completed. So, we went to Lorient [2 April]. Three Lancasters, just three. It was a clear, moonlit night and the first time I'd ever flown so high. The old Whitley could only struggle up to 12,000ft, and here we were in the top of the sky, millions of stars, and I thought if this is war, it's a picture. And the next night we were on for Essen which, the grapevine said, was just about the most heavily defended place we could go to. Only Berlin was worse. Then it was Kiel the following night, when our rear gunner Charlie Stewart shot off a few rounds at a fighter which apparently didn't want to fight.

SECRET No. 9 Squadron Combat Report

Date: 4th/5th April 1943. Pos. Hëide. Lancaster 'W'. Captain Sgt McCubbin.

Interception by a S/E E/A took place very shortly after bombing the target, Kiel. The pilot was carrying out continuous weaving at 21,000 feet. The E/A, believed to be Me109, was seen 200 feet below and directly astern at 100 yards by the rear gunner [Sergeant Stewart]. He warned the captain who executed a diving turn to starboard while the rear gunner fired two three-second bursts at the E/A, the second of which was seen to hit. The fighter immediately dived away and disappeared while still at 100 yards range without opening fire.

No moon, visibility fairly good. Layer of 10/10 cloud at 6,000 feet illuminated a little astern of our aircraft by searchlights.

Rear turret 450 rounds, no stoppages.

That was the first time we went in W-William, which we christened Cutty Sark after the frigate that picked us out of the sea. We found out that cutty sark was Scottish for short skirt, so we had a picture of a wicked witch wearing one painted on W's nose. And that was three ops on the trot so they gave us a week's leave.

The squadron lost six aircraft in action in the first nine days of April (plus one in training). We suddenly became one of the senior crews and we'd only been on four operations. The Wingco had us all assembled in a room for briefing [Frankfurt, 10 April]. Normally, a squadron should be a hundred-

ED654 WS/W-William, renamed Cutty Sark II, flew on to complete sixty-two ops, surviving a night-fighter attack at Nürnburg, 11 August 1943, in which rear gunner Sergeant Percy 'Dicky' Lynam was killed, and another, 3 October, Kassel, when mid-upper Sergeant Angus Leslie was killed. Cutty Sark II failed to return from Stuttgart, 20 February 1944, when all the crew died.

Operation Bellicose, 20 June, aimed at the Zeppelin sheds at Friedrichshafen, where the enemy was making radar sets, was the first of a new kind of raid called shuttle: go, bomb, fly on, land far away, hit somewhere else on the way back. In this case, far away was the north African base at Blida, on the coastal strip near Algiers, and somewhere else would be La Spézia. Five specially trained crews went from No. IX – here being briefed – including McCubbin's.

plus men needing the village hall to meet in. We fitted in somewhere like your dining room at home. He said, 'I'm going with you tonight, to find out what's wrong'. Which was a bit daft. He wasn't going to find out what was wrong that way. What was wrong was that Jerry was shooting us down, that's what was wrong.

Well, he didn't come back [all crew killed]. The Wingco might have been like quite a few of them, I think, senior officers brought up on biplanes and Empire business, you know, fighting the old fuzzy wuzzies in the Middle East somewhere. They were fearless and determined but perhaps not all of them had grasped the essentials of flying at 20,000ft at night over Germany.

The new CO, Burnett, supervised our move to Bardney, and still managed to send six of us to Italy, to La Spézia [13 April]. We took off from Waddington and landed at Bardney, and we were were a bit shocked at Spézia. There was a terrific anti-aircraft barrage, really heavy. And then, as soon as our first bomb hit, everything stopped.

We went gardening [mine laying, 22 April, Bayonne/Biarritz] and there was only half a dozen Lancs there and the moon was shining brightly. We circled twice around a lighthouse on the Spanish border, then we started in on our run, which was 1 minute 48 seconds. We could see the anti-aircraft fire ahead. They were throwing everything at us, light flak, heavy flak, machine guns, everything. The aircraft in front of us was blown out of the sky and we flew right through the explosion. We were shitting bricks, absolutely shitting bricks, and they never hit us with a single round. Not a bullet.

I was taken out of this world as we came back across the Alps from Algeria. We were at something like 18,000ft and it was a beautiful moonlight night, with a white ocean of cotton wool below, and sticking out of the cotton wool was the top of Mont Blanc. I couldn't help but watch it, on the port bow, until it vanished.

The next big thing was Hamburg. We missed the first two, with the special treat of going to Essen instead, but went on the third. We were flying along and there was a Lanc right next to us. I said to Jim [McCubbin], isn't that Fox? Jim said, 'By god, I think it is'. It was really unusual to spot anyone from your own squadron on a night raid, much less actually know who it was. Anyway, we looked down at our instruments again and bang. Flak. Direct hit. And we knew who was in there [Flight Lieutenant Charles Fox and crew, all killed].

SECRET No. 9 Squadron Combat Report
Date: 10/11th August 1943. Pos. Nürnburg. Lancaster 'W'. Captain Sgt McCubbin.

As Lancaster was running up to bomb, a Ju88 attacked from the port quarter up. The rear gunner opened fire and told the pilot to commence diving to port. The Ju88 continued firing and shells hit the rear turret, rendering it u/s and injuring the rear gunner [Sergeant Stewart]. The mid-upper gunner [Sergeant Lynam] had been killed, probably in the initial burst of fire from the fighter. The enemy aircraft then dived to port and took up position beneath the Lancaster approx. 600 feet below. It then continued to move from port to starboard and from starboard to port, and the front gunner [Sergeant Dagnall] was able to get in several good bursts, the last of which brought sparks from the enemy aircraft which dived and disappeared below.

I was down, ready for bombing. There was no noise, no warning, you just saw it, a line of tracer going right through the aircraft, and it hit Dicky Lynam. On the intercom I heard him make his last sound, like a sort of breathy retching, and then this German fighter flashed past us. I should say he was a new boy, or not very experienced anyway. He'd overshot and he was looking round, wondering where we'd got to. I grabbed my guns and blasted at him. Well, you've never seen such a hopeless mess. He was over there and my tracer was nowhere near. Jim had gone into the corkscrew, the fighter was swinging from side to side, and all those instructions we'd had about getting your target in the sights were a load of rubbish. I tried to imagine the fighter's flight path. I aimed for the sky where I hoped he would turn up, and he flew right through my bullets.

As soon as I'd seen the tracer, I'd pressed the tit (bomb release) and scrambled for my turret, not realising that the release hadn't worked. The attacks lasted 11 minutes with a full bomb bay. We were in a hell of a state. Everything was u/s for navigation and we found our way home by watching the defence boxes, the groups of searchlights and guns, and working out which city they belonged to. We threw everything out we could into the sea, including the bombs which were stuck and had to be released by hand, and we scraped in at Tangmere. I walked back through after we'd landed and saw Dicky. He was splattered all around the inside of the aircraft.

Charlie [Stewart, rear gunner] was badly wounded in his legs and there was high activity getting him out. What we'd been through must have hit me, because I was standing there in a daze. A ground crew flight sergeant came up to me and gave me my first taste of counselling. He belted me across the face and said 'Sergeant, get on with your job. You're all right.' I felt so ashamed.

Two replacement gunners had to be found. You had to get on with it. Here was somebody coming in for a dead friend, but you just did your job. So you're here for Dicky, you'd say. Well, I hope you bring us some luck. And we'd be off as a crew next time they wanted us.

McCubbin's last was Mannheim. I called 'bombs gone' at 23.30 and 2 minutes later we were hit.

SECRET No. 9 Squadron Combat Report
Date: 5/6th September 1943. Pos. Mannheim. Time 23.32. Height 20,000 ft. Target Mannheim. Lancaster 'R'. Captain P/O McCubbin.

S/E E/A sighted by RG [Sergeant Elliott] following Lancaster. Pilot informed and Lancaster commenced to corkscrew. E/A closed on

Lancaster from port quarter and RG opened up with a long burst at a range of 400 yards. E/A continued on a course to attack and broke away to port quarter after firing a long burst. MU [Flight Sergeant Houbert] fired a few rounds only before being hit and took no further part in the combat. More attacks ensued making five in all, firing long bursts in each attack and the Lancaster's RG also firing long bursts. During the final attack the E/A burst into flames as shots from the rear turret hit him. He dived beneath the starboard wing obviously on fire, this was confirmed by the flight engineer and bomb aimer. This E/A is claimed as destroyed. No searchlights or flares were seen to be connected with this attack. The Lancaster suffered considerable damage, the bullet holes being too numerous to count.

MU gunner 20 rounds.

Rear gunner 3000 rounds.

SECRET No. 9 Squadron Combat Report
27/28th Sept 1943. 00.17 hours. 1,500ft. Bardney-Horncastle area. Lancaster 'O'. Captain W/Cdr Burnett DFC

As Lancaster approached Bardney outer circuit lights, with navigation lights on, an unseen aircraft attacked from port bow slightly below and opened fire with cannon and machine guns. Attacking aircraft was not seen by any member of the crew. The visibility was very bad at the time and it was raining heavily. Three engines were damaged and both mid-upper and rear turrets put out of action owing to severed pipelines, and there were numerous holes in the machine.

I was looking for two trips as spare bod to fill my quota, and I went with the CO. We were coming into the circuit when tracer flew across and the runway lights went off. Burnett got on the radio. 'Put the bloody lights on,' he said, 'I'm coming in to land'. Our starboard outer went, which was not too bad because we were circling clockwise, then the port inner went, and just as he turned in on the landing approach, the port outer packed in. There was no panic. He said 'Ambulance, fire engine ready,' and touched down as the last engine stopped. He told them we needed dragging off the runway and said something about a pretty close thing, which I certainly agreed with, then I stood up and something started running down my leg. Skip, I said, I've been wounded, and he said all right, and that was that. Never saw him again. They gave him the DSO. He certainly could fly a Lancaster.

Wing Commander Burnett is here on the right with Squadron Leader 'Tubby' Fry. Pat Burnett DSO, DFC, forty-five ops completed, later became head of Air Ministry intelligence when the war was cold and the enemy Soviet Russia.

The doc slammed me on the table and started poking around, no anaesthetic or anything, hole here, hole there, but he couldn't find any bullets or bits of shrapnel. He had this metal probe with a little ball on the end, which he pushed into my wounds. There was a nurse there so I couldn't say anything. They put a sticking plaster over each hole and I had a message to say I'd finished my tour.

They made me an instructor for a year then I joined 227 Squadron, where my skipper was Wing Commander Balme DSO, DFC and Bar, a brilliant flyer who always put himself in the way of the worst jobs. He was an expert at the Immelmann Turn, a German First World War fighter manoeuvre. You were in your 10ft-long Fokker Triplane and you found you had a Sopwith Camel on your tail. You did an instant half loop followed by a half roll and you were on his tail instead. Balme used to execute it in a Lancaster to get us out of a searchlight cone. They did say that when you were coned you had 10 seconds to get out of it or you were dead.

Tommy Overend, Lancasters, 1943
Drink, women and leave were the three subjects uppermost in our minds, usually in that order, and drinking at the local was a big part of our lives. In fact, the RAF could have saved themselves a great deal of trouble had they sent our pay direct to the landlord of the Jolly Sailor. I was strolling one night down the garden to the outside toilet when I espied three pairs of ladies' nether undergarments, red, white and blue, hanging on the line. How patriotic, I thought. My intention of course when I unpegged the blue pair was simply to show them to my crewmates Eddie [Oakes, w/op] and Fred [Cole, mid upper], hoping to improve my dull image, and then to repeg them unbeknown. Alas, my short-term memory was affected by the cameraderie of the evening and it was not until after the fish and chips that I put my hand in my pocket and felt something silky.

'Aha!' I cried. 'Look what I got this evening.'

'Bloody hell,' said Fred, sheepishly withdrawing the white pair.

We looked expectantly at Eddie who, very slowly, produced the red ones. Next morning when we went out to the aircraft, Fred had been before. The white pair fluttered from the whip aerial. From then on, whenever we [Squadron Leader Derbyshire's crew] were on ops, one of the pairs similarly fluttered and Fred used to fly the red pair as a flag out of his turret as we took off.

Harold 'Jimmy' Parsons, Lancasters 1944–5
I thought I was very lucky because I didn't have much in the way of nerves. A bit of flak here and there didn't bother me, so long as it wasn't right in my face.

In bombing practice over southern England, on the Salisbury ranges, we'd bombed red and green target indicators from 7,000ft and these were the sort of heights we'd bombed at in France, so we could be super-accurate and avoid hitting our French allies. Over Germany [Scholven-Buer, 21 June], we were way up there at almost 20,000ft, as far away as possible from the flak and never mind about allies, there weren't any. At this height, the way the TIs behaved in the bomb sight was quite different. I was looking and I could see the markers but, as we flew towards them, they didn't seem to be moving much. Then I realised I'd picked up on the second target, Wesseling, several miles further on. Much to Ray's [Harris, pilot] disgust, this became a dummy run and he had to turn around, not the wisest thing to do in a bomber stream, and come in again to bomb.

On the run-up to the target [5 August, Étaples bridge] I saw two bombs hit the bridge. When I released my stick, I saw my first bomb hit. We were bombing from 10,000ft. The PRU took a picture the next day and we'd breached it in several places. This was with the Mark 14A bombsight, the 'old-fashioned bombsight used to hit cities', as an expert from a certain other squadron put it, as opposed to SABS presumably, which they'd used to miss it the day before. [SABS, Stabilised Automatic Bomb Sight Mark 2A, was used exclusively in wartime by 617 Squadron.]

Ray got into line [landing at Kegostrov, first Tirpitz raid]. I was having to guide him in because he couldn't see anything below. There were flares going up, which could have been meant to tell us we were coming in across the wind, which we were, or this was the wrong airfield, or what. Well, Ray just kept going and almost scraped a few scattering Russian guards off the top of the perimeter wall as we roared in and landed about halfway along the grass runway. I told Ray on the intercom that we were taxiing directly for a small building, a sentry post perhaps, so to turn to port, although there wasn't much airfield left before the farmland started.

Well, we hit a ditch and tipped up, nose first. I could see how well the spud crop was doing, and I was caught by the foot and couldn't get out. The others tried the side door but didn't fancy a 20ft drop without a parachute so they came back down again and climbed out through the pilot's hatch. They left me to get out on my own.

We were taken to Yagodnik and quartered in a kind of underground Nissen hut, which had just as many bed bugs as the riverboat where some of the crews were. We also had a Russian army batwoman, a quite elderly lady in the uniform of the marines, who pressed our uniforms using her own ironing technique, taking a mouthful of water and spraying it on the cloth as she went.

The stove's clay chimney stuck up above ground and was visible from the outside lavatory where seating arrangements were primitive and communal. Two of our crew, who shall remain nameless, were sitting there taking pot shots at the chimney with their Smith & Wesson .38 service revolvers when, out of their sight line, our fearsome batwoman came along with two full buckets of water on a yoke.

I was standing in the hut doorway, looking out, when a shot was fired and, to my horror, the woman went down. I ran over to her. She wouldn't let me touch her but I could tell she wasn't dead, anyway. I shouted to the two in the midden to go and get the vodka we had in our hut, and I waved at a near-by Russian to come and help. It turned out to be a false alarm. She'd heard the shot and felt something, but the something was a chip of clay off the chimney. Not knowing that you are never killed by the shot you hear, she had given herself up for dead. A couple of vodkas revived her.

At Yagodnik, in similar digs to Jimmy Parsons is Kenny Burns, w/op with Flying Officer Taylor, flanked by the Russian navy and a less fearsome type of domestic aide.

[At Bergen] We'd been hit all over by the fighters and I'd been uncoupling my intercom so I could move from my bomb-aimer's position to my other job, which was manning the forward pair of guns, when suddenly we were going very fast downhill. It was like being in an express lift in a skyscraper, or weightless in space. The thing went down and left me where I was, with a gap between me and where I'd been, which was fortunate because, where I had been, holes appeared simultaneously in both sides of the nose section and a pipe, fractured, started spilling pink hydraulic fluid.

It was a bit one-sided. The FW190 had two 20mm and two 30mm cannon, respectively three and four times the calibre of our Browning machine-gun bullets, but we got away somehow and levelled off. I went to the back end to find Bill Gabriel almost as smashed up as his turret but I had to lug him over the main spar to the rest bed and do what I could for him.

That was a long old way to Carnaby. We sent Bill off to the hospital and went to the pub.

Jim Brookbank, Lancasters 1944–5

[At Brest, 14 August] On our second op [Flying Officer W Scott and crew], we'd just finished our bombing run when a salvo of ack-ack hit us, which killed Johnny Tollast [w/op] instantly and wounded Scotty. The piece of flak which gouged a groove in our captain's head was only a few fractions of an inch from slicing it right off, and it took him a few moments to regain control as the Lanc dropped several thousand feet. He was concerned about Johnny so he decided to land at a nearby airfield. I assured him that there was nothing to be done, our friend was dead, and I pointed out that coming in to land at an enemy airfield would differ in no noticeable way to the defending gunners from coming in to bomb it. We would be shot to pieces.

The rest of the crew heartily concurred. Democracy and common sense prevailed and we set off back to Blighty, aiming for the nearest aerodrome at Exeter. When an instruction to steer 10 degrees to starboard was met with a steer 10 degrees to port, we realised that Scotty's headwound was perhaps worse than it looked. We had no wireless so I fired off a couple of Very lights above the airfield, red distress flares, the sight of which brought the local

This photograph was taken in July 1944. Coming home from Münster, 23 September, just two ops short of their tour, six of these men were killed but the new IX Squadron Scott crew were initially posted as missing. Back row, from left: Sergeant Jack Simkin, engineer, Flight Sergeant Louis Harding, navigator, Flight Sergeant L W Langley, bomb aimer, taken prisoner, Sergeant Les Hambly, rear gunner; front row: Sergeant Maurice Hayward, w/op, Flight Lieutenant Charles Berrie Scott, pilot, Sergeant Frank Saunders, MU gunner. Louis Harding was father of the entertainer Mike Harding.

blood wagon racing down the runway. Scotty landed on the grass, the undercart stayed put and all, apart from poor Johnny, was well.

A week later, we were posted as killed when the crew lost was Flight Lieutenant Charles B Scott's, who were almost at the end of their tour. When the SPs came to clear up our quarters and started taking our stuff, it was a stroke of luck that some of us 'dead' men were there or the telegrams would surely have gone out to the wrong crew's families. A few days after that I was walking down Lincoln High Street and a lad I knew from training in Canada came up to me and asked me what I was doing there, seeing as I was dead. I said no I wasn't, which I thought was clear enough despite what had apparently been printed in the 5 Group news sheet.

Karlsruhe, 26 September, was our reintroduction after Brest and the death of Johnny Tollast. We were a sprog crew, only on our third, and the mark of a sprog crew was not knowing what to expect. This was our first over Germany and we approached it with our usual optimism. We had our replacement wireless operator, Mossie the Aussie [Pilot Officer Mossenson].

He'd come into our hut when I was the only one there and introduced himself in his special Australian way.

I said that he should be warned, we killed off our wireless operators. He said that was all right, he'd killed off his entire crew. Mossie had his burns very visible still, including a purple band across his forehead. He told the story that when he got out after his crash, he'd tried to clamber back in to the aircraft and the firefighters stopped him, thinking he was bent on rescuing dead men. In fact, he'd forgotten his hat and wanted to get it. That's what a crash could do to you, and then as soon as they classified you physically fit, you were flying again at night over Germany.

Our CO, Jimmy Bazin, had this attitude that we were flying on an op, we were going to be the best at the job, and the enemy was just a nuisance getting in the way. There was never any let-up in the training and practice bombing, no let-up at all. You would think you had the afternoon off and suddenly you were off to Wainfleet. Bazin made us very conscious of the bombing ladder and one

Pilot Officer Mossenson, Mossie the Aussie, replaced Sergeant John Tollast as w/op in Flying Officer W Scott's crew.

time when the squadron was top of 5 Group and took the Camrose Trophy off 617, I knew that our crew was top of our squadron's ladder, which I calculated made me, a mere sergeant, the best bomb aimer in 5 Group, and so much for Dennis Nolan and 'Tosspots' Philpott and the other officer bomb aimers. Well, I reckoned so anyhow.

We were in Lincoln one night, in a hotel bar, probably the White Hart, and perched on a tall stool was a very good looking blonde with her nylon clad legs on display, a long cigarette holder and a fascinating air. She was certainly fascinating one of our group, a pilot officer, and she appeared fascinated enough by him until a flying officer upstaged him. She was entirely concentrating on the new chap when a flight looey muscled in and now he was the bee's knees. We weren't watching this so much as what one of our flight commanders was doing, standing there at the bar, apparently unconcerned, with his raincoat on. Anyway, he let the flight looey get thoroughly comfortable with this girl then said 'My, it's warm in here,' and

Bridge at Bremen – a very thin target, as Sergeant Brookbank observed.

took his mac off revealing his recently acquired squadron leader's uniform. 'Care for a drink, miss?' he said.

Altenbeken viaduct [14 February 1945], daylight of course, and we saw Johnny Dunne go down. We all saw it, all the squadron, and everybody in our aircraft and I'm sure everybody in every other aircraft was shouting jump, jump, jump you fools! But nobody did. They were hit by flak, a single shot on the way back from bombing. We were in a loose gaggle, very loose, kind of scattered about the sky, and one little German flak gun had one pot shot and that was it. They went down rather slowly, not a screaming dive. They couldn't all have been killed in the aircraft because the Lanc wasn't a mess all over. A mystery, that one, and the end of old Tosspots Philpott.

We were going with Tallboys to these very thin targets, like the bridge across the river Weser, at Bremen [22 March]. When we dropped the bomb we peeled off to starboard as we had to do, because of the situation of the target and the way we were attacking it. The Germans soon had this worked out and were ready for us. We took four flak hits at once, all superficial damage luckily, except one that hit me. As far as I knew, I had one foot fewer than before. I couldn't feel it at all. Scotty checked around, everybody OK, and I mumbled something about my foot and he sent Booster [Baker, flight engineer] to look.

The 'Scotty' Scott crew, looking cool with a Tallboy bomb. The man who aimed it, Jim Brookbank, stands on the far right.

Flying Officer Buckley's crew soon after joining IX Squadron. Dennis Nolan stands second from left.

Nurse Booster attacked my flying boot in much the same way as a rugby forward tackles an opposing halfback. He pulled my stocking off and I was expecting a right mess, but there was nothing except a nasty bruise on my little toe. The flak piece had punctured my boot and travelled down my leg, hit my toe a glancing blow and lodged there. My captain asked me to bring the toe up to the flight deck where he promised to lance it with his escape knife and then I'd have a war wound.

Dennis Nolan, Lancasters, 1944–5
The Tallboy was a wonderful weapon. When it dropped it was horizontal, of course, then it would slowly dip its nose and start to rotate, to spin on its own axis, and you knew it was going to cause havoc.

As well as the Tallboy we had the 12,000-pound cookie, the HC bomb, which used to roll and tumble and corkscrew and do all sorts of funny things on the way down. It had all the aerodynamic qualities of a London bus.

Our first op was the canal [23 September]. We saw about six-tenths cloud and they went ahead and marked it, so we went right down below the cloud, green as grass we were, looking around at all the pretty colours. When we got back and went into interrogation, I said it hadn't been as bad as I expected. I wasn't as frightened as I thought I would be, then when we talked to the other crews they were saying 'What a nightmare', 'Christ that was bloody rough'.

I went with Tweddle on the third *Tirpitz* op. A long period of boredom on the way in was interrupted by flying over a flak ship at 2,000ft in one of the big fjords. We were low, ready to hop over the mountains at the last minute and down into Swedish territory, keeping out of sight of the radar. That ship didn't half open up. It was only 30 seconds but it was a very hairy 30 seconds. Anyway, we rendezvoused over a lake, 20 minutes south of Tromsøfjord.

We were on dead reckoning and I was supposed to help the navigator by map-referencing from what I could see. Well, when dawn broke and I did see it, it was a whole series of pointy mountain tops covered in snow, and a load of little valleys all filled with white mist. No distinguishing features whatsoever.

On the run up, I spotted the ship from some distance and there were gouts of flame coming from it. They'd opened up with their main armament at maximum elevation, to try and frighten us off, I suppose. Then suddenly in front of us was the biggest burst of flak you've ever seen in your life. Never mind, that was the end of the *Tirpitz*.

Come the New Year and it was the canal again. We saw Harry Denton take off, then Cliff Newton. Instead of a green from the caravan, there was a huge Wooomph! and a great flash of fire, some distance away. I just said on the intercom what everyone thought. Some poor sod at Woodhall had gone in. Woodhall Spa, base for 617 Squadron, was 6 or 7 miles away. But it wasn't. It was Newton, not that we knew.

We sat and we sat, then we got the green and off we went. We were on the point of leaving the ground when red lights came on from both port engines.

At the same instant, the aircraft gave a mighty lurch as she hit the ground and the pilot shouted 'Cut!'. Ken Dawes [engineer] instantly did as he was told realising, like we all did, that we had been only a couple of seconds away from an almighty prang. If we had been a foot or two higher in the air it would have been a wingtip which grounded, not the undercarriage, and we would have been cartwheeling down the runway, spilling bombs and bodies everywhere.

As it was, we were still almost at airspeed, veering sharply to port and flitting across the grass. The Lancaster was a great aircraft for flying. Just as she had to be reined in hard on landing, so she was keen to get up there when she was moving fast enough. As the speed dropped, the ride got bumpier, from near-hover to jolting and banging along. Another Lancaster was at dispersal with her nav lights on. We watched them and they watched us in mutual horror, as A-Able bore down on their stationary aircraft with nobody able to do a single thing about it.

We were doing about 60mph in a very large vehicle, completely out of control. At the edge of the airfield ran the stream. It had originally been in an inconvenient place so, when RAF Bardney was built, a steam shovel dug a new watercourse and piled the soil up on the airfield side. The pile was about 3ft high and it made a nice launching ramp for a speeding Lanc.

We hit the ramp, tore our wheels off, waffled through the air for quite a few yards and hit the young pine trees of the plantation rather higher up their trunks than would otherwise have been the case. The trees bent, instead of making a barrier of posts, as we tore into them ripping off Perspex and other bits and pieces but we didn't get the explosion we were expecting. Finally, we stopped.

I'd seen the clearview panel next to me snatched off by a tree so I climbed through it, onto the wing. Next problem was, where could I go? It was dark and we were in the trees. I could hear the w/op, Flight Sergeant Moore and the mid-upper, Sergeant Round, behind me. They were leaping for safety, convinced that she was about to blow. There was an overpowering smell of petrol and the exhaust stubs of the engines were glowing red hot.

Our rear gunner, Sergeant Copperwaite, was trapped. Buckley was sitting on the rim of his escape hatch, above his normal position, heaving the engineer upwards who was shouting like mad because his leg was broken. Somebody grabbed an axe from inside the aircraft and chopped Copperwaite out of his turret, and we all cleared off and waited for help, which was a while coming because everything had gone to Newton's crash. They never did identify the cause of the engine failure, ours and Newton's, but frozen water in the fuel seemed the most likely possibility.

At Bergen, thirteen days later, our Lancaster and another [Flying Officer Ernie Redfern DFC] were flying on a similar course but the other was about 2,000ft lower, and we had three more aircraft in our view, which were FW190s. They stooged about while we watched them make up their minds. They were choosing. The sods were selecting which bomber to go for, us or him. They chose him.

PB368 WS/A, 1 January 1945. Dennis Nolan sits third from left. Rear gunner Sergeant Copperwaite, far left, looks suitably impressed by the experience.

He corkscrewed and appeared to be getting free when one of his engines caught fire, and then another. That Lanc hit the sea in a way which clearly said to us, watching from above, that there would be no survivors but the fighters carried on shooting into the burning wreckage until they had no ammunition left. They couldn't attack any more Lancasters, such as ours for example, so they flew away. I thought that here were three of the best fighter aircraft of the war, operated by three of the worst or least experienced pilots.

All the crew of American volunteer Flying Officer Cliff Newton were killed in the crash. Connie Grant received the dreaded telegram to tell her that her husband, Percy, aged 30 was one such. Given on the telegram as Flight Sergeant, Grant had recently been made up to Pilot Officer. The family picture was taken while Percy was in training.

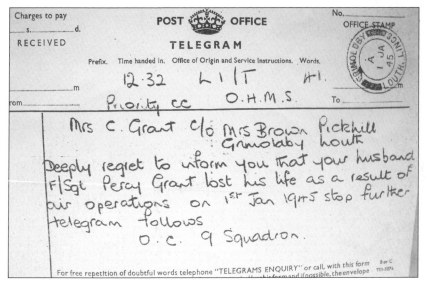

201

CHAPTER 14

Flight Engineers

Frank Belben, Lancasters, 1943–4

I joined the RAF as a ground-crew fitter/engineer in 1940, posted to a Coastal Command squadron in Cornwall flying Lockheed Hudsons, which were long-range reconnaissance bombers developed from a pre-war airliner. They still had their windows along the side. When our four-engined heavies started coming in, they asked for volunteer flight engineers from among us ground lads because we knew part of the job already.

I arrived at Number IX with Flight Sergeant Lou Glover's crew, expecting my first op in the normal way after the skipper had had his second Dickies, but the captain [Flight Lieutenant Ervine] due to take Lou on his learner trip

Paddy Ervine, who took Frank Belben on his most unorthodox debut op, sits centre at debriefing after Stettin, 5 January 1944, a few weeks before finishing his tour. Note the plentiful mugs of tea and the authentic period intelligence officer on the right.

[Leipzig, 20 October] was suddenly short of a flight engineer. He'd gone sick. So I had to fill in at the last minute. It must have been very rare, maybe even a squadron one-off, for a raw rookie to be acting as a fully functional member of an experienced crew while his skipper stood behind the seat and watched.

It was reassuring for me having an old hand like Ervine as my driver on my first, but I don't know what he thought about it. He didn't say anything but I guess he might have had the odd worry. He let me get on with my job, though, not checking up on me. The weather was utterly dreadful. We weren't shot up as such although there were some near misses, but you had to expect it over that type of target. I was glad to get it over, my first one.

Something similar happened soon after, but the other way around. A pilot called Froud was on his first op and his flight engineer wasn't available so I was drafted in. I'd had four trips by then and here I was going back to square one with a sprog crew. Froud went down at Leipzig [19 February 1944]. Losses were very high and it was rare for a crew to get through a tour, but we'd known that all along.

While I was out with a back injury, I missed Lou Glover being attacked by a fighter. They told me all about it, of course, and how I'd missed a treat, and Lou got the DFC.

SECRET No. 9 Squadron Combat Report
Date: 20 December 1943. Time: 19.45. Height: 20,000 ft. Target: Frankfurt.
Lancaster: 'G'. Captain: P/O Glover.

Shortly before approaching the target the bomber was swept by cannon and machine gun fire, which set fire to the rear turret and the port inner engine and damaged the intercommunication system. The rear gunner was injured by splinters in the face and slightly burnt and the mid-upper was hit by a machine-gun bullet in the leg. The attack came from astern well down and as soon as the pilot saw the tracer he commenced a corkscrew port, losing height rapidly to gain extra speed, having a full load on. Both gunners saw a Ju88 come in from astern down but rear gunner could not fire as guns had been damaged and MU could not get guns to bear. E/A broke away down and again attacked from same position opening fire at 600 yards and closing in to 100 yards. E/A's trace all passed above the bomber and he broke away astern down and was not seen again. The pilot resumed course on three engines and bombed the target from a very low altitude before returning to base.

Visibility clear but dark. No moon, flares or searchlights. No indication on any special apparatus. Damage to own aircraft: rear turret badly smashed. Port inner engine u/s. MU turret and fuselage holed in many places. Intercom shot away. No rounds fired by either gunner.

We did five Berlins [first one, 29 December]. Berlin was very frightening. You knew it would be a sticky one, inevitably, by its very nature. You'd often be locked onto by fighters, or you'd be coned, and it was always doubtful if you'd get out of it if you didn't escape straight away. They were skilled professionals, the men with the searchlights. It was always touch and go who would win. Your pilot had to react instantly. It was the one time when the team didn't come into it. It was all up to him, and it was a regular thing over Berlin.

There was another fighter attack at Stuttgart [1 March 1944]. We'd finished our bombing run, slow, straight and level, and were turning for home when Harry [Wood, rear gunner] shouted 'Corkscrew port, go'. Lou put her into the dive and as he did, our cockpit canopy disappeared. The whole aircraft was riddled. How the rest of the crew weren't killed I don't know. Nobody was hit. I'd been standing up when the shells hit the canopy and the dive flung me back and threw me against the main spar. I was a bit dazed, frankly, and I crawled down to my position and saw that the starboard inner tank was losing petrol very fast. The self-sealing we had was helpful but no good if you got cannon shells through. The rear gunner could smell petrol, which they always could with a leak because it whipped back in the slipstream, so I cross-fed all the engines onto the leaking tank. Of course, you have to watch that or you'll empty the thing and all the engines'll stop, and you have to use up the other inner tank to balance the aircraft.

We'd lost 10,000ft and hundreds of gallons of petrol, and I had to make an assessment of how long we could keep airborne. We'd normally have been going back in the stream on a set course but we didn't have the fuel, so we had to go directly from A to B on our own and hope we weren't attacked again. So John [Middleton, navigator] had to work out the best route allowing for the winds, and I had to work out if we could make it at certain revs at a low height, with the extra drag from our open-air cockpit. We all discussed if we should bale out or have a go. We got to a fighter station, West Malling, in Kent.

There was a huge raid on Nürnburg [30 March]. It was terrible. We lost one [W5006 WS/X, Flying Officer James Ling], and Bernie Utting, a gunner who had been with us for a while, was killed in a fighter attack [DV395 WS/V, Pilot Officer Harry Forrest]. That was a very stressful flight in, and even worse over what we thought was the target. From what we saw, we knew it was a night of heavy losses (95 out of 795). We had a couple of fighter attacks but our gunners drove them off and we never got hit.

There were a lot of French targets after that, some not so bad, but Mailly-le-Camp [3 May], well, that was something else again. And they still counted it as a third. The fighters were there, waiting for us, before we got anywhere near the target. It was terrible. You could see aircraft going down all around you in flames, and you'd see when they hit the ground and exploded. Terrible. There were fires burning all over the place and not from bombs, from our aircraft. You had to think, am I next? Then we got to the target and the fighters were there as well.

I'd done ops to fill in my missing ones, so I finished my tour at Nantes [27 May] with Lou Glover and most of the originals. I had thirty-six ops in my log book and the CO signed it, tour completed, twenty-nine and a third. We couldn't believe we'd finished. We never expected to survive. Like most crews, because of the dangerous life we led, we functioned as a unit socially as well as professionally. We'd go to the pub, go into Lincoln to a dance, and sometimes roller skating at Boston rink. Then we'd be back to it and all those meals after ops when we sat and ate bacon and egg and looked at the empty tables and chairs.

Lou Glover got us through. He was an excellent pilot – good take-offs and landings, obviously, but on ops his reactions were superb. He reacted on the instant when the gunners shouted to corkscrew. He'd be into the dive before anybody knew what was happening. Some of them weren't so quick and they were ones whose empty chairs we were looking at. Of course, there was no way of knowing, when you crewed up, which sort you'd got. Anyway, everyone was there on the last one, then they gave us seven days leave, which was kind of them.

James Pinning
[On the third *Tirpitz* raid] We [Flying Officer Coster and crew] were about to begin our bombing run when we were hit by heavy flak. It didn't seem enough to put us off so we carried on, when Taffy Jones [rear gunner] came over the intercom. 'Jim,' he said. 'Your starboard outer's on fire.' We followed the routine: open the radiator wide, dive and try and blow it out. Didn't work, close the throttle, feather the prop, press the extinguisher button, and it went out. Other flak damage had petrol leaking badly and the starboard

inner was running rough. I assessed the fuel situation. We were not going to get home.

We didn't have any proper maps but we knew where Sweden was. Our plan was to fly down the Norwegian coast and turn left, and it went wrong from the start. We flew over an aerodrome and they sent up a load of flak which did some more damage, then we ran into German fighters. One came in from the starboard quarter – my side of the ship – and Coster corkscrewed for our lives on two-and-a-half engines. Sounds impossible but he did it. Taffy was firing, I saw some smoke and the fighter gave up. Whether he was out of ammo, or hit, I don't know. It may be that just at that point we crossed into Swedish airspace, and the Germans would not violate that on any account.

We were flying over dense pine forests alternating with snowy peaks, the cloud was low and it was getting dark. There was hardly any petrol left at all and there seemed no end to trees and mountains, mountains and trees. We didn't know it but, as well as petrol, we were also running out of Sweden. We were in danger of having to make a choice between the Gulf of Bothnia and Finland, where there was all sorts of confusion with the Russians.

The Swedish holiday-makers back in Blighty – Taff Jones is second from left, back row. Jim Pinning is standing right, and Dave Coster, the Kiwi pilot, is sitting with his newly acquired RAF moustache.

Lancaster LM448 WS/M has made her final landing and is being guarded by Swedish soldiers in rather fetching hats.

Then we saw a bare patch. We went down to have a look and it turned out to be an island in a river. Coster took her in on our two and a bit engines, undercart up, bellyflop, knowing he only had one shot at it. Good pilot, Coster. It turned out we'd landed at a place called Vandnasberget, on the River Kalix, hardly 30 miles from the Finnish border. We were in Lapland. The aircraft half filled with slush as we ploughed along but we were all fine, and the locals took us in and gave us some reindeer meat or whatever it was, and some hot water to wash in.

We expected we'd be arrested by the Swedish police but, before that, the local schoolmaster and his wife had us round for dinner and wine, a lot of wine, and then we were interned at an army camp for two nights.

Things got better and better. They took us to Stockholm, put us up in an hotel, gave us full civilian kit, and we just wandered around the city. Nobody bothered about us, except we often noticed one particular policeman who, we were told, had German sympathies. We were issued with ration coupons and it wasn't like back home where, if you could afford it, you could go into a smart hotel and get a meal without coupons. In Sweden, it was always coupons everywhere you went. The British assistant military attaché looked after us very well and when it came to our time to go home he was choked. 'Well done, chaps,' he said. 'You got the *Tirpitz* by the balls.'

As we'd been shot down and interned, we were offered the choice of a desk job or going back on ops. We went back to Bardney, walked into the Mess, and got 'Where the hell have you lot been for three weeks?'.

Coster and crew's photograph of the raid on Heligoland, 19 April 1945, IX Squadron's penultimate of the war. There wasn't much left there to bomb after a massive main-force raid the previous day but IX and 617 took thirty-six Tallboys.

CHAPTER 15

Ground Crew

Aileen Walker

I wasn't 18 when I started, waiting on in the Officers' Mess at Waddington. It was just 44 Squadron then, before IX arrived. I worked to give them breakfast, lunch and dinner. I had the afternoons off.

When IX moved to Bardney, some of the 44 Squadron people went as well, like the adjutant, Flying Officer Rushton, who was the funny man Willy Rushton's dad. He was rather posh, Rushton. He said to me, are you coming with us to IX Squadron? I said I didn't know, sir. He checked the list and he said, Aileen, your name's not on it, but it will be in 10 minutes. You're coming with us.

Another one who transferred was Flight Lieutenant Wakeford. So I was in the Officers' Mess in the dining room, waiting at table, and Wakeford was there with his back to me. He was a big man, great mop of red hair, they called him Red, and an educated man. Without looking round, he said 'Aileen, are you there?' I said yes, sir. He said 'I'm bringing a dog back from leave, and when I go on ops I'm taking that bomb aimer with me, the one you're going out with. So you can look after my dog.' That bomb aimer was Harry Hawkridge, from Leeds.

Red Wakeford had been the first officer I served in the Mess at Waddington. My first lunch, and I walked through the door of the dining room with two plates of soup, expecting maybe a dozen or twenty men and there seemed to be hundreds, and they all gave wolf whistles which they always did with a new WAAF. I put this soup down in front of Wakeford and nearly spilled it all over him. He asked me if I was all right, and I put the other soup down and walked out and kept walking until I was in the rest room. The sergeant in charge of me asked me what on earth, and I said I'm not going back in there. She said oh yes you are, you're going to get some more soup, and you're going in, and you're going to give them back what they give you.

Flight Lieutenant John 'Red' Wakeford DFC, third from right, and crew board the aircraft in which they would die, ED689 WS/K. At the top of the ladder is American volunteer Flying Officer Jonah Reeves, navigator. Harry Hawkridge is there but cannot be identified.

They went on a special op that meant them landing in Algeria [Friedrichshaven, 20 June 1943]. We were all waiting for them to come back and when Red Wakeford's crew came in, they were all carrying bunches of bananas except my young man, Harold Hawkridge from Harehills. Nobody had seen a banana for years. They were like treasure. The wireless op, Alec Backler, he'd brought some for my friend Muriel. They were very close, Alec and Muriel, not like me and Harold. Anyway, I said to him, well, if you can't be bothered to bring me some bananas back, I can't be bothered to see you any more. He said, I've sent you something a lot better than bananas but you'll have to wait for it. Just a couple of weeks.

Well, it was less than a couple of weeks when they were shot down [Cologne, 3 July], and I had Wakeford's little dog, who was called Snifter. I wanted to keep him, and my mother in Nottingham wanted him as well, but he had to go to Wakeford's mother in Devon and I was given the job of sending him. I had to put him in a box and take him to the railway station, and I had to walk all the way because I couldn't get the box balanced on my bike. When I got there I handed him over and I had to apologise for how wet the box was with my crying tears. And that wasn't the end of it.

I was setting up the tables in the dining room when a letter came for me. It had stamps and postmarks all over it and it was in Harold's writing and it was from Algiers. I shouted 'Muriel! They're alive!' but when I opened it, it said that by the time I got it, Harold would be on leave at home. His mother had already lost two sons in the war. Harold wrote that he'd kept his distance long enough and he was coming back for me and we were going to get married. I was reading this, and he was dead. And still I wasn't finished with the tears, because a few days later there was a little box in the post and it was from his mother. The letter said thank you for making her son's last hours happy ones, and hoped that I'd accept this necklace as a small token.

I got a telephone call saying there were two officers coming back off leave who were on ops that night and could I get them some lunch. I hung around and gave them their lunch. They'd been there since the middle of May but I hadn't got to know them. One was a New Zealander, Flying Officer Head, and one was from Nottingham like me, well, he was Beeston actually, Flying Officer Shaw. He said when they got back we'd have a lot to talk about. Needless to say, they didn't come back [Reggio nell'Emilia, 15 July. Flying Officer Head evaded, see p. 229].

There'd be a call to say such an aircraft was home, two officers, so we'd get the bacon and eggs ready. We'd hear them come in, then the toilet door would go, then they'd drag themselves into the dining room, flying boots undone, hardly able to walk upright, and they'd flop into chairs. Tea and cigarettes they mostly wanted. Some wanted their food right away, and one might say 'I want so-and-so's egg. He got the chop'. You had to wonder how they could adjust their minds and be ready to do it all again tomorrow.

They were a mixed lot, the officers. For instance, Squadron Leader Derbyshire was a perfect charmer, a real gentleman. We could always spot the gentlemen. If they got a knife which had a mark on it, they'd discreetly give it a rub. The other sort would say here, polish this. Derbyshire was tall and thin, little black moustache. Some of the officers would talk to us, tell us about their girls back home, but he was very quiet, a very reserved person.

Not at all thin, in fact quite the opposite, was a visiting Group Captain. He was fat enough for two chairs. As a visitor of course he had to be served first, so I was walking up with a tureen of cauliflower in white sauce when I caught Muriel's foot and stumbled forwards. The cauliflower shot out of the pot like a missile and landed right in his lap, white sauce and all. I had no idea what to do. I took a spoon and started ladling the cauli back into the

211

tureen from beneath the overhang of his great stomach. Well, I was only 18, I didn't know what Group Captains kept in their trousers. Anyway, I hadn't got very far with it when he shouted 'That's enough, WAAF, that's enough!'.

That man, Turnbull, I did look after him [Pilot Officer W W W Turnbull, American volunteer known as 'Tex']. He was so, so thin and spoke so, so slowly. I'd go to him and ask him if he'd like some second helpings and he'd say no, he'd had quite sufficient, so we could never feed him up. One night I came off duty and there he was, leaning on my bike. I said, what are you doing. He said 'I'm holding your bike for you. I'm going to walk you home'. Well, he walked me home, he was blind drunk, and when he stumbled and

Tex Turnbull may have had a certain reputation with the ladies, but he had a reputation as a bomber pilot too. The quiet American flew a full tour of ops – here he is at Mannheim, 24 September 1943 – and earned the DFC for 'high skill, fortitude and devotion to duty'.

fell I took my tie-pin off and held it ready in my hand. He had a certain reputation, did Tex Turnbull.

The bar and restaurant were under the charge of Squadron Leader Burns, station adjutant. He was the old-fashioned type, RAF since childhood, and he had standards. We were the last squadron in Bomber Command, possibly in the entire RAF, to go over to self-service. He just wouldn't have it.

They had their rations like everybody else and the cooks had to do what they could with that. I went on a motorbike with sidecar, with the PMC (President of the Messing Committee) to Waddington to get it. Flight Lieutenant Doig, that was. But they must have had other resources. Anyway, Burns would never have stood for the bread sausages and so on that the other ranks had. We who worked in the Officers' Mess had a very good fringe benefit because we ate there, and we had a better class of joke to put up with if the menu said potato balls. The sergeant cook was a chef from a London hotel and he was a dreadful man for jokes. If it was chicken, he used to make us go and ask the officers 'Do you want stuffing?'.

I nudged his arm once when he was icing a cake and he said he'd get his own back and he did when I was on night duty. We were waiting for them to come home and I went in the kitchen and he was sitting there plucking a goose. I'd just washed my hair and it was still wet. Come and look at this, he said, and like a fool I did and got my head covered in goosedown. And I had to stand on duty in the Mess with a thousand white feathers sticking to my hair.

Another time we were entertaining a load of Yanks and Arthur, the cook, gave me a tray of sausages on sticks and said to take them round. I went in the anteroom, which was where the bar was, and they were half of them drunk, and I had to go round saying 'Chipolata, sir? Chipolata, sir?' and when I got back Arthur said where were the sticks. He wanted the sticks back. I was just a girl, I couldn't stand up to him, so I went back in and crawled about picking up all the sticks.

The telephone rang in the Officers' Mess and it was the CO. 'Wing Commander Bazin here. Can you get Morrison for me?' I looked about and couldn't see him. Where's Eddie Morrison, I said. Somebody piped up 'He's in the windsock'. That's how naive I was and they knew it. Sorry, sir, I said. Flying Officer Morrison isn't here but you'll find him in the windsock.

A certain officer rang and asked to speak to one of the WAAFs. I could hear the conversation. He said 'Slip into something loose and we'll go mushrooming'. I asked her, what are you going mushrooming for at this time of year?

The MO at this time was called Napier, and he came to me one day with a plateful of Crooke's cod liver oil capsules. I was to stand by the big table which was on the left of the door as you came in, with all the cups and saucers and tea urns on it, and I was to give a capsule every day to every member of aircrew who came in for breakfast. Ray Harris said 'What are they for, Aileen?' in a very cheeky way, and half of the officers wouldn't have them. So I used to take them away, and I had them. I was fighting fit, I can tell you.

Nancy Bower

My job was behind the bar at Bardney Officers' Mess. Flying Officer Rushton drank pink gin. Well, I didn't know what it was and he obviously expected me to know, so the first time he just ordered it and said nothing. I got the gin and wondered how to make it pink and Rushton pointed to the bottle of Angostura bitters. I thought, it must be like the Worcester sauce in a Bloody Mary so I poured it in. When he settled down, Rushton told me, four drops only. Ever after that he used to say, four drops, Nancy, four drops.

Joe Skinner was one of the cheeky ones. He had a big RAF moustache, a big smile and a famous glint in his eye. Phil Plowright always wore his striped scarf, which was in his college colours, green and orange. That was his good luck charm, and it worked for him. Tweddle was married and his wife used to ring up, which was a difficulty most of them didn't have. We weren't allowed of course to say where he was, but we'd say 'He's just not around at the moment,' and she knew by that he was flying.

Keeley was a very popular chap, and he was another of the cheeky ones like Ray Harris. There were many different types, it was no indicator of whether they'd last or not. You could have the anything-goes sort like Keeley and Harris, or the top-drawer officer like Melrose, but they got the same results. Bill Williams was a gentleman, too, like Melrose. Some of them treated us like ladies and, well, some of them didn't. Williams and Melrose were among those who did.

Squadron Leader Burns was our boss and, in his view, officers had to be treated in a certain way and they had to have the best of everything. The food, for wartime, was outstandingly good. There was usually a breakfast menu although they might be told the night before if it was kippers or something different.

The big thing was a Dining In Night. Squadron Leader Burns would decide when there was to be one and all the officers had to attend. Sometimes there would be men who'd been promoted that day, and we'd end up sewing the new badges of rank on their uniforms. It was absolutely best dress and

Some of Nancy's customers in the Officers' Mess, late 1944. From the left, McDonnell, the American Ed Stowell, Keeley and Laws.

best behaviour, and no women, only us. It was quite an atmosphere, and very hard not to clatter the cups when you were serving the coffee. One time there was a band in the corner, playing very quietly, and there was celery on the tables. Every officer except Burns got hold of a stick and started conducting the band. I don't think the Squadron Leader thought much of it.

Pip Beck

The King was coming to inspect us at Waddington and so we had a rehearsal parade. Everybody put on their best kit, then Andy Storey, who was a very tall American pilot, turned up with a little dog on a string, and with carpet slippers on because he said the RAF could not provide uniform shoes big enough for him. Anyway, when the real thing happened, he'd found some shoes and lost the dog, but I didn't go. I'd been up all night in Flying Control and I got myself all annoyed about them using gallons of petrol to scrub out a hangar, just so the King could see it as it never was. I stayed in bed.

I knew Flight Sergeant Storey's name and voice from my job in Flying Control, of bringing the boys in to land, and everybody knew what he looked like, and then I met him at the Sergeants' Mess NAAFI do on New Year's Eve (1942/3). Everyone who wasn't commissioned went to those things. They were good, the dances in the Sergeants' Mess. There was a band, playing Glen Miller and all the popular tunes, and the bar, and lots of tiddly blokes wandering around. This very tall, non-tiddly man asked me to dance and we did, and we were sitting later with a drink and he was telling me about his life in America without a trace of an American accent. One of his gunners came up and grabbed his leg and gave it a twist, and ran off. It must have happened regularly. Andy just said that he was big but not very well put together, and that there would be no more dancing. He hobbled across to the bar for more drinks and that was the way the evening went.

I had no sense of premonition with him. Sometimes air crew seemed to have the Black Spot almost visible on them. I once had the eerie experience of dancing with a quiet, pleasant Scottish sergeant pilot and suddenly knowing he was for the chop. I knew it with a certainty. I wondered if he had any suspicion of it himself. Sure enough, on his next op, he didn't come back.

Andy told me about his family, his school days at Deerfield and college days at Harvard. There might have been romance in the air, I don't really know. In any case, I already had a boyfriend. Perhaps Andy felt that a bomber pilot was not the best of propositions. After the ball was over, he walked me back to my billet. He dropped a chaste kiss on my forehead, stroked my hair and turned quickly back to the road.

I met Andy around the camp sometimes, stopping to exchange news but nothing more. His tour was almost complete. I asked him one day if he'd take me

Anderson Storey was one of thousands of Americans who volunteered for the RAF before Pearl Harbor. He came from a wealthy professional Boston family and had had holidays in Britain before the war. Here he is seen at home on leave from training in Canada, 1941.

up in his Lanc. He promised he'd take me for a flip when his tour was finished. I had a forty-eight (hour pass) due. When I got back, Andy would almost certainly have done his last op. [The squadron lost four Lancasters on a Berlin raid, night of 17/18 January 1943, among them Flying Officer Storey's; he was on his thirtieth op.]

So, I wasn't on duty that awful night, but if I had been, I'd have had to be impersonal. You had to be cool and calm. You couldn't start flapping about, and if your boyfriend didn't come back, well, you had to carry on. If you were heartbroken, you had to leave it til afterwards. You couldn't burst into tears and go all hysterical on duty. And nobody did. It was very hard sometimes but you had to get used to it and quick. Off duty, you were more vulnerable. Three of us had little breakdowns one night at a choir practice. A piercing sense of sadness flooded through me. Oh god, what was the matter with us all? I ran for the corridor where I sobbed my heart out.

The routine was always the same. Stack them up, bring them in. You might have a complication if the runway became blocked or there were some other special instructions to make you depart from the script. If someone was very late, we might get a phone call from another aerodrome to say they were down there. We might get a stray from another squadron, with wounded or dead maybe, or a shot-up aircraft, and he would make a Darky call.

I would say 'Hello Darky, this is Bardney,' and we'd find out what the matter was and sort him out accordingly. Whatever it was, there was nothing personal about it. You couldn't. That was just not on.

We might overhear a conversation between the CO and the Flying Control Officer. 'So-and-so's very late. Doesn't look good. If we don't hear something soon, I suppose that's it.' It was a very saddening thing and there was nothing anyone could do. The air crews went to bed. They knew what the chances were and the war had to go on. It was no good waiting up and biting your nails. You'd never cope if you did that.

John 'Mick' Maguire

I was Acting Pilot Officer Maguire, suddenly plucked from an Air Ministry job and told I was armaments officer for IX Squadron, report immediately to Waddington. I'd been out of Bomber Command for a while, and when I'd been in it we'd had light bombers. Up there in Lincolnshire I knew it was one big brawl, heavy losses, constant losses, unremitting battle. I thought I could imagine the pressure but I didn't have a clue.

Legendary IX Squadron armaments officer Mick Maguire, with a raid-load of Tallboy bombs.

First I had to report to a senior armaments man who shall remain nameless, and he was in a panic. I'd been in the air force for seven years by this point and I'd seen a fair amount of the war, and I knew a flap when I saw one. It was a maximum effort op that night, clearly causing him maximum anxiety, which I had to sit there and watch. Eventually he dropped it all and took me in a little van across the dark Lincolnshire countryside, in the black-out, to Bardney airfield and into a tiny shoebox of an office with the standard dim blue light.

He scuttled round and round this office to no purpose. From the noise of engines, an op was imminent. He shouted 'I've got to go. There's trouble at Skellingthorpe,' and left me alone. I'd been there 2 minutes. The whole place was palpitating with noise. I'd been on stations with a hundred Spitfires but a dozen or so Lancs at night seemed a lot noisier.

The phone rang. Every instinct said 'Don't answer it,' but I answered it: 'Maguire, armaments officer.' A voice said 'What?' I said 'Acting Pilot Officer Maguire, new armaments officer, just arrived'. The voice, which could only have been the CO, shouted 'Well, get over here right away,' and then the phone went dead. I didn't know where over here was, or how to get there in the dark.

At a time like this, the CO would be in the control tower and, if I got down on my knees I could just make out an outline which had to be the tower. There were stairs up the back, and inside I found a little Group Captain, striding up and down, demented. 'Who are you?' he said. 'Where are you from?' Well, I guessed he wasn't expecting me to say 'Belfast, sir,' so I told him, 'Fighter Command'.

'Fighter Command?' he said. 'Fighter Command?' I thought he was going to burst. 'There's an aircraft out there with a u/s rear turret and you've got 45 minutes'. I didn't like to mention that I'd never been close to a Lancaster before, so I asked if this one could be held back to be the last to take off. He gave me that look again, only with extra steam. The other people in the tower were studying the night sky with enormous concentration. The Group Captain, whom I soon found out was paradoxically called Pleasance, took two steps towards me and almost screamed 'It's already done!' and I half fell backwards down the stairs.

The Lancs were warming up their engines. Take-off looked rather less than 45 minutes away as I stumbled back towards the only place I knew, that office with the blue light and the telephone. There I bumped into a large sergeant with a dog end dangling from his bottom lip and an air of exhaustion and frustration about him. 'Who are you?' I said. He looked at me, clearly at the end of his tether, and spoke in a strong Liverpool accent. 'I'm Sergeant Gallant, but more to the point, who the ****ing hell are you?' So I told him and said we had to fix this turret and I'd never seen one before.

'Follow me,' says he, and off he went with me straining to keep up. We passed a little crane with a man inside and the engine running. 'Don't ****ing move,' said Sergeant Gallant and next thing we were diving into the MT section and a truck. In two ticks we were beside some hangars and another crane came out with a rear turret hanging from its jib, and a small low-loader appeared, spun around, and the turret was put on it. The other little crane turned up, hoisted the turret to the aircraft's rear end and two corporals got stuck into it.

They had the new turret on and were connecting up the hydraulics and servos when the aircraft started sliding out of the dispersal. There was nothing I could do except watch as the corporals finished their work on the move, and Gallant suddenly appeared in the turret doorway with a can of hydraulic oil and jumped to the ground. I was just thinking that the whole exercise was pointless because the hydraulics would be full of air, when Gallant said 'He'll bleed the bastard in the air. It's all right. He knows what he's doing.' When I asked Corporals Meadows and Delaney about Form 700 (which certified the aircraft serviceable and without which it could not take off) they said they'd signed it in advance.

We went back to the office. There was a bunch of armourers in there, smoking, loafing about, and I was the object of mild curiosity while they carried on talking about the problems they'd been having, and they did have problems. That turret business was just an example. I hadn't slept for 24 hours so I was half dozing when the CO walked in, Shorty Pleasance, and everybody kind of shuffled to attention, and he said to me 'Sorry about all that. You managed.' I said I hadn't managed, they had, pointing to my new colleagues.

Life in Bomber Command was very tough, and tough enough without any extras. My blokes told me that everything was always the armourers' fault. If an aircraft didn't take off on time, it was the armourers. The station armaments officer, who was theoretically responsible for the bomb dump, the shooting range and other non-aircraft matters, had been having to do my job as well, squadron armaments, and he hadn't been making a great success of it, they said, and we get blamed for it all. The general opinion was that this man was afraid of explosives and hated aeroplanes, which was an odd combination for an armaments officer. 'Well,' I told them, 'from now on, if anyone gets any blame, it will be me.'

Every time a new Lancaster arrived, which was often, we had to fit some special deep incendiary holders, part of the modifications which had gone on to double the Lanc's bomb load from the original spec. I was watching Corporal Willing, and he was dabbing a blob of red paint onto the corners of these things, and then they closed the bomb doors and opened them again. Wherever there was a spot of red on the inside metal skin of the doors, Willing attacked it with an axe. To me this was treasonable damage of His Majesty's aircraft.

'What are you doing?' I said. He looked and said 'Bomb doors have got to shut. It's the quickest way,' and this was the essence of everything. We never had any time. It led to magnificent achievement being routine, because the job had to be done whether we had the time or not. For instance, the armourers found that standard tools weren't adequate, so they designed and made their own. They could change a rotation motor in a turret faster than I could give the order.

I was in the office with Chiefy Harrison, who was earnestly filling in his private operations record book for the night before, his glasses on the end of his nose. Some of the armourers were playing cards. We were finished for the night. The squadron was taking off. So, the door opened. It was Corporal Steel, a very quiet chap, unobtrusive. He said 'There's an aircraft burning on the runway'. The card school looked up. Chiefy looked over the tops of his glasses. I said 'Say again?' He said 'There's an aircraft burning on the runway'. We pelted outside, and I dashed into my superior's office and shouted 'Aircraft burning on the runway' and a voice from beneath the desk said 'I know.'

I thought, no help from this quarter so I dashed outside again. I could see the aircrew, running flat out, Jack Maule [pilot] in the lead by a short head with the last man in his Taylor suit which made him look like a Michelin man, so he was Charlesworth the rear gunner. I counted them, they were all out. We ducked down behind something concrete when one of the electricians came up and tried to go past. Sergeant Gallant grabbed him and asked what the hell, and he said he had to get to the aircraft because he was on fire duty. We pointed out that even the regular firemen with their fire engine were waiting until the bombs went off, so he'd better do the same.

It was a new load, first time, being a 2,000lb HC, a smaller version of the cookie, and J-bombs, a new type of incendiary inside a tube of methane which acted like a giant flamethrower at 1,500 °C. The HC exploded and sent a shower of J-bombs arcing into the bomb dump. We knew all about these J bombs. We'd had one to pieces and we'd test-fired them, so we knew they weren't going to explode. We had various kinds of fire-fighting gear all around the bomb dump so we just ran there and started putting out the fires, and the fire tender arrived with no water, and the new station CO came up, Group Captain McMullen, in his staff car.

'How's it going?' he said. 'Oh, we're beating the fires out, sir. I've got people all over the dump. Nothing to worry about.' 'Well,' he said, 'you'd better tell that to your immediate superior. He's evacuated the Waffery and the villagers are moving out with their furniture.'

I had a Matchless 350cc and Doug Melrose had a 500cc Beezer. He preferred the looks of mine and said he was going to swap with me. I said like hell you are. He said 'I'm a Flight Commander'. I said stuff the flight commander. I'm the armourer and I'll blow you up next time you go on ops. So Dougie said he would race me round the perimeter track and the winner would have the choice of machines. I couldn't see what was in it for me but I rode round that track a hundred times a week. I'd no fear of losing to Mr Melrose. We set off in front of Flying Control and by the time I got to the end of the main runway, Dougie was nowhere near.

I stopped to look and there he was, halfway along the track, stranded. His spark plug lead had come off and the silly sod had tried to put it back on from the saddle, while the wheels were still going round, so he got a severe electric shock. I rode slowly back to find him rubbing his arm and looking decidedly fed up. 'You all right?' I said, and Dougie replied 'You can keep your bloody Matchless'.

W4964, the centurion J-Johnny Walker, is seen here in late June 1944, when Melrose had taken possession. Note the motorcycle. It's a Matchless 350cc, belonging to armaments officer Mick Maguire.

Ken McClure

I was in signals ground crew. A bicycle was an absolute necessity. Our living quarters were a long way from our workshops and even further from the dispersals. A lot of the everyday repair and maintenance work was done at the dispersals, and we hardly knew what leave was. A seven-day week was normal. We had to work whatever hours were required to get the aircraft operational on time. A 14-hour day was not exceptional although a standard day was probably 08.00 to 18.00, but on top of that we still had to fit in our station duties like airfield guard and firewatch.

We had three of what you might call bottom lines. Time of take-off, time of return, and the special views of a given skipper and crew on 'their' aircraft. Some crews, and some members of crews, were very fussy and were forever checking their own positions. If the skipper had a different opinion from the official one on how, what and when to test, we had to follow the skipper.

Often without the proper spares and official tools, our one aim in life was to keep our Latin motto for ever holy: 'Ubendum wemendum'.

CHAPTER 16

Escapes, Evasions and Captures

John Shore and crew, 1941

Operation: Cologne. Date: 27 March. Captain: Flight Lieutenant J T L Shore. Wellington R1335 WS/K shot down over Belgium on return from target by Oberleutenant Walter Fenske of III/JG1. Message received at 22.48: 'I am forced to land GN [goodnight]'.

At 12,000ft my starboard engine packed up. It started again then, 5 seconds later, both engines stopped. It was impossible to start them again and at 8,000ft I began getting rid of my crew, leaving the aircraft myself at 1,500ft.

I landed in a football field, spraining my ankle, about 6 miles from Heusden en Maas, the Netherlands. I tried to destroy my parachute by burning it but they appear to be treated with some fire-resisting substance. It is best to cut them into shreds with a knife. I kept about 12yd of my parachute cord concealed at the back of my tunic. I started walking along a road heading west; it was then about 23.30 English time.

By 03.00 I reached a small village and tried the church, which was locked, and could not find the vicarage. At a farm I tried and failed to rouse the inmates by throwing gravel at a window, so I went to sleep in a barn. In the morning, the farmer's wife gave me something to eat while the farmer fetched the local padre, who advised me to hand myself in to the Dutch police but also obtained a lift for me into Heusden on a vegetable cart.

At a cavalry officer's house, when I went to wash upstairs, I found civilian clothes, papers and money had been put out for me, and the window left open, but I had to decline this obvious invitation due to the state of my ankle.

With my permission, the officer telephoned the police. A policeman arrived and, about half an hour later, a German major, who asked me if I had any firearms but did not search me, and asked about my aircraft but did not press me when I refused to answer.

I was taken to a police station where I found the rest of my crew with the exception of Sergeant Tomkins. Tomkins had a 4.5 Smith & Wesson on him and, as he was a navigator, he would know where he was. He could speak good French and was always determined to get away in the event of capture. He also had the rations as they had been laid out on the navigator's table in front of him.

His parachute had been found by the Germans and I should like to draw attention to the fact that every parachute is stencilled with the owner's name, number and rank, so that the Germans knew that one of the crew was missing [Sergeant H J Tomkins was arrested and spent the rest of the war at Stalag Luft VI, Hydekrug].

We were taken on a bus to a barracks in Amsterdam, where we were put in separate cells. Personal effects were confiscated but not kit and, after breakfast next morning, my crew and four Sergeants of a Whitley crew were put in a bus for the railway station. On our journey to the station the Dutch waved and cheered. We went by train to Frankfurt-am-Main, arriving there at about 20.00 hours, travelling in second-class carriages and being issued with bread, sausage and margarine. The guards were very lax and put their rifles on the rack. We did not see any bomb damage at Cologne. At Frankfurt I noticed that one of the Germans was carrying the navigation bag of my aircraft. I cannot think how they could have got this but they said it had been found 20yd from the crash. In the Red Cross buffet we were given water while some twenty German soldiers came in and out and were given soup. Though we asked for some of this we were refused.

Our guards were young and of the Luftwaffe, and they did not enforce the no-talking rule in the buffet

Second pilot in John Shore's crew was Pilot Officer James R 'Cookie' Long, who had only arrived from OTU three weeks before. A fellow prisoner in Stalag Luft III took this photograph. Two years after being shot down, Cookie Long, with fellow IX Squadron pilots Jimmy James, Tom Kirby-Green and Les Bull, emerged from a tunnel in what came to be known as 'The Great Escape', 24 March 1944. James Long was the last of the fifty escapers to be executed by the Gestapo, at Breslau, on 13 April.

or on the bus that took us to Dulag Luft. While driving through Frankfurt I noticed that the black-out was fairly good but not so good as ours. At the camp we were issued with bed clothes and food and assigned to rooms.

The commandant, Major Rumpel, came to see me the next afternoon. I did not answer any of his questions and he said it did not matter what squadron I came from, nine, ten or eleven. He tried to put me at my ease and asked me about the bombing of our towns, my mission, place from where I started, etc. His attitude was deliberately friendly and casual.

The Security Officer, *Hauptman* von Actzen, tried to elicit the same information with a fake Red Cross form, with name of squadron commander, etc. but I refused. I was issued with a Polish greatcoat and Polish tunic and trousers but had my own underwear. I gave my parole to go out on walks. Discipline was lax and there was no searching of rooms. Interpreters usually dropped in for a chat around tea-time, about our letters from home, bomb damage, new aircraft types, etc. We were issued with Rhine wine and Dunkirk whisky. We also had beer at the little inns on our walks. Everybody seemed very happy at Dulag Luft, although two tunnels were being built.

We were given 48 hours' notice of leaving. I was given back all my RAF kit including flying boots.

On 15 April we were taken to the goods yard at Frankfurt station, where we boarded a carriage in a goods and mail train with the camp guards. The train started and I went into the lavatory. There was a small window on two hinges and I loosened the screws, leaving the window like this until I needed it. There were ordinary railway maps in the carriage and we were allowed to look at these for a while. As I wanted to go to the Swiss frontier I had to get out of the train fairly soon, during the day time. I jumped out of the window but unfortunately they heard me and pulled the alarm cord while I made for a wooded bank, crossing the line to get there. The guards came out of the train and started firing their revolvers. I was caught by a *Feldwebel* who was very annoyed when he got hold of me and pushed me down a bank. We arrived late at Kassell and missed our connection. When the next train came in at about 6 o'clock we [the officers] were put in one carriage and locked in. We could go and speak to the sergeants if we wanted to. Going through Berlin we saw one lot of bomb damage. We arrived at Barth [Stalag Luft I] on the morning of 17 April.

We were searched and personal items were taken away. We were issued with a bowl, knife, fork and spoon and given a number. The rations were very poor. Red Cross parcels were coming in at a rate of one per man per month. Suggestions for Red Cross parcels. No carrots or Maconochie stew should be sent. Too much tea is sent. Too much bramble jelly, which is insipid. Provisions which would be appreciated are self-raising flour, dried eggs, custard powder, coffee, cocoa, raisins and currants, salt and pepper mixed in waterproof packets, thin transparent lavatory paper, curry powder.

Maconochie stew was a delicacy familiar to members of all the British armed forces as well as POWs in receipt of Red Cross parcels. It was made by Maconochie Brothers, contractors to the War Office and suppliers of rations – tinned meat and vegetables – during the Boer War and onwards. The statement on the label, 'The meat in this tin is prepared in its natural juices', caused much discussion.

[After two failed escape attempts] I noticed there was a tunnel started from the rubbish bin so I approached the man who had started it. At 10.30 every day there was a football match and the boys watching used to stand on the sloping top of the incinerator. Under their cover we kicked open the trap door and dropped in. We left the door open a little for air and James [Pilot Officer Bertram 'Jimmy' James of IX Squadron, shot down 6 June 1940] and I worked from 10.30 to 17.00 when another twelve people stood there while we got out. On Sunday we could not dig as there were no football matches.

We used a table knife and took the earth out on a board and put the earth in the incinerator. The Germans had been told to look out for people hiding in the refuse cart so they paid no attention to the incinerator being half full with earth. It took us four days to dig the 25ft with just enough room to crawl along. I had to wash my clothes after each day's digging but luckily I had two pairs of trousers. The Germans emptied the incinerator during this time, throwing the earth and burned rubbish mixture into a cart and taking it away.

Once the tunnel was completed, the next thing was to wait for an air raid, when the guards were trebled but the lights were put out. I gave us a time limit of 5 minutes to get through the tunnel, entering through trap doors we had made. At 22.30, 19 October, bombers were heard and the lights went out. I started crawling through my trap door wearing my greatcoat, which prevented me going back so that a German guard came along and nearly stepped on me before walking towards the gate. I got up and walked after him, making my footsteps coincide with his. I went along to James's hut and called him and he came out just behind me. I got into the incinerator but James did not come [he had been spotted by torchlight and taken].

The tunnel had 6in of water in it but I got through, emerged into the football field, and crawled under the lowest strand of barbed wire which was buried just beneath the surface. I waited for James in a wood but saw lights and had to go on, after squeezing lemon on my boots and clothes to destroy the scent for the dogs that the Germans employ.

After finding that Sassnitz was 35 miles away instead of 6 as I had thought, I made an attempt to steal a bicycle, but was seen. My feet were very sore and painful when I reached Sassnitz. By this time I looked just like a German workman, very dirty and wearing a cap I had made myself in the camp.

I twice attempted to hide on trains that I expected to be shunted on to the ferry but on both occasions they set off in the opposite direction, towards Sassnitz station, and I had to jump off. I hid in some bushes and watched the ferry leave.

I decided to become a Swedish sailor looking for a berth and went to the docks. When an SS man came up and asked me for my papers, I said '*Ich bin Schweder. Nicht verstehen*'. He brought two Danes from a nearby ship so that they could show me what he meant by papers. Another Dane, drunk, appeared and put his arms around me and the SS man and I was able to slip away, making for the railway lines that led to where the ferry would dock in the morning. I saw two Pullman coaches and got in one and had a drink and a wash in the lavatory. I was feeling rather despondent by then and got into a second-class carriage and went to sleep, not caring much if I was discovered. I woke at about 03.00, went out, scrambled into a tarpaulin-covered truck full of piping, and saw the funnels of the ferry. A line of trucks was being taken aboard so I jumped out and ran 50yd to scramble onto a low truck with a German lorry on it. I spent the voyage sitting in the cab of the lorry.

In Trelleborg, I was seen by a Swedish guard and taken by police in a car to the police station. There I was made to write out a short report for the Swedish Foreign Office. I asked to see the British Consul but instead was given money and a first-class ticket to Stockholm. There, I paid for a taxi to the British Legation and was flown home to arrive in Britain on 29 October.

Having earned the nickname 'Death' for his escape attempts, Wing Commander Shore MC was killed in a post-war crash.

John Duncan and crew, 1943
Sergeant John Duncan of Saskatchewan and crew in ED480 WS/U-Uncle were hit by flak over Gelsenkirchen, 9/10 July, after yet another unsuccessful attempt to blast the oil refinery. As they had struggled through a dozen ops together, so they struggled as far as the Pas-de-Calais but the loss of fuel made home an impossibility and Duncan gave the order to abandon ship.

The ship fell and was completely destroyed near the village of Troisvilles. The engineer Sergeant Blunden, wounded, and the mid-upper Sergeant Warner were taken prisoner but the rest of the crew had a better time of it.

Flight Sergeant Henry Brown, navigator: I landed in a tree near Pommereuil, about 3 miles NE of Le Cateau. I cut myself free and ran off. After about 3 miles I went into a wood and slept until 05.00 hours, when I heard the wood being searched. I took off my tunic and was in the middle of cutting off my sergeant's stripes when I heard German voices quite close to me. I hurriedly pushed my tunic into some undergrowth and ran off. I stopped at a farmhouse where translators were called in. A man asked me if I knew of anyone who could help me or if I wanted to give myself up to the Germans. I told him I had no friends in France but that I intended to return to the UK. He gave me a complete set of civilian clothes, and a woman who spoke good English took me in her car to a house.

Sergeant Gerard Bartley, bomb aimer: I came down in a potato field about half a mile due east of Cambrai. I hid my parachute, Irving jacket and Mae West in a hedge, crawled a few hundred yards to a secluded spot and went to sleep. In Cambrai main street there were large numbers of French people about on their way to work. A youth told me to go back as there was a German control on the gate. [A farmer] hid me in the middle of a large cornfield. He, his father and sister brought me food and said the Germans were making a house-to-house search. I walked to a small village and went to the church. I left after the service and two youths followed me out of the village and gave me food but no other help. At the next village I had to pass two German sentries but neither challenged me. Another farmer gave me shelter and food and a road worker arranged for a van to come and pick me up and take me to Chauny.

Sergeant Sid Hughes, w/op: I landed several miles due north of Cambrai in a cornfield where I hid my parachute and Mae West. I went through my pockets and tore up any papers with writing on them as well as £3 10*s* in notes. I lit a cigarette with another pound note and walked to the nearest farm and spent the night in a woodshed. I had help from the farmer, who arranged for a tailor to come and measure me for a suit.

Sergeant John Duncan, pilot: I continued across country, passing through a small town where a boy gave me a loaf of bread and showed me on my map where I was. I went to a farmhouse and got food and shelter, and the next day another farmhouse, when I was taken to another house, given food and shelter then taken by car to Chauny.

228

Sergeant David McMillan, rear gunner: I landed badly in a meadow and sprained both my ankles. My legs for a while were quite inert from the shock but when I could move them freely I started off in the direction of a clock chime some distance off. I thought that if the chime came from a church I would try for help there, but a young German soldier found me and took me to a guardroom to be searched and documented. There was no transport to take me onwards so I set off on foot with the private who had found me. My ankles were paining me considerably and after going a little way I sat down on a low stone wall, took off my flying boots, showed my swollen ankles to the German and rubbed them. He was not sympathetic.

I accidentally knocked one of my boots off the wall and, feeling for it in the darkness I also felt a large stone. I put the boot on and reached back for the stone. Pretending severe pain and disability, I held out my left hand for help. The German offered me his left hand. I pulled him towards me and crashed the stone, which I had kept all the time in my right hand, against the left side of his head. He dropped with a clatter. I tried to get the bayonet off his rifle but failed. I searched him hurriedly and recovered my cigarettes and watch but found nothing else of use. He was quite senseless, bleeding a little from the nose, and I put him over the wall.

I was feeling shaken and left the town at once. I reached Busigny and went to the station. There was an elderly man in the ticket office. I said '*Un, Paris*', and put down four of the 50-franc notes from my purse. He gave me the ticket without comment, handing me back two of the notes and some small change. I asked him '*Train, quelle heure?*' and he wrote 4.30 on the back of the ticket.

At Chauny, Duncan, Bartley and Hughes were taken in hand by an organisation that spirited them away into Spain and on to Gibraltar. Brown reached Spain on his own through a French evaders' organisation. McMillan was picked up by some young Frenchmen while waiting for his train and had a journey to Spain arranged for him. Sergeant Duncan returned to IX Squadron and finished his tour of ops.

Malcolm Head and crew, 1943
The squadron was sent to bomb an electrical installation at Reggio nell' Emilia, 15 July, on a small venture of two-dozen Lancs with several north Italian targets between them. They would fly on to north Africa. Flying Officer Head in P-Peter sent a message from near the target saying he'd collided with another aircraft. This was DV167 VN/M of 50 Squadron, which

went in straight away killing all the crew. Head's message also said they were going to try and make Algeria. After a further 20 minutes, he gave orders to bale out, at about 05.00 hours. Flight engineer Ted Edwards was killed when his parachute failed to open but the rest fell to earth safely and were captured.

Flight Sergeant Johnny Merchant, w/op: I landed by a canal and hid my parachute and Mae West in a culvert. I saw the rear gunner [Flight Sergeant W J McCoombs] and we decided to hide in the bushes, but the Italians were out searching for us and we were picked up immediately and taken into Miràndola where we met the rest of the crew, excepting Sergeant Edwards who was killed in landing. We were taken to Bologna for one night and then Poggio quarantine camp. The treatment at this camp was good but the food was very scarce. From there we were sent to Rome and on to POW camp at Chieti.

During my stay the Italian Armistice was signed but the prisoners were forbidden to leave the camp. A small party of Germans arrived and took the camp over. There were three escape tunnels built and, when the Germans were moving us out, sixty POWs hid in these tunnels and were left behind. We went to Sulmona.

We were put on a train in box cars to be sent to a prison camp in Germany. During our trip north the men in our box car broke a hole in the side. In company with Sergeant G E Pearson [RASC] I escaped by jumping off the train close to San Benedetto val di Sambo where we contacted a civilian and stayed with him for a week.

Flying Officer Malcolm Head: [At Poggio] we were first placed in solitary confinement and then in pairs. We were also interrogated. In Rome we were in a large house, some sort of private residence. There were mostly RAF here but we suspected some so-called Army officers to be stool-pigeons. While at Sulmona, a Lieutenant Ward, eleven Sikhs and myself attempted to escape by climbing through the window of the latrine. We would only have had to penetrate the outside wire to get away but, as we saw that the Germans had observed us and had sub-machine guns trained on us, we gave up the attempt. We were placed in cells for three days.

[On the same train as Merchant] Myself, the eleven Sikhs, Lieutenant Ward and three army captains, King, Cheer and Wood, took the cover off a ventilator on the train and got out when it stopped before Goriano Sicoli. By the time Ward got out, the train was passing through the station and doing about 20 miles an hour. The eleven Sikhs ran for it while the rest of us went to find Ward.

We found him surrounded by Italians who were very helpful and took us to a deserted house, the idea being that we would remain hidden there until our own troops arrived. We were joined by two Sicilian officers who wanted to get down to our lines and fight with the British. We stayed in the hut for a fortnight, fed by the station master and his staff.

The Italians told us they did not think it safe to remain at Goriano any longer. We were walking along the railway line when we were called to halt by a German patrol with an officer in charge. We were taken back to Goriano and locked up in a barn. We were interrogated, chiefly with a view to discovering the names of those who had helped us. We gave no names away and the interrogation was not pressed. We were sent to an improvised POW camp at Castel di Sangro. Here, Ward escaped but was recaptured. We also commenced to dig a tunnel but it was discovered.

We were put on a train moving north, confined in a sort of sub-compartment of a guard's van, a *Feldwebel* and six men being in the main compartment. When the train was passing through a tunnel we lowered the window and felt for the latch on the outside of the door, which we released. After being in the train for about 2½ hours, it was dark enough and the train moving slowly enough for seven of us to get out. The Germans fired several shots at us and in the confusion I lost the others but soon picked up Lieutenant Ward and one of the Sicilian officers and we three moved together. Later we found Captain Cheer. We stayed about eight days in the mountains near where we had jumped, then moved south with a guide who took us across the Sangro River. Near Forli del Sannio we were shot at by Germans. I was hit in the left arm, which was broken, and Captain Cheer was hit in the arm and the leg and captured, as he could not run. Eventually the rest of us contacted British troops and, via hospital in Bari and Cairo, I reached the UK in February 1944.

On the run in Italy, John Merchant's civilian took him and his new pal to Milan, thence to Como, and found a guide to take them on into Switzerland. Merchant stayed in Switzerland for almost a year before making an expedition into France with two more soldiers where they contacted the Maquis and were smuggled to Casablanca. After a short stop-over in England, Merchant was repatriated to Canada.

Stalag Luft III, March 1944
Berlin, 24 March 1944; of the 800 bombers on that raid, including 16 from IX Squadron, 72 went down. Strong winds blew them about, the stream divided into streamlets which strayed all over, even into the Ruhr, and the flak men had a great night of it. This was the last major offensive in the battle

IX Squadron pilot Tom Kirby-Green, seen here with his wife, became Squadron Leader with 40 Squadron and the only survivor when his Wellington was shot down. He recovered from spinal injuries to join Bertram 'Jimmy' James, seen here in a prison-camp photograph, in tunnelling at Stalag Luft III.

PAMIĘTAMY
BOCHATEROM ALİANCKİCH LOTNİKÓW OFİCEROM
ROSTRZELANYCH PRZEZ GESTAPO
ZAGAŃ MARZEC 1944

F. O	BIRKLAND. H	Can	Fl. Lt	HAYTER. A	Br	F. O	PICARD. H	Belg
Fl. Lt	BRETTEL. G	Br	Fl. Lt	HUMPHRIES. E	Br	F. O	POHE. J	N. Z
Fl. Lt	BULL. L	Br	F. O	KIDDER. G	Can	Por	SCHEIDHAUER. B	Fr
Sq. Ldr	BUSHELL. R	Br	Fl. Lt	KEIRATH. R	Aus	F. O	SKANZIKLAS. S	Grc
Fl. Lt	CASEY. M	Br	Major	KIEWNARSKI. A	Polak	F. O	STEVENS. R	S. A
Sq. Ldr	CATANACH. J	Aus	Sq. Ldr	KIRBY-GREEN. T	Br	F. O	STEWART. R	Br
F. O	CHRISTENSEN. A	N. Z	Por	KOLANOWSKI. W	Polak	F. O	STOWER. J	Br
F. O	COCHRAN. D	Br	Por	KROL. S	Polak	F. O	STREET. D	Br
Sq. Ldr	CROSS. I	Br	Fl. Lt	LANGFORD. P	Can	Fl. Lt	SWAIN. C	Br
Por	ESPELID. H	Nor	Fl. Lt	LEIGH. T	Br	Por	TOBOLSKI. P	Polak
Fl. Lt	EVANS. B	Br	Fl. Lt	LONG. J	Br	Fl. Lt	VALENTA. A	Cz
Por	FUGELSANG. N	Nor	Fl. Lt	McGARR. C	S. A	Fl. Lt	WALENN. G	Br
Fl. Lt	GOUWS. J	S. A	Fl. Lt	McGILL. G	Can	Fl. Lt	WERNHAM. J	Can
Fl. Lt	GRISMAN. W	Br	Fl. Lt	MARCINKUS. R	Lit	Fl. Lt	WILLEY. G	Can
Fl. Lt	GUNN. A	Br	Fl. Lt	MILFORD. H	Br	Sq. Ldr	WILLIAMS. J	Aus
Fl. Lt	HAKE. A	Aus	Por	MONDSCHEIN. J	Polak	Fl. Lt	WILLIAMS. J. F	Br
Fl. Lt	HALL. C	Br	Por	PAWLUK. K	Polak			

HONOUR THE BRAVE

The list of escapers shot by the Gestapo includes three IX Squadron men: Bull, Kirby-Green and Long.

for the Big City, which was a mess but not a write-off. Many, many aircraft had been lost over the months of the battle, more than 600, with 3,000 men killed and 750 taken prisoner or, looked at another way, 25 entire squadrons in 16 attacks.

The prisoners in Stalag Luft III, Sagan, Silesia (Zagan, Poland), on that night had no idea it was the end of the Battle of Berlin. Flight Lieutenant Les Bull DFC, who as Sergeant Bull had flown his first ops with IX Squadron in the spring of 1940, was now known as Johnny after the portly, waistcoated chap who supposedly represented the British spirit. Bull was at the exit hatchway of a tunnel called Harry which he, Conk Canton (Flight Lieutenant Norman Canton DFC, IX Squadron pilot 1942) and hundreds of other inmates had built over many painstaking weeks. His job was to open the hatch, climb out, lie in the snow and control the escapes of the first lot of men.

British spirit was in great demand just then because the hatch wouldn't open, swollen in the wet and, when they did manage it, Bull popped his head out to find that the tunnel, instead of emerging in the woods, was 3yd or more short. Everybody would have to crawl across open ground, in full view of the guards in the tower.

Bull solved the problem with a system of rope tugs, one end of the rope tied to the tunnel ladder, the other in his hand as he lay in the undergrowth at the edge of the woods, watching the guards. Everything went well at first if much too slowly, until the air-raid sirens signalled the Berlin raid 60 miles away and all the camp lights were switched off. Their tunnel lights went off too but at least it was black dark outside. More men pushed themselves along the tunnel floor on the little trolley carts running on wooden rails and it came to the turn of Squadron Leader Thomas Gresham Kirby-Green, Bull's contemporary in IX Squadron days. Judging by the passionate letter he'd written that morning to his wife Maria, his thoughts of her would have been making him utterly determined to succeed.

He was a big man, Tom Kirby-Green, 6ft 4in and still big after months of Stalag diet, and when he unbalanced and derailed his trolley in mid-journey he dislodged some of the planks lining the tunnel. The roof caved in. Kirby-Green was entirely buried except for his head and it was a good hour before he was free and the tunnel repaired. The Lancs and Halifaxes had turned away from Berlin by this time and were into their next round with the night-fighters, the camp lights were back on and around fifty men, including IX Squadron man Jimmy James at Number 39, had gone through the tunnel.

James: I stood at the bottom of the exit shaft and looked up and saw stars framed in the rough outline of the hole 20ft above me. There had been much toil but worth every moment, I thought as I climbed the ladder.

James and a group of colleagues had a 3½-hour walk in the perishing cold, through woods and open country, to a tiny rural railway station.

Back at the tunnel there was another disaster, a second roof fall. Under it this time was another IX Squadron man, Cookie Long. Luckily the collapse wasn't anything like as bad as the first and more men struggled through until the first signs of dawn around 05.00 when they decided to stop. The eightieth man was about to emerge but discovery came before the halt was called. The previous three and the eightieth were marched back into camp by a truly astounded sentry and the escapers' expected 4-hour start, between dawn and roll-call, was gone.

Canadian IX Squadron observer Graham Welsh (see p. 141): That left 120 of us who didn't get out, including me. My job until then had been intelligence, working in a team led by Roman Marcinkus, the only Lithuanian RAF officer in the camp. I knew German and so I was assigned to read the daily newspapers from Berlin, Frankfurt, Hamburg and Vienna for any little snippets about transport and communications which might help us make our escape good. Now we prayed that our work had been good enough. Roman was out, anyway.

Also out was Jimmy James: We were supposed to be a party of twelve on leave from a woodmill. The booking clerk at the little station couldn't believe we wanted twelve tickets but we got them eventually and travelled without incident to Boberöhrsdorf.

By 06.00 a *Grossfahndung* (hue and cry throughout Germany) had been ordered and every available member of the armed forces, the police forces and the local militias were out looking for British and Commonwealth airmen and more from occupied Europe including Poles, Norwegians and Dutch, seventy-six altogether. Kirby-Green was buying a ticket at Sagan station when they caught quite a few of the others; he managed to make it a little further. Jimmy James was away too, climbing through waist-deep freezing snow up the mountains which lay between him and the Czech border. Survival in thin clothes seemed unlikely. A tactical switch was made, to a railway station at Hirschberg.

James: As we [James and Greek airman Nick Skanziklas] approached the ticket office I saw two figures move towards us. We converged at the barrier. A policeman in teapot helmet and a civilian stood in front of us. We produced our passes confidently on demand but the policeman merely glanced at them, put them in his pocket, inspected the contents of our packs, and said 'Komm mit'. I protested that we were foreign workers on legitimate business and that our old mothers were waiting to see us, but we were marched away.

The end was almost inevitable. In twos and threes and fours they were rounded up. On the 27th, the score of escapers held at Sagan's town jail were taken to another jail at Görlitz where they were interrogated singly and, in the cells, found more of their fellows. It seemed they were not going back to camp yet. They were being collected.

Hitler, in a mad rage, had ordered all the escapers to be shot. Göring, with practical objections, succeeded in modifying this to 'more than half' and the executions began on the 29th with shootings of twos and threes in the back. Les Bull was among the first day's cull, and Tom Kirby-Green. Later, eight of Jimmy James's woodmill party were shot, including Nick Skanziklas.

Of the seventy-six, only three succeeded in disappearing from Germany; one Dutchman and two Norwegians. Fifteen were sent back to Sagan, four more to concentration camps, and Jimmy James was one of another four who, for reasons not understood, disappeared in a different way.

> Order for the transfer of Prominent Prisoners to Camp 'A' Sachsenhausen Concentration Camp. The following officers – Wing Commander Day, Major Dodge, Flight Lieutenant Dowse and Flight Lieutenant James are to be transferred to Camp 'A' Sachsenhausen. To the outside world they are to be considered as escaped and not recaptured. The Commandant and his representatives are responsible with their heads for their secure housing and treatment.

Jimmy James: I had no idea why Dowse and I were considered to be in this category of Prominent Prisoners.

Come September, these four plus the famous Commando officer Jack Churchill MC, DSO and Bar, would tunnel out yet again, and yet again be the subject of a *Grossfahndung*, and yet again be recaptured but spared execution despite Himmler's direct order.

As for the 'more than half', by mid-April fifty men had been shot. They faced firing squads, six at a time, ten at a time, but many took a bullet in the back, in secret, out of the way, or sometimes openly by the side of the autobahn. The favourite trick was to put a couple of them in a car, drive them supposedly to a new prison and on the way offer them the chance to take a leak. All were 'trying to escape' or 'offering resistance', even when the orders for their cremation had been signed before they were dead. The last one, Cookie Long, was executed alone by the Gestapo at Breslauon 13 April.

Russ Gradwell and crew
See p. 127. Gradwell set off towards the north west where the front line was. He knew he was somewhere north of Paris (in fact, near Beauvais in Oise, hardly 15 miles back from the target), probably 50 or 60 miles from the English Channel coast.

Progress was very slow, with much bumping into trees, stumbling about and falling over, until I found a country lane. I heard a vehicle, dived into the ditch and peered nervously at the steel helmets of the passengers in the truck which came past.

When they'd gone, I carried on and came to a village, took off down a side road and turned into a cornfield. I walked with great care through the ripe corn so I didn't leave a trail and, strangely considering my circumstances, I also didn't want to spoil any of the crop by flattening it. My thoughts turned to the common sense which so far seemed to be lacking in my plan. If Jerry was out looking for me, surely it would be better to hide until he'd moved well on? So I lay down in the corn and fell asleep.

I was woken by a group of Typhoon fighters flying very low. Resigned to a long, hot day with no food or water, I got up but had only taken a few steps when I heard the clatter of a reaping machine being pulled by two horses. I was very proud of the fact that I was that rare thing among aircrew, a man who could speak French, but I'd never tested it in a French cornfield before. 'Hey, Messieurs. Je suis Royal Air Force,' was the best I could manage, and it didn't seem to be good enough. The two French farm workers looked blank. I pointed to the wings on my uniform and the letters RAF. 'Ah!' they cried. '*Vous êtes Royal Air Force*'.

I was taken to a farm, a very big farm, and word had gone ahead of me because formed up outside the farmhouse were a dozen or more people, all anxious to shake hands and kiss both cheeks with the brave English flyer. As I worked my way down the line, I really did wonder at it all. If the Germans had arrived they'd have shot the lot of them. Anyway, with formalities complete and protocol satisfied, everyone went back to their work except for Madame Carron, the farmer's wife. Inside the house, she wanted to know if I was hungry. RAF procedure on an escape was to accept food only if you were desperate, because the French were themselves desperately short. So I said '*Non, non merci, je suis bien*'.

Madame Carron gave me a nod and a smile and went down the cellar steps. She came back with the biggest steak I had ever seen, which she began to fry in about half a pound of farm butter on top of the wood-burning stove.

While that was doing, she produced a gorgeous white loaf, more butter and a bottle of red wine. I hadn't seen white bread since the war broke out and I had a year's ration of butter in front of me.

Somehow, out of politeness, I managed to demolish it, plus the wine, plus the steak which, at home, would have been expected to feed a family of four for a fortnight. Madame Carron placed a large bowl of strawberries on the table with a jug of fresh cream. Cream was illegal in Britain.

A strange incident followed, when I was subjected to a close but wordless inspection by a small boy. I felt that my authenticity was being questioned so I placed my packet of Player's cigarettes on the table top. The boy examined this, seemed satisfied and left, still without a word, to be replaced as validator by an elderly lady, Madame Ravel, who was clearly not to do with farming but rather a gentlewoman, nobility maybe.

She spoke good English and had been to school in England, in Richmond, Surrey, of which my knowledge was limited having driven through it once with my parents before the war. Madame was happy to hear instead about my home town, Llandudno, and the Great Orme, and Mostyn Street and anything else I could bring to mind.

She didn't say but I felt that Llandudno had been among her visited places and that I was passing the exam. 'I am sure you are an officer in the Royal Air Force,' she announced. 'I will fetch assistance.'

Two men arrived, introduced themselves as M. Maigret and M. Thibou, and asked for the names of the rest of my crew. One took a camera from his pocket and photographed me. The Germans had recently changed the pattern of French ID cards so the pictures we carried in our escape kits were no longer any use. The French patriots were well ahead of the game, being supplied directly with ID card blank originals by the same printer who produced them for the occupying forces, and with official stamps by a lady who worked as a cleaner at German headquarters.

Thibout and Maigret told me they had found six of my crew. I became Roger l'Anglais, which Thibout and Maigret thought frightfully witty since I came from Wales. They brought Atch Atkinson [bomb aimer] to the farm but there was quite a deal of traffic past us, including refugees from Paris begging food. Somewhere quieter was preferable and so we were moved in a covered cart, through the town of Auneuil to the tiny village of Villiers St Barthélemy where Marcel and Germaine Dubois had a three-roomed cottage. Marcel had been taken prisoner at the Maginot line, escaped, broke his leg in the process, had it fixed by a local doctor and walked home to Paris.

The couple had taken cover at Villiers. He worked on the land and she, having been a milliner of the film-star class, got work around the village sewing and mending. They managed, and they shared what they had with us, and we did what we could in return, chopping wood, pressing the cider apples, going out to the woods at dawn in search of snails and mushrooms. This carried on for six weeks and still our presence in the village was a complete secret. Even the people next door didn't know, nor did they know that Maigret and Thibou had moved four more airmen, my crew minus Price and Oldacre, into another house in the village. We had a reunion every Sunday.

Atch and I were totally French-looking by this time. We were setting off on our dawn snail and mushroom raid with Marcel when a truck came along full of German soldiers. Two NCOs jumped down and, pistols threatening, demanded in French to know what the three of us were doing out before curfew was up. Atch, who didn't speak French but had grasped what was going on, instinctively looked at his Bulova watch. Marcel and I froze in horror. If the Germans noticed the watch they would ask some very awkward questions. Where did a French peasant, apparently a deaf and dumb one, get the kind of Swiss watch favoured by the wealthy and those concerned with perfectly accurate time-keeping, such as Allied aircrew, who would be shot as spies if not in uniform?

The Germans could not be bothered to make anything of it and with a *Raus*! and a wave of their guns sent the three of us on our way. Mushrooms and snails were still to be got so we continued our mission by another route but, returning by the way we always used, coming out of the woods onto a main road, we were dumbfounded to see German army vehicles parked as far as the eye could see. The soldiers were lounging about in the sun having their breakfast. Marcel took the lead, Atch came next and I, with my French now fluent after many tutorials with Madame Dubois, brought up the rear.

This was the German army in retreat. They didn't care about three poor Frenchies carrying some rubbish out of the woods in their shirts. Nobody spoke to anybody as we threaded our way politely through men and vehicles, but the experience was quite enough for us. Two narrow scrapes in a day was pushing it. The third would surely see us taken. We were discussing this burning topic over our own breakfast – mushrooms – when two Germans walked past the window, then two more. It ended up with about fifty of them billeting themselves in the barn next door.

Two days passed without incident. On the third morning, Atch was giving Germaine a hand in the room they used as kitchen, diner and parlour. I was making the bed in our room with the door to the street open, to get some air in. The room darkened suddenly.

I turned to find a large German soldier in the doorway with a couple of eggs in each hand. He wanted me to make an omelette for him. I waved at him to say, stay where you are, and went into the kitchen, smuggled Atch into the Dubois' bedroom and persuaded Germaine to cook the eggs, on her condition that the soldier didn't eat them on the premises. I went to the window, called the man over and passed the eggs to Germaine. We stood there, enemies divided by a kitchen wall, although only one of us knew the whole of it, and conversed as best we could. My French was a lot better than his. He was a typical conscript squaddie. He didn't want a war. He didn't want to kill anybody or be killed for the Fatherland. All he wanted was to get back to Dresden, to his wife, his family and his rose garden.

Next day the Germans disappeared and the Allies replaced them in the street. Atch was taken to the village square to listen to the new soldiers' conversation. It had to be checked because it was common practice for Germans to appear in Allied uniforms, wait for the Resistance to appear out of the woodwork to welcome them, and shoot. Atch said that the British accents were authentic and the church bells rang out.

I walked with Marcel to the village square. Everyone called out 'Les Anglais sont ici', bottles and glasses were produced and I was quite squiffy by the time we got there. The reconnaissance unit told us to stay where we were until the infantry came through in force. Before that happened, Maigret and Thibou in a large and sumptuous motor car came to pick the six of us up and take us to the chateau where dwelled Madame Ravel.

The table was set for a magnificent luncheon with different wines in their own glasses to accompany the courses. At the end came brandy, real Cognac which we hadn't seen for years, and real coffee. Real coffee, made from coffee beans, costing goodness knows what on the black market.

The next day, amid many tears and kisses, we said our goodbyes and thank-yous and hitched an army lift to start our journey home, which included passage through areas where fighting had been fierce. In some places, the German bodies had been bulldozed to one side to open the road. In others, they still aimed their guns from their foxholes but could not see anything to shoot and never would. Once back in Blighty we found that, of course, we had been listed as missing and immediately sent off telegrams to our relatives, who had assumed – because there had been no news on the BBC of capture for all this time – that we had been killed, lost without trace.

The two Canadians, Atkinson and Best, were repatriated and the rest of us were counted as tour expired even though we were officially one short. As successful evaders, we could transfer wherever we wanted. Three of us went to Transport Command, 242 Squadron and the Middle East, flying the York, the wide-bodied version of the Lancaster. The squadron expanded and I assumed temporary command of a flight of ten crews. When the permanent officer arrived to take over the flight, it turned out to be a certain Squadron Leader Micky Martin, DSO and Bar, DFC and two Bars, ex-617 Squadron Dambuster, who insisted on doing his second Dicky as per proper procedure, so he went with me to Colombo, capital of Ceylon [Sri Lanka]. We had a fault with the aircraft so Pete Lynch – my old flight engineer – and I stayed to discuss this with the ground crew while Micky Martin went up to flight control.

Everyone sprang to attention when he walked in, saluting such a highly decorated officer. A WAAF got out the flight record and asked him to sign here. 'Oh no,' he said. 'I'm just the second pilot.' I walked in and sensed an atmosphere, which disappeared as soon as I said I was the skipper.

'What was all that about?' I asked Martin outside. Martin laughed. 'Well, I told them I was only the second pilot, so they were jumpy. They must have thought the pilot was going to be at least an Air Vice Marshal.'

Walter Oldacre also made contact with the Resistance and found his way home, to return to IX Squadron and fly Lancasters through to the end of the war. The body of Sergeant James Thomas Price, wireless operator, aged 21, whose parachute hadn't opened, was not found until February 1945.

Henry 'Tug' Wilson, 1944
Before joining No. IX, Tug Wilson was with sister squadron No. 61, based at Skellingthorpe, and went with them to Königsberg, on 29 August, a return trip of nearly 11 hours. He was navigator in Lancaster PB436 QR/D-Dog on her third trip.

The route home was sea all the way except for the Denmark part coming up and our mood was cheerful as we crossed the Danish coast near Ålborg. We'd been over Denmark hardly more than 2 minutes when there was a terrific thump and the aircraft lurched sharply to port.

Our starboard inner was on fire, really on fire. Our mid-upper, Sergeant Longhurst, saw the flames leap and begin to threaten the tailplane. It had been a good shot. We weren't flying through masses of flak. It had been a deliberately aimed, precision job, a pot shot. The Germans must have been

240

tracking us on radar. We'd had no warning, no range finding shells, just the one, bang.

Loneon [Australian pilot] pushed the graviner button for the starboard inner. This activated a stream of carbon tetrachloride, dry cleaning fluid, from a pair of bottles strapped to the engine. It was supposed to put the fire out and sometimes it did, but by the time he had the aircraft back on an even keel and Harris the engineer had the starboard inner prop feathered, the fire was raging. Given a few minutes, the starboard wing and tailplane would be blazing and that would be that.

Loneon on the intercom put all our thoughts into a few words, offering us a choice of ditching in the sea or parachuting onto dry land. The answers were prompt. I announced a change of course to due south. Loneon turned left and we were flying down the centre of Denmark.

Our skipper shouted his order into the intercom to jump, 'Abracadabra, jump, jump', plus something about Pommie bastards. The gunners went from the side door. Bomb aimer, flight engineer and wireless operator jumped from the front hatch. I sat for a second or two on the edge of the hatch then rolled out into nothing. Finally Loneon, who had been struggling to hold the aircraft level, jumped as well. None of us had ever done it before, nor even had a go at anything approximating. Parachute training for RAF Bomber Command aircrew in 1944 consisted of showing us (a) how to clip on the chute and (b) where the rip cord was.

At least 2,000ft wasn't all that high for a parachute jump but it was probably high enough for complete beginners, and at least we weren't dropping on a moonless night in the rain towards goodness knows what in the Ruhr. As it was now, at a quarter past four on a fine summer's morning, I could admire the sun rising over Denmark. I was still in the air when our Lancaster hit the ground and blew up into small pieces. I hit the ground in a field of cabbages, which didn't offer me much cover but I made half a fist of hiding my chute between the rows. I jumped in a ditch, threw off my Mae West and pushed it into the mud, and scraped some more mud over it.

Ever so carefully I peeped over the top of the ditch, and I was straight back down into it when I heard shots. The firing seemed some way away. I thought the Germans were shooting the other crew members. So, that made my own instructions clear. Unless I wanted to be shot, I had better get the bloody hell out of there.

I ran and ran, fell exhausted into some undergrowth, and reviewed the situation. I had my standard issue escape money, in Deutchmarks naturally.

Nobody would think to issue us with Danish krone, simply because we happened to be flying over Denmark. I had my photograph, for use in forging identity papers. I had my standard issue escape kit with its water sterilising tablets and length of fishing line with a hook. There was a compass and maps, except there was no map of Denmark so the compass was no more use than the sun. There was also a hacksaw blade, the main use for which, I had learned from talking to mates, was to cut off the tops of your flying boots so they looked more like ordinary shoes.

The escape lectures we'd had in training were still fresh in my mind. I'd only heard them a few weeks before. First, they said, get away from your aircraft. Second, hide your parachute and Mae West. Third, contact the Resistance movement. What? Come again?

I could see there were people about. There was a farmhouse but it wasn't flying a banner saying Welcome to the Royal Danish Resistance. On the other hand, neither were there any signs of the Wehrmacht. It looked very like an ordinary working farm, working an ordinary day.

Dusk was falling. A man who seemed to be the senior character on the farm came out for his last look around. He was an oldish chap, clearly a farmer all his life and someone who had seen all kinds of fashions go by while the farming stayed the same. As soon as this serene, untroubled man strolled near my hideyhole, I stood up.

The old fellow's jaw dropped and he took a pace back. Then he took a pace forward and peered. Here was a youth of about 20, he would say, dressed in pale blue, covered in mud and jabbering in tongues while pointing to himself and a piece of embroidery with a wing on it.

I wasn't getting very far so I did wavy hand movements and throaty engine noises, followed by Yeeee-ow! noises and Boooff! noises. He shoo'd me back into the trees, went into the farmhouse, and came out again with a large piece of sacking. He wrapped this around me and took me to his home.

After much pantomime, it was established that I was Tug Wilson, Royal Air Force, and they were Mr and Mrs Kjær, Danish farmers, and this was their son. They were by a place called Valgård, near Farsö. I would indeed like something to eat, and there were no Germans stationed nearby. At least, there was nobody stationed nearby who goose-stepped up and down farmhouse kitchens with his right hand extended aloft while two fingers of his left held his nose up.

It became clear that the supper was not the limit of the Kjærs' compassion. They would have been in no doubt about the penalty for discovery. It was the firing squad or worse. Even so, they were prepared to shelter me for as long as it took. My bed was to be among the straw in the barn, with underfloor heating provided by the cattle below, but before that I had to be inspected by the local veterinary, Mr Sonne. Mr Sonne spoke some English and knew about the crash. He seemed to think that I was genuine enough.

I spent my first full day in the straw while farming life went on, and managed to snooze a fair portion of the day away. The farmer brought me some lunch: black bread and boiled bacon. In the early evening, he came again and gestured for me to come down the ladder. We went together into the house. I was shown to a chair and the wireless was switched on to the BBC 6 o'clock news. At the sound of the familiar announcer's voice, my thoughts were transported to another kitchen, in a modest family house on Somerset Avenue, number 23, in Welling, Kent. My mother, father and elder sister Alice would be listening to the wireless too, while they were having their tea. I knew also that they'd have had a telegram by now.

They had. It read thus:

> = DEEPLY REGRET TO INFORM YOU THAT YOUR SON 1398593 SGT H W WILSON IS REPORTED MISSING AFTER AIR OPERATIONS ON 29TH–30TH AUGUST 44 STOP ANY FURTHER INFORMATION RECEIVED WILL BE COMMUNICATED TO YOU IMMEDIATELY PENDING RECEIPT OF WRITTEN NOTIFICATION FROM THE AIR MINISTRY NO INFORMATION SHOULD BE GIVEN TO THE PRESS = 61 ADJUTANT

After the news, Mrs Kjær showed me the sink and the tap and gave me a towel. While I washed, she dished up a meal. Boiled bacon, with potatoes this time. We ate in silence but not an awkward silence. We knew we couldn't communicate across the language barrier and Mr and Mrs Kjær were too polite to talk between themselves in Danish in front of their guest. I did feel awkward but not about that. I felt very, very awkward as long as I was in that house. If I was discovered in the barn, the Kjærs could claim they didn't know I was there. Sitting at their table, sharing their food, there could be only one result from the dreaded sound of rifle butt on door.

With the meal over I went back to my straw to resume my wait. The Kjærs were so calm about it all, I guessed that there was something to wait for. Mr Sonne turned up with his daughter Else and his assistant Hald, all speaking English. They had bits of the exploded wireless set from the Lancaster, and told me that the other crew members were all now prisoners of war. Well, at least they were alive.

There was some animated conversation in Danish between young Kjær and Sonne, pointing at me and discussing me as if trying to decide if I was a porker or a baconer. I deduced that these two, the leaders, must be active Resistance members, in which case they would be on the radio to London for confirmation of my identity. Mr Sonne explained that his own son had been among a group of eighteen Resistance members taken by the Germans. All of them had been shot 'while attempting to escape'. This was why Else was here, home on compassionate leave from her hospital in Copenhagen where she was a nurse. Sonne, the brave man, said he thought I was about the same build as his son had been and that the clothes still hanging in the cupboard would do very well.

After a week in my barn, with bacon and black bread for lunch every day and visits from Else and the others every evening, there came news that Loneon had contacted the Resistance and was being looked after. So, he was free too. It was time for the next stage. I said goodbye to my courageous friends, the Kjærs. Tears fell, kisses were exchanged, hands were shaken firmly and promises made in two languages before I mounted a bicycle, accompanied by Else and Hald, and set off for a certain house in Farsö.

In civilian clothes now, I was liable to be shot as a spy. I only hoped that if we met a German soldier, it would not be one who spoke Danish. My new identity card, using my escape-kit picture, showed me to be Jens Christian Hansen, born 11.10.1924 in Nodagir. It was beautifully produced, worn and used to perfection and overstamped by the police apparently in October 1943. This would be fine, so long as I wasn't asked what I did, where I lived or if I agreed that the weather was excellent for the time of year.

At the house, Loneon was waiting, desperate to tell me that one of the places he'd stayed in had been the hunting lodge of King Kristian, although he hadn't actually met the King who was under house arrest.

A car arrived to take us away. They drove us out of town, far, far into the country where, cheerily and with much jesting in Danish, we were placed under arrest by Constables Nielsen and Pietersen. They explained to us, the prisoners, that we were burglars, going for trial in Copenhagen, and this was the explanation also given to any citizens who asked why the four of us had a compartment on the train to ourselves while the common herd had to stand in the corridor. 'Only a couple of common burglars,' the police would say, 'but you never know with these criminal types.' This was thought to be a huge joke by the policemen and they kept repeating it in variations between themselves, roaring with laughter. Loneon and I thought we would never understand the Scandinavian sense of humour.

Hospitality in Copenhagen reached new heights. People were thrilled to meet the English heroes and vied with each other for the privilege of being shot by the Gestapo should they be found in association.

By day we were shown the sights, even though there were Germans everywhere. They constantly reminded us not to do anything English such as looking the wrong way when crossing the road. By night we were kept inside, often by serious Resistance fighters who never opened the door without a gun in their hand. A squadron of Mosquitos had raided the diesel engine factory in Copenhagen quite a while before, January '43, but everyone we met had their own story to tell of the great excitement, and they were all eager to encourage the English to bomb their home town more often.

One dark night, we were collected by a very dubious looking fellow, a swarthy type who might have been an arms smuggler or a Mafia hit-man if those professions had not seemed too tame. He ushered us into his large, shining, black saloon car. Perhaps, I thought, we were VIP guests being taken to meet the head of all organised crime in Scandinavia.

To our complete astonishment, this character turned on a siren and put the headlights on full beam. He drove as if in hot pursuit, tyres squealing, engine blasting, screeching around bends and flying down straights. He could not have been more noticeable. We couldn't believe it was happening. Anyway, after a few minutes of this, with his foot hard down and one finger on the wheel, he turned to us, sitting terrified in the back seat, and let us into a little secret. 'Not my car', he said. 'Gestapo. I steal him. Nobody try to stop us.'

This confidence was followed by huge guffaws. What a wizard wheeze, he thought, to spirit a couple of Englishes away in a luxury car belonging to an enormously powerful and totally ruthless gang of official murderers and torturers. Once more I failed to see the funny side of the Norseman and was much relieved to arrive at the dock gates, which opened up for us. The car came to a skidding halt beside a ship. Our swarthy chauffeur showed us up the gangplank to be welcomed aboard by the Swedish captain.

Aquavit being an essential component of running escaped enemies of Germany into neutral countries, many toasts were proposed, seconded and thirded before the two centres of attraction were allowed to retire for the night. Our chauffeur, unaffected by enough aquavit to render senseless an entire rugby league team, said his goodbyes and left, presumably to return the Gestapo car so that it might be refuelled, polished and maintained in peak condition, ready for when he needed it again.

We were allowed on deck the next morning, to watch the approach of the Swedish coast, and a small motor boat came alongside. The big ship hove to, we said thank you to the captain and his crew, and soon we and the motor boat were docking in Malmö. The British consul gave us £10 each. All that was left for us was a train ride to Stockholm, a trip to Scotland in the bomb bay of a Mosquito, and a lift back to our station at Skellingthorpe where, following tradition, we found the ladies who had packed our parachutes and gave them 10*s*.

CHAPTER 17

Brave New World

On the last day of the air war in Europe, 25 April 1945, a force including 360 Lancs attacked Hitler's holiday cottage at Berchtesgaden. The op was viewed by many air crew as a PR exercise, a needless risk and a potential waste of good men. Ken Dagnall was there: 'The planning was absolutely atrocious. They hadn't taken proper account of the mountains and we couldn't get a proper run. We were on top of the target before we knew it.'

It was something of an anticlimax on which to finish, for a squadron recently peaked at thirty-four operational crews. Some 6,000 sorties had been flown in that war - 2,500 in Wellingtons, with over 100 aircraft lost, and 3,500 in Lancasters, with 127 aircraft lost, one of the largest totals of Lancasters from a single squadron, plus 22 in accidents.

Training began on 1 June for the expected move to the Far East as part of Tiger Force. Many flights were made to repatriate POWs, and 'Cook's Tours' to show VIPs – and, rather more importantly, IX Squadron ground crew – the results of the bombing campaign in Germany.

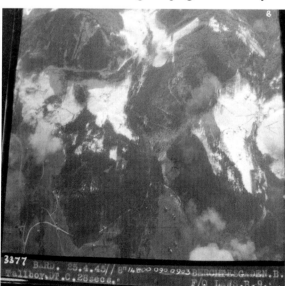

Berchtesgaden, 25 April. Hitler was not at home. He was in Berlin, trying to win the war with imaginary armies and a few boy scouts. Apart from the barracks of the SS there to guard the Führer, the target was of no military significance.

Another centurion: Lancaster EE136 flew 93 ops with IX, seen here with Flying Officer 'Tiger' Lyon, air crew and ground crew in her early days, transferred to 189 Squadron and finished the war with 109 ops.

Victory in Europe – ready for the party in a Bardney hangar.

The last farewell.

The squadron said goodbye to Bardney on 6 July, moving back to Waddington. Japan surrendered on 14 August but the move abroad did come about in another way in the new year when, re-equipped with the Lancaster Mark VII, sixteen machines, twenty-one crews and all supporting staff and kit flew to Salbani in West Bengal. It was a dangerous situation with India in turmoil but, apart from one short period of stand-by during a mutiny in the Indian navy, flying was largely to do with showing the flag.

It was also the last gasp for the Lanc. At their new base, Binbrook, shared with 12, 101 and 617 Squadrons, No. IX began taking delivery of the Lincoln in mid-July in its Mark II version, basically a higher/faster/further Lancaster as long-range bomber.

A few fortunate crews went on Operation Sunbronze, a fighter-affiliation exercise involving flights to Malta to escape the cold and snows of the 1946/7 winter. More crews and aircraft joined up with 617 for a spring tour of the USA. Otherwise there was little happening beyond routine until 3 April 1948 when six Lincolns went on a month's secondment to Shallufa, an RAF base in Egypt's Suez Canal zone. This was an intensive training programme of bombing and air firing; Harry Brittlebank was there, on National Service as ground crew:

> Those four weeks were very, very busy, plus sandstorms. There were no hangars so everything got covered in sand. My aircraft was C, flown by F/O 'Lucky' Lukins, and when it was time to leave I spent a whole day with a new paintbrush, clearing out every last grain of sand from it. I was hoping to fly back with him but I was listed to go with the CO [Squadron Leader L D Wilson DSO, DFC, AFC]. We stopped off in Malta, and the morning after we landed at Binbrook I heard Lucky Lukins and ten more men were dead in France, cause of crash unknown.

The cause was almost certainly bad weather. On 30 April 1948, Avro Lincoln B2 RF474 WS/C had only just crossed into southern France when it hit the turbulence of a cumulo-nimbus storm cloud, broke up and crashed at Verquires, Bouches-du-Rhône.

There was another Shallufa exercise, a goodwill tour to Pakistan, many flypast demonstrations, affiliation with jet fighters and intensive visual- and radar-bombing training with many flying hours demanded of a squadron equipped only with six Lincolns, which became eight by 1951.

One notable party was held in the Officers' Mess, 17 February 1950, when

Avro Lincoln SX958 WS/G was one of the last piston-engined bombers on IX Squadron, transferring to 617 Squadron in January 1952.

Something of a change for the squadron – the English Electric Canberra jet bomber replaced the Lincoln in 1952. At least the routine didn't change too much initially – from sunshine in Malta to the British winter and Canberras at Binbrook.

the C-in-C of the Norwegian air force presented a bulkhead from the *Tirpitz* to IX and 617 Squadrons, a trophy that was to cause several inter-squadron incidents over the next few years.

In May of 1952, the last piston-engined bombers departed the squadron and conversion began to the jet English Electric Canberra via practice in the Gloster Meteor. By this time it had been recognised that bombers were not going to be able to defend themselves against modern jet fighters such as the MIG 15, so the Canberra was designed to fly fast enough, and high enough, to avoid combat (later variants were armed for ground-attack roles).

Peacetime in a war-ready RAF squadron was a curious mixture of training, exercises, flying displays, goodwill visits to faraway places, bombing competitions (at which No. IX recorded many victories), new equipment trials, overseas detachments, and more training. The Soviet threat was ever present and the squadron had to be prepared for nuclear strikes, but the squadron's first operational action after the Second World War came from a different direction.

The Malayan government had been fighting a Soviet-backed communist insurgency for some years; in March 1956 IX Squadron was deployed to Butterworth base, Changi, for anti-terrorist duty. It was a stint of just under three months, including bombing raids, a goodwill tour to the Phillipines, and joint strikes with 101 Squadron who took over from IX towards the end of June. Pilot Derek Hopkins was flying with No. IX:

> Mosquito nets were essential, and a useful accessory to have in your room was a gecko. I had a nice creamy yellow one that lived behind my bedside light and popped out in the evenings to devour whatever insects were within his reach.
>
> On ops, there were two methods of dropping our bombs. One was by a map reference in the jungle, but the preferred method was for an Auster of the Army Air Corps to drop a smoke marker. Those boys knew the jungle very well and looked for signs of crops being grown. Our objective was to deprive the terrorists of food and supplies, so the AAC would order a strike and we'd go in with three aircraft in formation, each carrying six thousand-pounders, which we dropped from 4,000 feet. The updraught from the explosion gave us the sensation of driving over a 'sleeping policeman' in an old sports car with no springs.
>
> By the end of April, the emergency was all but over. We took part in the Queen's birthday flypast over Penang, and I flew a final strike on 12 June before saying goodbye to the curries that came in three grades: hot, very hot, and ******!!!, being taken home in a Hastings of Transport Command.

The squadron was hardly back to Binbrook when President Nasser nationalised the Suez Canal in July and tensions rose in the region. Israel invaded the Sinai Peninsula on 29 October; IX Squadron flew to Hal Far, Malta, on 30 October and bombed Abu Suier airfield, evening of 31 October. Abu Suier had been a British base since 1918; 84 Squadron had been stationed there until the April, and now IX was bombing it. Derek Hopkins:

At Hal Far we were issued with an escape kit, which comprised a silk map of north Africa, a length of wire that allegedly could cut through prison bars, six gold sovereigns, a .38 revolver and twelve rounds. I later found out that my gun was u/s and would only have been useful for throwing at potential captors.

The trip to Abu Suier was five hours fifteen minutes return, with four thousand-pounders. To have a chance of getting home we had to conserve fuel so cruise-climbed all the way there and back, up to 55,000 feet, which gave us temporary rheumatism in all joints. Our bomb aiming computer only operated up to 25,000 feet, and we were to drop from 44,000, above anything the Egyptian Meteors could reach. So, we had to go back to WW2 methods, of extremely careful and accurate straight-and-level flying while the bomb aimer [Sam Slatter] used the sighting head and the written table of settings provided.

It's a great tribute to Sam, and to our training, that we had a direct hit, two bombs either side of the marker flare, and we had good results again two nights later, bombing the Huckstep Barracks in Cairo.

This brief encounter ended with the ceasefire on 7 November. The squadron carried on with training at Hal Far, returning to Binbrook on 17 December.

Peace returned but the Cold War remained and, beginning in July 1957, the squadron's Canberras were modified to carry the atomic bomb and to deliver it by a new technique, the Low Altitude Bombing System. No. IX was the first squadron to become operational in LABS, training at Idris, Libya (previously Castel Benito). Pilot John 'Flash' Grindon remembered this procedure:

We flew at 250 feet and 360 knots, then pulled up into a loop at around four G. The bomb would be released and would shoot forwards some distance, while a roll off the top of the loop took the aircraft away, to be seven miles from the explosion. We practised with one eye covered in case the flash should blind us. At Coningsby [1959], 12 Squadron had the same role as we did, each with a QRA [Quick Reaction Alert] nuclear-armed Canberra on continuous stand-by. The bomb was an American one so we had US troops to guard it. Our Canberra sat in a white-painted circle at the end of the runway, a very strict no-go area. We – including our American guard – had secret war-codes; fortunately for humanity, we never had to use them.

Aircrew of No. IX pose with Canberra B2 at Binbrook, 1953. Commanding officer Squadron Leader J C M Mountford sits third from right. Standing left to right: Jeff Smith, Roy Spencer, Gordon Rondel, Tony Hollins, Dick Bedford, Wilton Philp, Barney Platt, Pete Elton, Taff Morgan, Wilf Crank, Jimmy Price, Ken Neate, Chick Whittle, Ken Hancock, George Bridson, Jimmy Noel, Rory; front row, left to right: Flight Lieutenants Clarke, Oram, Ted Flavell, Mountford, Colin Bell, Downey. Sergeant Neate and crew were the first in the RAF to bomb from a Canberra at 45,000ft.

Our target was an airfield near Moscow. Flying at high level would probably have meant that we'd be shot down, so low level was the answer, which needed reasonable weather and which gobbled up fuel. If we were to run out, there was a contingency plan to land on a Dutch motorway.

Shades of 1938 there, when IX Squadron air crew expected to parachute into Holland after the proposed raids on Germany, should the Munich peace talks fail.

Air Commodore 'Spike' Milligan was a 20-year-old Flying Officer when he joined No. IX just before the 1959 move to Coningsby:

My flight commander was Dougie Melrose DFC and Bar, whose long bombing experience was all to do with flying straight and level at high altitude. We were at the forefront of developing this new low-level method, so now Dougie found himself upside down at 7,000 feet at the top of a LABS maneouvre. When his undercarriage failed one day,

Canberras as art? Or it could be Canberra as UFO, demonstrated by Derek Hopkins. 'We flew into a 150-knot jet-stream over London at airspeed 150 knots, and so hovered over the city with our lights on for 10 minutes. When we turned 180 degrees, at full power we reached a groundspeed of about 650 knots. We made the papers next day – UFO over London.'

IX Squadron Vulcans flying over Boston, Mass. during a goodwill visit.

Designed for the atom-bomb age, the Avro Vulcan was the supreme bomber of its time. XM603 came on squadron in December 1963.

he made the perfect wheels-up, flapless landing. There was so little damage to the airframe that the engineers had Canberra WH974 flying again quite soon afterwards.

We still did 'normal' bombing, for instance on our Sunspot exercises, twice yearly to Malta and Libya, when we'd bomb from 30,000 feet on the practice range near Tobruk. Navigating over featureless desert was a challenge, as our only navaids were hardly much better than Dougie had had in his Lancaster. Air-to-air refuelling was not in vogue then, which meant my longest sortie was Coningsby to Akrotiri, five hours, as much as anyone would want when sitting on the supremely uncomfortable Martin-Baker ejector seat.

For almost ten years, the Canberra and IX Squadron had been serving the country in every way possible except, thankfully, in the one task for which, in the background, they were always ready. A brief hiatus came with the standing down of the old jet, when the squadron disbanded for a short time from July 1961, but the one task stayed uppermost when the reformation came in March 1962, and with it the Avro Vulcan.

The first Vulcan arrived at Coningsby in April 1962 and the squadron set about the exercises and other training to bring all crews up to the new standards required. The NATO deterrent role kept the squadron under strict constraints, oriented around the same three letters as before – QRA, Quick Reaction Alert, to the threat of Soviet attack on Europe, with the Yellow Sun Mk 2 nuclear bomb. As with the Canberra, a IX Squadron Vulcan, fully armed, was in continuous readiness for a 4-minute scramble.

The Vulcan was designed for QRA. It could be up and away very quickly in less than 5,000ft of runway, half the length needed by a B-52. At this time, the most likely threat was of a massive invasion of Western Europe by USSR ground forces, overwhelming the much smaller NATO armies. The V-bombers own threat deterred such action, when high-level operations at 0.86 Mach could be expected to be successful beyond the reach of Soviet fighters.

As one officer put it:

We were bored stiff on QRA, glad not to have to do it for real, but the practices were quite exciting, particularly with several aircraft in four-minute scrambles. Training otherwise was routine, with detachments to RAF El Adem, Libya, RCAF Goose Bay, Akrotiri and Singapore. What was it like to fly the Vulcan? Like sitting under the stairs with the lights out and the vacuum cleaner running.

Avro Vulcan of IX Squadron with full armament, including the nuclear bomb.

The Vulcan had a crew of five. On three rear-facing seats were the navigator radar, navigator plotter and air electronics officer; in the cockpit were the two pilots who had ejector seats and minimal vision forwards through a narrow windscreen and sideways through two small portholes.

As the backbone of the V-bomber force and therefore of the strategic nuclear deterrent, Vulcan squadrons were expecting to be re-equipped with the American Skybolt missile but President Kennedy cancelled it. Around the same time, effective Soviet anti-aircraft missiles were being deployed so, in 1963, IX and five other squadrons were switched to low-altitude attack and, from 1966, a new bomb, the WE177B.

Inevitably in the age of the ICBM, long-range strategic bombing from aircraft was becoming outdated and the deterrent was handed to the Royal Navy and their Polaris-armed submarines from 1968, while the V-bombers assumed a tactical responsibility.

Alastair Christie was the CO in 1967/8, when the squadron was based at Cottesmore:

The Vulcan was a magnificent aircraft to fly, powerful but easily controlled and surprisingly manoeuvrable, especially at extreme

256

altitude. Discipline had to be strict because of QRA and the nuclear role, and changes in alert states made life difficult at times. There were highlights, such as exercises to the Far East and winning bombing competitions, but all that is rather eclipsed in my mind by an event early in 1968.

Peter Tait was one of my senior captains. On a routine training flight in that January, he had had overheating in the weapons bay followed by two explosions, and set off for Cottesmore to burn off fuel before landing. While climbing away after a touch and go roller, the turbine disc of one of the engines broke off from the engine shaft. The fan blades, like a circular saw, cut through control lines, cables and hydraulic pipes.

Out of control at very low altitude, Peter ordered the crew to abandon the aircraft. The co-pilot ejected safely but the rest of the crew were in an impossible situation. The three in the back had no ejection seats, and there was an extra man, F/Lt Alistair Bennett, the NavRad Leader checking the aircraft's kit. They were expected to escape by parachute, really only possible in level flight at a reasonable height, by sliding out the way they came in, through the aircraft's door, but the Vulcan was inverted and very low. The skipper had no option but to eject, knowing his crew were stuck and he was too near the ground to have a hope of his parachute working.

By chance, he fell into some power cables and his streaming parachute, so far useless, wrapped around them and held him suspended from the death that befell F/Lt Bennett, F/Lt S R Sumpter, F/O B D Goodman and F/O M J Wheelan when the Vulcan crashed nearby.

In early 1969, two squadrons of Vulcans, Nos IX and 35, replaced the Canberra squadrons at Akrotiri, in that revised tactical nuclear role and to support UK conventional requirements for the Mediterranean and Gulf region. Areas for squadron duties extended west to Gibraltar and Italy, north to Turkey and Iran, east to Oman, Gan and Singapore and south to Kenya. Spike Milligan:

The Vulcan of course had a great deal more equipment and was much more sophisticated than the Canberra. When I was at Akrotiri, Iran was a CENTO ally and we flew from Mehrabad [near Tehran] on testing exercises with the Iranians' F4 fighters. We also had 'fights' with US Navy aircraft launched from carriers in the Med. The social life was pretty good on these overseas postings but there were also some exciting moments. We heard about the time when one pilot managed to land his Canberra smack on top of another one parked in dispersals – nobody hurt, not even the young technician inside the innocent machine – and Eddie Baker's Vulcan was totally wrecked when trying to land at Shiraz with some highly complex technical faults.

Exercises took them even further, to Australia for example, where they experimented with several attack profiles. One sent a single Vulcan towards the target, expecting to alert the defences including Mirage fighters. The Vulcan scattered a chaff screen and turned away from the target while the fighters looked for the chaff-simulated attackers. As they ran short of fuel and returned to base, more Vulcans, on different attack headings at low level, had a good chance of getting through.

There were detachments at various times to Masirah, Muharraq, Nairobi, Peshawar, Sharjah, Tehran and Tengah. At Masirah, a message from the tower asked three Vulcans to hold off for 10 minutes as they had fifty camels lying on the runway.

Kiwi Harry Denton DFC, pilot of the Lancaster in which Flight Sergeant George Thompson earned his VC, suggested a IX Squadron visit to New Zealand. This was arranged, to tie in with the 1972 air show at Hamilton air base, plus other flying displays, meetings with old IX men and the collection of a Second World War bat trophy from a squadron widow.

After twenty years with the Vulcan, the squadron became the first operational unit in the world flying the supersonic fighter-bomber, the Tornado, based where their Wellingtons began the Second World War, Honington. Crews came from flying fighters to join the old Vulcan boys, and Wing Commander Peter Gooding had the job of moulding them into No. IX's traditions of excellence:

We were still nuclear-capable but not on QRA in our NATO strike role, and some of our weapons rather lagged behind the development of the aircraft. Navigation kit offered impressive advances over what we'd had, and was ultra-reliable – which was as well, considering the faith we had to put in the terrain-following radar as we flew between mountains along the Scottish lochs in cloud and rain.

The Falklands War came too soon for us, but we could demonstrate the reach of the aircraft with an air-refuelled, non-stop flight to Cyprus

A little showmanship here, with the Vulcan doing a vertical climb with bomb doors open for the benefit of a crowd below.

Another dramatic change – from Lincoln to Canberra, from Canberra to Vulcan, and now Vulcan to Tornado. No. IX was the first operational unit in the world to be equipped with this most advanced machine.

and back, over ten hours. Our first three years established the capability of the aircraft and developed the new tactics that would be so valuable in the wars to come, and proved in many exercises including Green Flag in Nevada.

There were difficulties, of course, with such a sophisticated new machine. The avionics systems worked almost flawlessly but the more mechanical aspects of the aircraft gave problems in a very dense airframe. It is to the ground crew's great credit that we flew the required hours and could meet the demands of NATO Tacevals [Tactical Evaluations] and everything else we were asked to do.

On one of our early Tacevals, an aircraft returning from a night sortie suffered a total electrical – and therefore engine – failure over

These are the first operational Tornado air crew in the world. From left to right: Flight Lieutenant Peter Chandler, Flight Lieutenant Chris Davies, Wingco Peter Gooding, Squadron Leader Jim Ball, Flight Lieutenant Piet Lishman and Squadron Leader Dave Phillips. The simplified version of the IX Squadron bat seen on the Tornado's fin was Gooding's idea, and it's still in use.

the Wash. F/Lts Stephens and Nichols had to eject. Nigel Nichols did so successfully, but Mike Stephens did not leave the aircraft and was killed when it crashed on the Sandringham estate.

The squadron moved to Brüggen, near the German/Dutch border, in October 1986 and carried on with training for low-level ops; likely scenario, Central Europe, likely enemy, Warsaw Pact. Once again, action came from an unexpected quarter and the squadron had to make some rapid adjustments.

In August 1990, the Iraqi army invaded Kuwait. The quarrel had been rumbling for some time, over oil revenues, and a US-led consortium of nations was quick to make preparations for what became known as Operation Desert Storm. The UN Security Council voted unanimously for military action to enforce sanctions, 25 August, and mobilisation began. No. IX trained with new types of guided weapon. UN Resolution 678, 29 November, gave Iraq until 15 January to get out of Kuwait. Nothing happened, nor looked like happening, so IX was deployed to Dhahran, Saudi Arabia, 3 January 1991 and was flying war-training missions two days later, little knowing that Mesopotamia and the Gulf states would become such familiar territory over the next nineteen years. The briefing on 15 January put forty-eight RAF Tornados on war footing (Operation Granby) and, on the 17th, IX flew their first operation for many years from Dhahran, Saudi Arabia, to drop JP233 mines on Wadi Al Khirr airfield, south-west Iraq.

With pilot Flight Lieutenant Paul 'Chimpo' Simpson was navigator Flying Officer Paul 'Leanman' Lenihan:

> The Boss [Wing Commander Evans] called us in on the 16th saying we would go to work for a couple of hours, no major snags, then on the bus told us 'It's a goer. 31 Squadron go tonight. We go tomorrow.' When the 31 Squadron boys came back, it was all euphoria, yet pictures on CNN News of the AAA made it look like nobody could survive it. For our trip, Met gave us good weather all the way. We'd have preferred bad. In the briefing the professionalism clocked in and it seemed like a training sortie, well, almost. Then the intelligence officer invited us to empty our pockets of personal effects and checked that we had our war ID cards, silk maps, gold coins and goolie chits, none of which we'd ever seen before. The more sombre mood returned.

The goolie chit is a piece of paper promising a substantial reward in several languages for whoever helps a downed airman to get home. It is thus a ticket to ride and save one's integrity.

> It was second nature again as we walked to the jets and crewed in. The routine of ops forced all other thoughts away. Chimpo asked 'All set

Leanman?' All tickity-boo back here, all toys working nicely, I said. We got airborne and RV'd with the tanker, all to plan, and flew along for an hour as usual. We tanked, we nattered, we listened to Dire Straits, then number four said he was u/s and returning to base. We dropped off the tanker about 150 miles out and went down to 200 feet. Fifty miles out and the boss in the lead aircraft said he too was u/s and going home. Fluff [Flying Officer Andy Jeffery] asked if he wanted an escort.

It was quite a junior formation of two that crossed into enemy airspace in the black night. 'T-Dot E-Dot three whites' said Chimpo (automatic terrain-following radar is working OK). Nothing on RHWR, Skyshadow not seeing anything, I said (radar warning not showing any threats, countermeasures pod not detecting anything and therefore not jamming or spoofing). We saw AAA miles away but it seemed closer. No matter, I had to aim the weapons as we ran up to target and concentrate on the early warning system.

Fluff's bombs should go now – and they did, to the second, and lit up the sky. Our weapons ejected at 200 feet, we dropped to 100 and accelerated. We were going through 550 knots – but we were at seventy feet. I mentioned this to the pilot who said that, on the contrary, he had not turned on the heaters (afterburners) but would climb to 110 feet if that would make me any happier. I know this is so because it was the first time the radar altimeter had locked in.

Back in friendly airspace, we realised we didn't know the correct radio frequency to go home on. Fluff came on to say that he hadn't quite caught what Dicky [Flight Lieutenant James, lead navigator on the op] had said about that, so we said we hadn't listened either and tried getting gen from the American AWACs.

Tornado of IX Squadron on an exercise over the Woomera range in Australia.

We landed after four hours. There was more euphoria, beer, questions, congratulations, hugs and tears, and pizza in the crew room. The warrant officer said 'Welcome back Mr Simpson, Mr Lenihan. I hope you haven't bent my aeroplane.'

In the nine days of the air campaign, total air superiority was gained, much more quickly than expected; seven RAF Tornados were lost, none from IX.

Pilot Stew Gillies and navigator Pete Rochelle flew in the leading formation of two four-ships, 24 January. Gillies:

Our task was to destroy Mirage F1 and MiG 23 aircraft in soft shelters at Ar Rumaylah, dropping five thousand pounders from medium altitude. We took off at 0350 and joined a massed tanker fleet with some aircraft already in tow – a spectacular sight. We were to fly out into the western desert, missing the missile rings defending Kuwait. Two of our formation had technical problems and went home. As we crossed the border into Iraq, our radar showed that an enemy I-Hawk missile installation had locked on to us [Target Acquisition, TA], which was a weapons system we had no counter-measures for. It stayed at TA [no launch] so we pressed on, then a TA came up for another Soviet missile, the SA-3.

This was more worrying because we had started our attack run and we knew this was probably real. We dropped the correct chaff and, at about ten seconds to release, we had SA-3 guidance indications. I hadn't seen a launch. Calculating that we had 20 seconds before it hit us, I decided to drop our bombs and evade when we were lighter.

The bombs went and I pulled and rolled with maximum reheat. Almost immediately there was a huge orange flash and a very loud bang. The aircraft rolled violently left and pitched nose down, and of course we thought we'd been hit by the SA-3.

'Don't eject,' I said to Pete. 'I can still fly.' My plan was to limp to the Saudi border, or at least the open desert away from the Republican Guard, and then eject. There were multiple flashes from the ground and a missile with a bright orange flame appeared to be tracking us and manoeuvring. Pete deployed more chaff, I broke low and the missile exploded in three flashes well away from us.

At the same time, I saw the canopy, front seat and back seat ejections from the aircraft of Burgess and Ankerson, and we heard nothing more from them.

Dawn was breaking and we could see white vapour coming off the top of our port wing and some ragged metal flapping, and not a lot else was working at 10,000 feet. I had an amber caption, no RHWR, no reheat on either engine and the left nozzle was stuck open. We were on the wrong side of the drag curve and slowing down. We went lower to try and get some speed up, and reached 300 knots before starting a very slow climb.

An amber caption is a warning that could mean all kinds of trouble. There was no warning of incoming weaponry from the radar, however, and a stuck nozzle means that the thrust of the engine could not be directed. If you find you have more drag than thrust, you are on the wrong side of the drag curve, in a developing dangerous situation which may result in the aircraft stalling. The usual remedy is to fire up the power and get the nose down, only some of which the pilot could achieve.

We were not sure where we were, being without functioning navigation kit, and needed someone to look at us from the outside. We also needed more fuel if we looked fit enough to get home.

Via the AWACS, the leader of the following formation arranged to find us with a tanker. He told me he could see daylight through the fin and tailplane, that I shouldn't expect thrust reverse on landing, but otherwise we should do the trip. The tanker came down to our level and, flying on one engine, we took sufficient fuel to get to Dhahran.

A visual straight-in landing seemed the best option. The undercarriage didn't come down but responded to the emergency handle. We got down on a very wet runway, taxi'd very slowly with the aircraft settled low on the left, and reached dispersal. Our own exterior inspection showed shrapnel under Pete's seat, holes through the cockpit, left wing, spoiler, left engine nozzle and fin, and a hole the size of Desperate Dan in the tailplane. The warrant officer suggested we went for a strong cup of tea.

It turned out that we hadn't been hit by the SA-3 after all. One of our own bombs had detonated prematurely and almost blown us out of the sky. 'Budgie' Burgess and Bob Ankerson had been captured and would spend six weeks at Saddam's pleasure. Meanwhile we flew fifteen more missions, none quite so eventful as this one.

Operation Engadine was the RAF codename for the liberation of Kosovo. Crews of IX Squadron flew from Brüggen, the first squadron to be re-equipped with the new Tornado GR4, armed with thermal imaging equipment and Paveway laser-guided bombs. These were long ops, 7 or 8 hours, accompanied by VC10 tankers. Kosovo itself is only about the size of Devon and Cornwall, but the Serbian air defences were spread widely around and were very efficient with ground-to-air missiles and fighter aircraft. Flying over France, across the Alps, down through Italy and still with some way to go, these were fatiguing missions, with springtime storms to contend with while keeping formation at night.

There was a move to the French base at Solenzara on Corsica in May 1999, with day and night operations, but diplomatic negotiations soon solved the problem and the squadron had to return to Brüggen.

Pressure on Iraq and Saddam Hussein's nuclear programme built up over the whole of 1998, and the phrase 'weapons of mass destruction' was used so frequently it could be abbreviated to WMD and everyone knew what was meant. Eventually, patience was exhausted and Operation Desert Fox was launched in mid-December 2003. Squadron Leader James Linter was there, as IX Squadron Weapons Leader, crewed with the CO, Wing Commander Derek Watson, and together they led the squadron formation through the four-day conflict. Linter:

No Fly Zones had been operated since the first Gulf war, and had remained essentially peaceful until Desert Fox, after which the NFZs became more hotly contested, and anti-aircraft fire, counter-attacked by us, became a regular feature. Full-scale war was yet to come, and we trained for it, for example in the Arizona desert, with the new satellite-guided, all-weather bomb, and in Cyprus with target marking by thermal imaging, used with laser-guided bombs.

The war became a near certainty at the start of 2003 and twelve crews of the squadron were ordered to Ali Al Salem in Kuwait in the February, to be part of a combat wing of thirty-six crews. The base had become home to hundreds of American helicopters and it was a busy place as we built up to our full combat strength and covered the normal NFZ operations. It was also a strange period of waiting and wondering. Would we go into action (Operation Telic) or would there be a diplomatic solution? When it became clear that war was inevitable, we began examining the first night plans which, for us, meant attacking enemy air defences, 10 minutes after the first cruise missile strikes.

Plans went awry when an opportunity attack was mounted against targets in Baghdad. The Iraqis reacted by launching missiles against Kuwait every two hours, crudely aimed but we never knew what kind of warhead they might have. Sirens sounded, there were dashes to the bunkers in protective gear, but the novelty wore off and we were keen to retaliate. We got our chance on the night of 21 March.

As we flew across the desert we could see convoys of Allied vehicles driving up the road towards An Nasiriyah. It had definitely started. We split the formation into two elements to fire against different targets in Baghdad, as we saw the first cruise missile explosions in the city centre. Radar warning receivers showed no sign that the enemy was waiting for us. Our aircraft rocked as a ripple of five missiles snaked up into the night sky and a hard turn pointed us back at the dark desert, when an enemy missile arced across the sky in our direction. Our equipment told us that we were safe at this height from a missile of that type but we took evasive action anyway. We had several more sightings of enemy missiles but they seemed unguided and passed safely behind the formation.

The next night, we flew a four-ship with ALARM missiles and satellite-guided bombs to targets in Baghdad. Soon after we split, my pair was engaged by missiles that we believed to be two Rolands and

Tornado of IX Squadron equipped with ALARM – Air Launched Anti Radar Missile, a specialised weapon to suppress enemy defences by destroying radar installations.

one SA-8. As we climbed to avoid these, heavy calibre anti-aircraft artillery and rockets were aimed at us. With fire all around, we headed for our launch point where all went quiet again and our firings went well. As we crossed back into Kuwait we talked to our wingman about completing recovery checks and descended towards the base. As we did so, a bright flash illuminated the desert ahead. Who could be firing at us? We banked hard to avoid what was clearly a missile and I saw it past us. I have never seen anything so fast in my life. There was an explosion behind and about 10,000 feet above.

On the ground, we learned that a US Patriot had engaged a probable Iraqi missile just north of the base at the time we were recovering. The 'probable' was a IX Squadron Tornado, and Flight Lieutenant Dave Williams and Flight Lieutenant Kevin Main were dead. The padre organised a moving memorial service. Someone played 'The Last Post' on his bugle as the crowd, all in desert uniforms, stood silently in the evening air, a very emotional occasion for all.

We soon embarked on a cycle of ops based on a thirty-hour day and never established a settled sleep pattern. As the ground troops rapidly advanced, our task changed to attacking the Iraqi army and in particular the Republican Guard units between our chaps and Baghdad. We had attacked Tallil in the first Gulf War and photographed this enemy airbase for a decade; now it was our diversion airfield. As the targets dried up, sorties became longer, often requiring two refuellings in the air, with the first half of the mission wearing night-vision goggles, to watch dawn rise over Mesopotamia and land in mid-morning.

I dropped my final two bombs on an ammunition dump near Tikrit, 14 April. These were to be the last weapons dropped in the campaign.

A night meeting of the UN Security Council, 17 March 2011, approved the creation of a no-fly zone over Gaddafi's Libya and demanded an immediate end to the government's attacks on its own civilians. No. IX's Tornados were loaded with Storm Shadow missiles and made ready to fly at short notice, while crews rapidly went through intensive updates in their missile training.

Storm Shadow, a highly complex weapon to load and fire, required a great deal of difficult engineering work in a very short time. Mission planning was similarly complicated by many unknown factors in a swiftly changing situation, but crews were briefed and standing by on the night of 18 March, only to be stood down after Gaddafi's ploy of a ceasefire call.

Next evening, four IX Squadron Tornados took off from Marham, to be refuelled in the air and assemble over southern Italy for the strike. This was a 3,000-mile round trip, and the first RAF bombing mission launched from the UK since the Second World War. Andy Turk, squadron CO, was leader of this mission:

> The tactical phase was pretty uneventful. There was quite a lot of cloud which we punched through at about 4,000 feet. Everyone confirmed their systems were on line and all the missiles came off as advertised. It was really quite a straightforward first-night-of-war sortie, if there is such a thing. All the missiles hit their targets, which was testament to the work done at home by ground crew and training officers.

Two days later, four IX Squadron GR4s left Marham for Gioia del Colle in southern Italy, each carrying three dual-mode seeker Brimstone air-to-ground missiles, two Paveway IV precision-guided bombs and a Litening radar defence pod. Four more left the following day, two of them with RAPTOR reconnaissance pods.

The first sorties over Libya were flown from Gioia on Wednesday 23 March. Andy Turk:

> Very few of the squadron's engineers had got to Gioia by the time the first aircraft arrived. They were using the equipment they'd been able to carry with them to Italy to get the aircraft turned in a safe manner. They got the oils and lubrication into the aircraft, refuelled them and were ready to go within hours, and we flew two days of operations with minimal support equipment.

Gaddafi's forces were threatening Benghazi and Ajdabiya. No. IX sent two GR4s to look for armour at Ajdabiya. Andy Turk: 'My wingman spotted a number of T-62 tanks spread out alongside the highway with their barrels facing towards the town. Dual-mode Brimstone missiles destroyed all of them. The effects of the weapon are contained in the hull of the tank, so it's an exceptional weapon for firing in an urban environment.'

On another sortie, a self-propelled gun and nine vehicles were driving through the town of Misratah. The gun started firing into houses. The crew had only a few moments to fix target position, load co-ordinates into the

Tornado ready for take-off with Storm Shadow missiles, and Tornado landing at IX Squadron base, RAF Marham, Norfolk.

bomb, swing round and drop the bomb before the artillery moved off. Andy Turk: 'Paveway was accurate enough to destroy the gun with no effect on the houses, similarly when we hit more tanks driving down the streets of Misratah with the Brimstone missile, an extremely precise weapon using laser seeker and radar to find its target.'

The squadron's deployment to Italy was as temporary pioneers, to establish an RAF presence on operations until other units could gear up for a longer stay. After three weeks, No. IX came home to Marham to resume training for Afghanistan.

Like Iraq, Afghanistan has provided a much longer commitment than ever anticipated. Many, many close-air support, intelligence, surveillance and reconnaissance missions have been flown in the years since the first ops in 2008. Ken McLean, navigator with IX Squadron, has been to Kandahar Airfield (KAF) on four tours.

> Kandahar is huge, home to 26,000 personnel, and the busiest single runway airfield in the world, supporting helicopters, fast jets, unmanned aerial vehicles, and big machines like the Hercules transporter. There is even a civilian side to it, with a passenger terminal for domestic and international flights. The heat takes some getting used to for us Marham boys – forty-five degrees is not exceptional.
>
> Our main role is in supporting the troops on the ground, various nationalities as well as the Afghan security forces. Flying in Afghanistan is spectacular. The scenery is quite unlike anything else, as is the weather. When any rain appears, people are so baffled by it that everything stops while they stare up at the sky.
>
> Day to day life in KAF becomes routine very quickly. The engineers work twenty-four hours a day on twelve-hour shifts while aircrew plan, brief and fly sorties every day. On reconnaissance missions we have RAPTOR [Reconnaissance Air Pod for TORnado], essentially a one-ton camera that dominates the under-fuselage. It takes infra-red and monochrome photos and is primarily used to spot IEDs. The ground troops find the images from RAPTOR extremely useful and Tactical Imagery Wing [TIW] likewise.

Or, to put it another way, during one three-month tour on Operation Herrick [general term for British involvement in Afghanistan] the squadron flew 463 sorties, clocking up 1,581 hours flying time, supporting 300 individual requests for close-air support at 30 minutes' readiness, although many missions were launched in much less time. As Helmand is less than 10 minutes' flying time from Kandahar, quick reaction aircraft were usually over friendly forces well within 30 minutes of their first call for assistance.

With RAPTOR, the squadron imaged over 2,600 locations looking for suspicious activity and IEDs, plus another considerable number of images were made using the Litening III targeting pod. There were only four direct engagements using Paveway, Brimstone and cannon, as the enemy was almost always deterred from engaging land forces by the mere proximity of a GR4, or following the shows of force that were executed at extremely high speed and very low level, by day and night.

There will probably be no more deployments to Afghanistan for No. IX, and what's next for the squadron is not clear. There will be overseas exercises, and training to be ready for anything that might be required of Britain's senior bomber squadron.

A century on from the 50mph weather-slave machines of IX Squadron's beginnings, navigated by eye to drop 20lb bombs from the hand and send messages by Morse, with no counter measures beyond a service revolver, the Tornado GR4 flies faster than the speed of sound, navigates automatically over any kind of country in any weather, day or night, and finds its targets to the inch – hitting the right building, as *The Times* put it in 1914.

Anti-aircraft artillery these days is not aimed by eye either, but equipment in the GR4 tells the crew when they are about to be attacked and what kind of Mach 3 guided missile is being aimed at them.

There's one thing that has not changed, however. Air crew and ground crew remain utterly loyal to the cause and extend themselves beyond measure to do whatever has to be done. There's always bloody something.

APPENDIX

Specifications of
IX Squadron's Main Aircraft

In France, from formation to March 1915

Armament is stated as none where no armament was fitted ex-factory or specified in the design. Squadron armourers fitted machine guns and bombing apparatus where possible.

Blériot XI – 8 aircraft

Wingspan:	25ft 7in
Length:	25ft
Height:	8ft 10in
Top speed:	approx. 50mph
Ceiling:	approx. 3,000ft
Engine:	Gnôme 80hp
Armament:	none

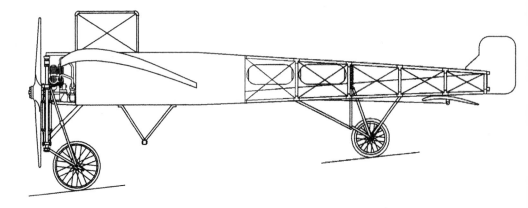

APPENDIX

Farman MF7 'Longhorn' – 2 aircraft

Wingspan:	50ft 6in upper, 37ft lower
Length:	39ft 10in
Height:	11ft 4in
Top speed:	approx. 60mph
Ceiling:	approx. 13,000ft
Engine:	Renault 70hp
Armament:	none

This one was captured by the Germans and recycled.

Farman MF11 'Shorthorn' – 9 aircraft

Wingspan:	51ft 9in
Length:	30ft 6in
Height:	10ft 4in
Top speed:	approx. 70mph
Ceiling:	approx. 12,500ft
Engine:	Renault 70hp
Armament:	none

The Shorthorn was one of the few very early aircraft deemed capable of carrying armament. A machine gun could be fitted for the observer to use in the front cockpit and, depending on the weather, up to a dozen or so small bombs were also carried.

Royal Aircraft Factory BE2A – 8 aircraft
Wingspan: 36ft 11in
Length: 28ft 4in
Height: 10ft 2in
Top speed: approx. 75mph
Ceiling: approx. 10,000ft
Engine: Renault 70hp
Armament: none

This is the BE2A. Early in 1915, the squadron also had the BE2B, two aircraft, which was the BE2A with the fuselage built up a little around the crew to give more protection from the elements, and the BE2C, see p. 276.

Avro 504 – 1 aircraft
Wingspan: 36ft
Length: 29ft 6in
Height: 10ft 5in
Top speed: approx. 80mph
Ceiling: approx. 13,000ft
Engine: Gnôme 80hp
Armament: none; Lewis .303 machine gun fitted to later models

In England, April to December 1915
Royal Aircraft Factory BE8A – 5 aircraft
Wingspan: 37ft 9in
Length: 27ft 5in
Height: 10ft 4in
Top speed: approx. 75mph
Ceiling: approx. 10,000ft
Engine: Gnôme 80hp
Armament: none

Martinsyde Scout – 1 aircraft
Wingspan: 27ft 8in
Length: 21ft
Top speed: approx. 85mph
Engine: Gnôme 80hp
Armament: Lewis .303 machine gun

During this period, the squadron also had two Avro 504 and the use of three more, single examples of BE2, Blériot XI, MF7 'Longhorn'. Briefly also, No. IX flew the Royal Aircraft Factory Reconnaissance Experimental 5 and the RE7. These latter two were experiments that failed. The RE7 was an attempt at a high-altitude, heavy-

bomber version of the RE5 with a much bigger upper wing (57ft span rather than 42ft), meant to carry a single three-hundredweight bomb (336lb, 150k). The RE5 was dismissed by an RNAS commander in 1914 as not suitable for use, and the underpowered RE7 was described by Trenchard as useless in the field, although both were used in France in small numbers.

In France, Belgium and Germany, December 1915 to July 1919
Royal Aircraft Factory BE2C – 38 aircraft
Wingspan:	36ft 10in
Length:	27ft 3in
Height:	11ft 2in
Top speed:	approx. 80mph
Ceiling:	approx. 10,000ft
Engine:	RAF1A 90hp
Armament:	none

Royal Aircraft Factory BE2D – 16 aircraft
The BE2D was a dual-control version of the BE2C with larger fuel capacity. It had a lower ceiling at 7,000ft and was said to be slightly faster, but with a much slower climbing rate.

Royal Aircraft Factory BE2E – 51 aircraft
Wingspan:	40ft 9in upper, 30ft 6in lower
Length:	27ft 3in
Height:	11ft 2in
Top speed:	approx. 90mph
Ceiling:	approx. 9,000ft
Engine:	RAF1A 90hp
Armament:	none

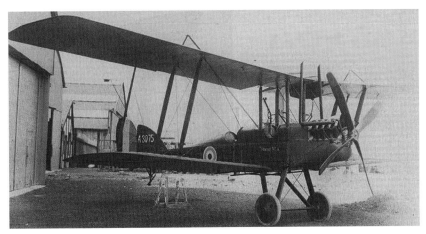

A BE2E.

Royal Aircraft Factory RE8 – 158 aircraft

Wingspan:	42ft 7in upper, 32ft 8in lower
Length:	27ft 11in
Height:	11ft 5in
Top speed:	approx. 100mph
Ceiling:	approx. 13,500ft
Engine:	RAF4A 140hp
Armament:	Vickers .303 fixed to fire through propellor, Lewis .303 on observer's cockpit

Bristol F2B – 3 aircraft in wartime, 18 post-war

Wingspan:	39ft 3in
Length:	25ft 10in
Height:	9ft 9in
Top speed:	approx. 120mph
Ceiling:	approx. 18,000ft

Engine: Rolls-Royce Falcon 275hp
Armament: Vickers .303 fixed to fire through propellor, twin Lewis
                .303 on observer's cockpit

Royal Aircraft Factory SE5A – 1 aircraft post-war
Wingspan: 26ft 7in
Length: 20ft 11in
Height: 9ft 6in
Top speed: approx. 140mph
Ceiling: approx. 17,000ft
Engine: Hispano-Suiza 8/Wolseley Viper 200hp
Armament: Vickers .303 fixed to fire through propellor, Lewis .303 on
                upper wing

E5903, the squadron's only SE5A, was in service for three months in 1919.

After the First World War to January 1939

Vickers Vimy – 11 aircraft 1924–5

Wingspan:	68ft 1in
Length:	43ft 6½in
Height:	15ft 7½in
Top speed:	103mph
Ceiling:	12,000ft
Engine:	Two Rolls-Royce Eagle VIII 360hp
Armament:	Lewis .303 on nose cockpit, ditto on rear cockpit. 2,500lb bombs

Avro 504K – 9 aircraft 1924–8

Wingspan:	36ft
Length:	29ft 5in
Height:	10ft 5in
Top speed:	95mph
Ceiling:	16,000ft
Engine:	Clerget 9 130hp and others
Armament:	none

Vickers Virginia – 74 aircraft 1925–36; specification Mark X

Wingspan:	87ft 8in
Length:	62ft 3in
Height:	18ft 2in
Top speed:	108mph
Ceiling:	15,500ft
Engine:	Two Napier Lion VBW-12 580hp
Armament:	Lewis .303 on nose turret; two ditto in tail turret; 3,000lb bombs

Vickers Victoria V – 3 aircraft 1930, 2 1932

Wingspan:	87ft 4in
Length:	59ft 6in
Height:	17ft 9in
Top speed:	130mph
Ceiling:	16,200ft
Engine:	Two Napier Lion XI 570hp
Armament:	none

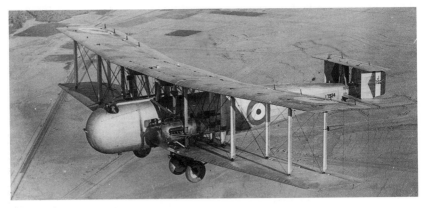

Handley Page Heyford – 21 aircraft 1936–9

Wingspan:	75ft
Length:	58ft
Height:	17ft 6in
Top speed:	142mph
Ceiling:	21,000ft
Engine:	Two Rolls-Royce Kestrel IIIS 575hp
Armament:	Single Lewis .303 on front and rear cockpits and in retractable ventral (dustbin) turret; 2,660lb bombs

APPENDIX

Vickers Wellington – 202 aircraft 1939–42: 18 Mark I, 36 IA, 73 IC, 4 II,
71 III; specification Mark III
Wingspan: 86ft 2in
Length: 64ft 7in
Height: 17ft 5in
Top speed: 255mph
Ceiling: 19,000ft
Engine: Two Bristol Hercules IX 1,590hp
Armament: Two Browning .303 in front turret, four in rear turret;
                4,500lb bombs

Avro Lancaster I and III – 188 aircraft 1942–5; specification Mark III
Wingspan: 102ft
Length: 69ft 6in
Height: 19ft 7in
Top speed: 275mph
Ceiling: 24,000ft
Engine: Four Rolls-Royce Merlin various 1,390/1,610hp
Armament: Two Browning .303 in front and mid-upper turrets, four in
                rear turret; 12,000lb bombs

Avro Lancaster VII – 188 aircraft 1945–6
As above with 1,610hp engines

Avro Lincoln B2 – 23 aircraft 1946–52
Wingspan: 120ft
Length: 78ft 3½in
Height: 17ft 3½in

Top speed: 319mph
Ceiling: 30,500ft
Engine: Four Rolls-Royce Merlin 85V 1,750hp
Armament: Two Browning .303 in front and rear turrets, ditto mid-upper turret or two 20mm Hispano cannon; 14,000lb bombs

Airspeed Oxford II – 1 aircraft 1949–52
Wingspan: 53ft 4in
Length: 34ft 6in
Height: 11ft 1in
Top speed: 192mph
Ceiling: 23,550ft
Engine: Two Armstrong Siddeley Cheetah 350hp
Armament: none

English Electric Canberra – 44 aircraft: 23 B2, 21 B6
Wingspan: 64ft
Length: 65ft 6in
Height: 15ft 8in
Top speed: 605mph
Ceiling: 48,000ft
Engine: Two Rolls-Royce Avon 109 7,400lb thrust
Armament: 8,000lb bombs/nuclear bomb

APPENDIX

Avro Vulcan – 36 aircraft 1963–82

Wingspan:	111ft
Length:	99ft 11in
Height:	27ft 2in
Top speed:	645mph
Ceiling:	65,000ft
Engine:	Four Bristol-Siddeley Olympus 301 20,000lb thrust
Armament:	21,000lb bombs/nuclear bomb

Panavia Tornado GR1/GR4; specification GR4

Wingspan:	45ft 8in (28ft 3in swept)
Length:	54ft 10in
Height:	19ft 6in
Top speed:	Mach 2.2/1,490mph
Ceiling:	50,000ft
Engine:	Two Rolls-Royce RB 199 Mk 103 9,850lb thrust
Armament:	(typically) Five 500lb Paveway IV smart bombs or 2 Stormshadow cruise missiles; single 27mm Mauser
cannon	(1700rpm); other configurations include Dual Mode Seeker (DMS) Brimstone, ALARM Mk2 missile, Litening III and RAPTOR

Bibliography and Sources

Publications

Air Power Review, various articles, including Air Commodore Peter Dye, 'The Aviator as Superhero?'

Becker, Cajus. *The Luftwaffe War Diaries*, 1964

Bowyer, Chaz. *Wellington at War*, 1982

Chorley, Bill. 'No. 9 Squadron Diary', *Aviation News*

Chorley, W R. *RAF Bomber Command Losses of the Second World War*, Vols 1 to 6

Dee, Mike. *The Third Son as Night Bomber*, 2002

Florentin, Eddy. *Quand les Alliés bombardaient la France*

Garbett, Mike and Brian Goulding. *The Lancaster at War*, Vols 1, 2, 3, 5, 1971

Harris, Sir Arthur T. *Despatch on War Operations*, 1995

Holmes, Harry. *Avro Lancaster, the definitive record*, 1997

Holmes, Robin. *The Battle of Heligoland Bight*, 2009

Hopkins, D B. *To Stroke a Cheetah*, 2002

Jacobs, Peter. *The Lancaster Story*, 2002

James, B A 'Jimmy', *Moonless Night*, 1983

Mackay, Alan. *313 Days to Christmas*, 1998

Mason, T. *9 Squadron*, 1965

Middlebrook, Martin and Chris Everitt. *The Bomber Command War Diaries*, 1985

Neitzel, Sönke. *Die deutschen Ubootbunker und Bunkerwerften*

Turner, John Frayn. *VCs of the air*, 1993

Websites

www.467463raafsquadrons.com

www.rafcommands.com

Archives and Accounts

IX Squadron Operations Record Book and various other documents held by The National Archives

First-hand reports by IX Squadron members

Index